Visions of the Grand Staircase–Escalante

Examining Utah's Newest National Monument

D1616578

Visions
of the
Grand Staircase- Escalante

**Examining Utah's
Newest National Monument**

EDITED BY

Robert B. Keiter

Sarah B. George

Joro Walker

Utah Museum of Natural History and Wallace Stegner Center, publishers

Salt Lake City, Utah

Cover and text design by Nona McAlpin. The text of this book is set in Goudy. Printed in the United States of America by Publishers Press, Salt Lake City, Utah, on recycled paper with agricultural-based inks.

Library of Congress Cataloging-in-Publication Data

Visions of the Grand Staircase–Escalante : examining Utah's newest national monument / edited by Robert B. Keiter, Sarah B. George, and Joro Walker.
    p.   cm.
Includes bibliographical references.

ISBN 0-940378-12-4 (alk. paper)

1. Grand Staircase–Escalante National Monument (Utah)—Management—History.
I. Keiter, Robert B., 1946–   . II. George, Sarah B. III. Walker, Joro, 1961–

F835.G66V57   1998
333.78′3′0979251—dc21

                 98–6818
                 CIP

10   9   8   7   6   5   4   3   2   1

Cover photo: Kenneth B. Castleton, *The Gulch* from Kenneth B. Castleton, **Petroglyphs and Pictographs of Utah, Volume 2** (1979) (courtesy of Manuscripts Division, J. Willard Marriott Library, University of Utah).

To

Wallace Stegner

and his

geography of hope

Wallace Stegner Center

Located at the University of Utah College of Law, the Wallace Stegner Center for Land, Resources and the Environment provides interdisciplinary opportunities for classroom and clinical education, scholarly and applied research and community service in the areas of natural resources and environmental law and policy.

Utah Museum of Natural History

As the state museum of natural history, the Utah Museum of Natural History at the University of Utah seeks to acquire, maintain and disseminate knowledge about the natural systems and cultures of the earth and to collect, preserve and hold in trust natural and cultural history objects for the people of Utah and its visitors.

TABLE OF CONTENTS

Acknowledgments

We are indebted to several people who were instrumental in bringing this book to fruition in a relatively short time. The authors whose work is represented in these pages each provided us with timely, well-crafted manuscripts of their conference presentations. University of Utah professors Bob Benedict and Dinah Davidson played key roles in organizing the conference from which these papers emerged. The College of Law staff, including Lisa Stewart, Kathleen Morgan, Karen McLeese, and Pamela Starley, brought the conference off flawlessly. College of Law Dean Lee Teitelbaum and Associate Vice President for Academic Affairs John Francis provided critical financial and moral support for the conference. Elizabeth Kirschen and Marilyn Ellingson put in many long hours assembling and preparing the final manuscript. Durrae Johanek's editorial assistance significantly improved the final product. Nona McAlpin's production work and advice has greatly enhanced the book's design and appearance. In addition, the R. Harold Burton Foundation provided much appreciated financial support for the book. We are enormously grateful to all.

Introduction

The Grand Staircase–Escalante region of southern Utah has a distinctly enigmatic quality. The area's dry, stark terrain, interlaced with myriad geological formations and deep riverine canyons, has never supported large-scale human habitation. Originally home to the Anasazi and Fremont peoples, the region contains numerous Native American artifacts and other reminders of these ancient cultures, which mysteriously disappeared almost seven centuries ago. Although intermittently inhabited by the Paiute people and then resettled by Mormon pioneers in the 1870s, the area was not fully explored or mapped until well after John Wesley Powell made his epic journey down the Colorado River. Powell's famous arid-lands report vividly depicted the difficulties involved in settling these desert lands.

For much of the 20th century, the area could perhaps be labeled the lands that time forgot. A few thousand residents scratched a living from the area's mineral, grass, and timber resources, just as their ancestors had. Yet the Grand Staircase–Escalante region did not long remain unnoticed. The surrounding national parks brought visitors in ever increasing numbers, and burgeoning interest in the Colorado Plateau's recreational opportunities introduced urban Utahns and others to the area. And the region's mineral resources attracted national attention in the aftermath of the Arab oil embargo and growing public concern over energy shortages. Indeed, during the latter part of this century, the region became a public lands battleground: first during the 1970s with the uranium exploration frenzy and proposed coal development on the remote Kaiparowits Plateau, and then since the 1980s over wilderness designation for its public lands.

With many of these debates still unresolved, President Clinton intervened in September 1996 and used his power under the Antiquities Act of 1906 to designate the Grand Staircase–Escalante region as a new 1.7-million-acre national monument. Most environmental organizations applauded the Monument designation, but state and local interests deplored the decision and have sought both legislative and judicial redress. In the meantime, the president's decision has dramatically refocused the immediate debate over the region's future on planning for management of the new Monument.

The Grand Staircase–Escalante National Monument Proclamation breaks new ground on the public domain. The proclamation vests management responsibility for the new Monument, for the first time ever, with the Bureau of Land Management (BLM) rather than the National Park Service. The proclamation also expressly sanctions the continuation of grazing and other preexisting multiple-use activities within the Monument. And the proclamation establishes a three-year public planning process designed to address how the new Monument will be managed. In his Monument designation speech, the president challenged everyone concerned about the region's fate to engage in this planning process. Governor Mike Leavitt has declared that the state of Utah will be an active participant in the planning process.

To promote understanding about the new Monument and the planning process, the University of Utah hosted a day-long conference in May 1997 titled "Visions of the Grand Staircase–Escalante: Exploring the Future of Utah's Newest National Monument." Sponsored jointly by the College of Law's Wallace Stegner Center for Land, Resources and the Environment, the University's Faculty Environmental Committee, and the Utah Museum of Natural History, the conference was conceived as an interdisciplinary gathering to inform and encourage public participation in the Monument planning process. This book represents a compilation of the conference presentations; it is designed to provide a comprehensive review of the new Monument's natural and human attributes, the planning framework, and the issues of paramount concern.

The book is organized into four sections. The first section describes the Monument's physical setting, specifically the geological, biological, paleontological, and archaeological resources that are the basis for the designation itself and that must now be preserved through the planning process. The second section addresses the socioeconomic setting, describing the region's history, the cultural context, emerging economic trends, and the potential role of tourism and recreation. The third section focuses on legal and planning issues, providing an overview of the Antiquities Act, the legal framework governing Monument management, the BLM's approach to its new planning responsibilities, and public participation opportunities and concerns. The final section outlines the principal concerns that must be addressed in the planning process from the perspective of an economist, private industry, environmental groups, Native Americans, the state of Utah, and the local populace.

Several themes recur throughout the assembled papers. First, because scientists generally agree that the Monument's large size is vital to ensure effective preservation of its manifold resources, the Grand Staircase–Escalante's vastness offers rare research opportunities while simultaneously presenting significant management challenges. Second, the planning process affords both the BLM and the public an unprecedented opportunity to define how national monument preservation responsibilities can be reconciled with the multiple-use activities still sanctioned within the Monument's boundaries. The planning process also presents a unique opportunity for often-conflicting national and local interests to engage in a joint effort to define future resource priorities. Third, the national monument designation provides local residents with an opportunity to define a more stable and sustainable future for the region, something that has eluded nearly everyone since this arid landscape was first inhabited over 10,000 years ago. Finally, it is clear that the Monument designation has not ended all conflict over these lands and their inherent value—widely divergent estimates persist over the value of local mineral resources, the potential benefits and costs that might flow from an enhanced tourism-based economy, and the degree to which intensive mineral or recreational development should be allowed within the new Monument.

Translating this new national monument concept into a practical reality will not be easy. Initial answers to many of these conflicts and questions can be found in the chapters that follow. Even when answers are not evident, the authors offer valuable insights into the region's past, its natural and human components, and the forces and choices that will shape its future. Although the Monument's natural resources are now ostensibly protected by the new designation, the lands will be managed by a multiple-use federal agency under a charter that contemplates an ongoing human presence. Reconciling preservation and use will plainly present the BLM with manifold challenges. But as Wallace Stegner recognized, "The natural world is a screen onto which we project our own images." For the Grand Staircase–Escalante, this book aims to sharpen and focus those images.

PART ONE

Hewn Out of the Rock

The Physical Setting

"This high, rugged, and remote region, where bold plateaus and multi-hued cliffs run for distances that defy human perspective, was the last place in the continental United States to be mapped."

President William J. Clinton
Proclamation No. 6920

"...the geological record in the Plateau Province is probably as clear as it is anywhere on the earth..."

Wallace Stegner
Beyond the Hundredth Meridian

◆◆◆

GROSVENOR ARCH

Photograph by Jerry Sintz, courtesy of the BLM, Utah State Office.

Previous page: Big horn sheep petroglyph from Calf Creek confluence, Site 3
from Kenneth B. Castleton, **Petroglyphs and Pictographs of Utah, Volume 2** *(1979).*

CHAPTER ONE

The Geography and Geology

M. Lee Allison

The Grand Staircase–Escalante National Monument is composed of approximately 1.7 million acres of federal lands administered by the U.S. Bureau of Land Management. The Monument also encompasses state lands managed by Utah School and Institutional Trust Lands Administration (SITLA), totaling approximately 176,000 acres of surface and 200,000 acres of mineral estate. In addition, the Monument is bordered by several other federally administered land units (Figure 1.1). The Dixie National Forest lies to the north of the Monument. The southern boundary abuts the Glen Canyon National Recreation area. Bryce Canyon National Park is located adjacent to the west of the Monument, and Capitol Reef National Park is adjacent to the east. About 275 square miles of school trust lands are scattered throughout the Monument as in-holdings (Allison, 1997; Figure 1.2).

The Monument is located in the west-central part of the Colorado Plateau's physio-graphic province (Allison, 1997; Figure 1.1) and is divided into three regions. In general, the exposed rock units are younger and topographically higher from east to west.

The Escalante Canyons region comprises roughly the eastern third of the Monument, from Capitol Reef National Park on the east to the Straight Cliffs or Fiftymile Mountain on the west. The topography of the region is formed of a series of north-south- to north-west-southeast-trending anticlines and synclines (rocks folded into elongated domes and basins) controlled by the underlying geology (Doelling, 1975). The region is dominated by the Circle Cliffs, the largest of the anticlines. Colorful sandstones of the Triassic and Jurassic periods (245 to 145 million years ago) are exposed, and erosion by tributaries of the Escalante River has carved deep canyons into them (Davidson, 1967). A broad valley extending south from the town of Escalante and bordered by the Straight Cliffs on the west, is underlain by relatively soft and thus easily eroded Jurassic-aged Entrada Sand-stone, resulting in an area conducive to grasslands that have been used for livestock grazing.

The Kaiparowits Plateau region extends from the Straight Cliffs to the Cockscomb on the west. It is characterized by a series of plateaus, buttes, and mesas underlain by the relatively undeformed Cretaceous-aged Straight Cliffs Formation (Doelling and Davis, 1989). The Kaiparowits Plateau covers approximately 1,650 square miles in the central

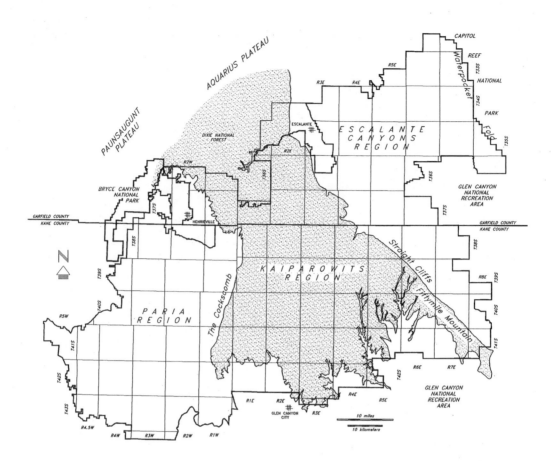

Figure 1.1. Physiographic features within the Grand Staircase–Escalante National Monument, Garfield and Kane Counties, Utah (Allison, 1997).

part of the Monument (Figure 1.2). The feature is a broad structural basin; however, the topographic expression is that of a northward-tilted plateau (Doelling and Davis, 1989). The Kaiparowits Plateau merges to the north with the Aquarius Plateau, and to the northwest with the Paunsaugunt Plateau. Elsewhere, the edge of the Kaiparowits Plateau is defined by the outcrop of Cretaceous-aged (85 million years ago) strata (Hettinger et al., 1996). The plateau is a dissected mesa that rises as much as 6,500 feet above the surrounding terrain. The landscape is defined by four sets of cliffs and benches that form a steplike topography between the Aquarius Plateau and Lake Powell (Sargent and Hansen, 1980). The Straight Cliffs form a prominent escarpment that extends northwest to southeast along the plateau's eastern flank; the escarpment is as high as 1,100 feet along Fiftymile Mountain (Figure 1.2).

The westernmost area is the Paria region and includes the eastern extent of the Grand Staircase. The Cockscomb, which forms the eastern boundary of the region, is a

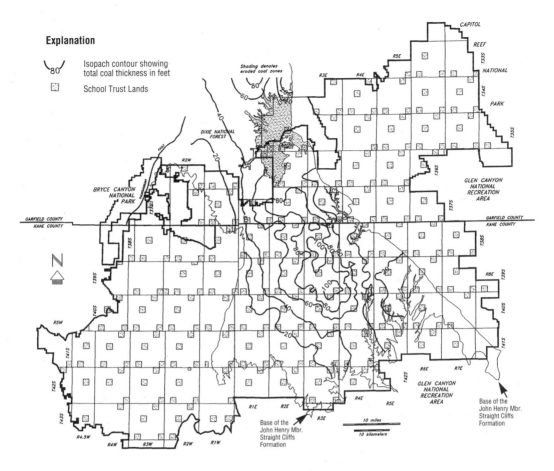

Explanation

$\searrow$80$\swarrow$ Isopach contour showing total coal thickness in feet

☐   School Trust Lands

Figure 1.2. Generalized contours of total coal thickness in the Kaiparowits coal field, and the location of School and Institutional Trust Lands within the Grand Staircase–Escalante National Monument.

prominent and spectacular geologic fold in which rock units are bent down from west to east. The Paria region consists of a series of terraces and benches both geologically younger and topographically higher than the two monument areas to the east. Superimposed on this terrain is the Paunsaugunt fault, a through-going north-south feature that downdrops the region to the west.

The Grand Staircase consists of a series of topographic benches and cliffs that step progressively down in elevation over a distance of about 150 miles, from the Pink Cliffs near Bryce Canyon in the north to the Chocolate Cliffs of the North Rim of the Grand Canyon in the south (Allison, 1997; Figure 1.3). These stairsteplike features include the Paria Terrace and the White and Vermilion Cliffs, which extend southward decreasing in elevation from the Paunsaugunt Plateau near Bryce Canyon (greater than 9,000 feet) to the Shinarump Flats (less than 5,000 feet).

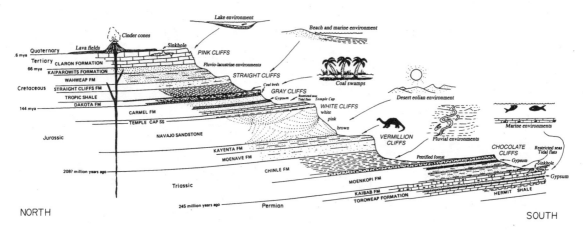

Figure 1.3. Diagrammatic cross-section of the Grand Staircase in western Kane County, Utah. Reference is made to geologic formations, the age and environments of deposition, and famous lines of cliffs, which build the "steps" of the staircase. "It is the most colorful exposed geologic section in the world" (Doelling and Davis, 1989).

A Billion Years of History

Rocks representing the Permian through Quaternary periods (286 million years ago to the present) are exposed at the surface in the Monument. Rocks older than Permian, dating back to the Precambrian era, approximately 1.1 billion years old, have been encountered in the subsurface by drill holes. The Precambrian rocks, belonging to the Chuar (pronounced "chew-are") Group, crop out in the Grand Canyon, and extend northward under the Monument. These "basement" rocks were at least partly deposited in a marine environment and some layers are composed of up to 10 percent organic material, derived from the decomposition of mostly soft-bodied early life-forms.

The Precambrian rocks were uplifted, broken, faulted, and eroded following their deposition, leaving a hiatus in the geologic record of hundreds of millions of years. Starting about 600 million years ago, Cambrian-aged sandstones and shales were laid down over much of North America. As a result, the distribution of Precambrian rocks under the Colorado Plateau is irregular and poorly known.

Following the Precambrian era, the Colorado Plateau region was an area of relative calm that preserved much of the subsequent history of the Paleozoic era (640 to 245 million years ago). Vast deposits of marine sandstones and limestones formed in shallow seas. These geologic units are relatively extensive and uniform.

During the following Mesozoic era (245 to 65 million years ago, also known as the Age of Dinosaurs) the region became more terrestrial with environments dominated by sand dunes, rivers, floodplains, swamps, beaches, and coastal plains. During the Cretaceous period (145 to 65 million years ago) a shallow sea invaded the continent, extending from the present Gulf of Mexico to Alaska. The western margin of this sea ran through

---

Utah, developing a prominent coastline with sandy beaches and barrier islands. To the west of these beaches were swamps similar to those seen today in southern Louisiana. Over time the beaches and swamps slowly subsided as new deposits buried them. Trees and other vegetation in the swamps were protected from rapid decay, eventually turning into coal from the heat and pressure.

The coastline remained relatively stable in the Kaiparowits region resulting in unusually thick deposits in the swamps. Cumulative coal thickness in the center of the Kaiparowits coal field exceeds 140 feet. The fossilized beaches to the east are more resistant to erosion than other geologic units and thus form the Straight Cliffs.

The Tertiary and Quaternary periods (65 million years ago to the present) have been dominated more by deformation, uplift, and erosion, than by deposition. However, in the northwest part of the Monument, the Tertiary Claron Formation forms the uppermost step in the Grand Staircase as the Pink Cliffs. Deposited in a large freshwater lake and associated river systems, the unit is composed of limestones, sandstones, and conglomerates. It is the geologic unit that forms the beautiful spires and cliffs in Bryce Canyon National Park.

Deformation and Uplift

The Colorado Plateau is characterized by relatively flat-lying strata that have been locally offset and folded during vertical movements along north-south-oriented blocks in the earth's crust. Forty to 50 million years ago these crustal movements compressed and folded the overlying strata into many asymmetrical or monoclinal folds that have one gently dipping side and one steeply dipping side. The two most prominent monoclines are the Waterpocket Fold (east side of the Circle Cliffs uplift) and the Cockscomb (east limb of the East Kaibab monocline). These features form the boundaries of the Monument's three physiographic regions.

About 15 to 18 million years ago, the crust in western Utah and Nevada starting undergoing extension (stretching) that continues to the present (Basin & Range orogeny). Extension caused the overlying strata along the west side of the Monument to break along faults.

Geologic Resources

The Utah Geological Survey is statutorily directed to carry out activities having as a purpose the "development and exploitation of natural resources in the state of Utah." The UGS also serves as geologic adviser to the Utah School and Institutional Trust Lands Administration. The immediate goal of the UGS is to ensure that the fullest possible understanding of the geologic resources potential in the Monument is made available to the Monument planners and others, and is considered in the Monument management plan. In addition, the UGS will provide the best possible scientific and technical data to be used to defend the value of school trust lands considered for exchange or sale.

Coal. Coal in the Kaiparowits Plateau was first mined by settlers in the late 1800s near the town of Escalante, and small mines produced coal for local needs until the early 1960s. Coal investigations were first reported in the Kaiparowits Plateau by Gregory and Moore (1931), but it was not until the early 1960s that energy companies expressed interest to commercially develop coal in the region. As many as twenty-three companies acquired coal leases, and drilled about 1,000 coal test holes (Doelling and Graham, 1972). Plans made in 1965 to develop a 5,000-megawatt coal-burning power plant were revised in the mid-1970s to construct only a 3,000-megawatt plant after controversy over environmental issues. Construction plans were finally discontinued because of government action and pending lawsuits over environmental concerns (Sargent, 1984). In the latter part of the 1980s, Andalex Resources began formulating plans to mine underground and ship up to 3.5 million tons of coal annually from their leasehold in the southern part of the Kaiparowits coal field. Environmental analyses for the proposed mine, required as part of the permitting process, were under way at the time of the proclaiming of the Monument. Following establishment of the Monument, and the President's stated opposition to coal mining there, Andalex withdrew its application and entered into negotiations with the U.S. Department of the Interior to exchange its coal leases for leases outside the Monument.

The U.S. Geological Survey (USGS) recently performed an assessment of coal resources in the Kaiparowits Plateau coal field as part of a national coal availability assessment (Hettinger et al., 1996). The USGS study builds on the classic study of the Kaiparowits Plateau coal field by the Utah Geological Survey (UGS; Doelling and Graham, 1972) and is based on data from geologic mapping, outcrop measurements of stratigraphic sections, and drilling that has been conducted in the region since the late 1960s (Figure 1.2). Although the distribution of coal was well documented on outcrop (Doelling and Graham, 1972; Blackett, 1995), coal distribution in the subsurface remained largely unknown due to the proprietary status of company data. Recently released company drill hole data and drilling by the USGS provided new insight into the subsurface aspects of these coals allowing a more complete and accurate calculation of the coal resources, which they determined to be 62.3 billion tons of coal in place (Hettinger et al., 1996). A preliminary estimate of recoverable coal is 11.3 billion tons, with 880 million tons coming from school trust lands (Allison, 1997). The economic value of the coal will be debated, especially since Andalex's withdrawal will preclude determination of any actual production costs.

Coal-bed Gas. Most of the Kaiparowits Plateau coal field has potential for development of coal-bed methane gas, even though no definitive studies have been done to date. Based on research in other Utah coal fields and extrapolating to the Kaiparowits field, the UGS estimates that the coal beds of the Straight Cliffs Formation contain between 2.6 and 10.5 trillion cubic feet of methane.

Oil and Gas Potential. The Monument contains all the elements necessary for major oil and gas accumulations: source rocks, reservoirs, and trapping mechanisms.

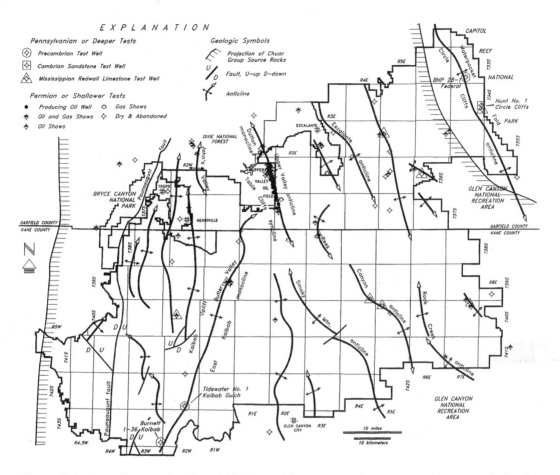

Figure 1.4. Axes of principal geologic folds that could serve as petroleum traps, and locations of oil and gas wells in the Grand Staircase–Escalante National Monument (Allison, 1997, after Montgomery, 1984).

Commercial deposits of oil have been discovered both within and along the margins of the Monument at Upper Valley field (Peterson, 1973). Although the characteristics of the Monument and Kaiparowits basin as a whole are favorable for the accumulation of oil and gas, wildcat density is extremely sparse. Only forty-seven exploratory wells have been drilled within the Monument, or an average of fifty-seven square miles per well (Figure 1.4). The postulated reasons for this apparent lack of exploratory activity are: (1) inaccessibility, (2) lack of oil and gas pipelines, (3) low success rates, (4) the collapse of world oil prices in 1986 and a nationwide oversupply of natural gas, and (5) environmental concerns and restrictions. Although the exploration risk is high, the Monument could contain major accumulations of oil or gas based on the production history of Upper Valley field and geologic evidence (Montgomery, 1984; Rauzi, 1990; Uphoff, 1997).

Circle Cliffs Tar Sand. Solid hydrocarbons impregnate Triassic-age sandstone and siltstone along the flanks of the breached, Circle Cliffs anticline in the northeastern part of the Monument. Known as tar sand, such deposits are essentially exhumed fossil oil reservoirs where the lighter, more volatile fractions have been removed due to exposure. The entire west flank of the Circle Cliffs tar-sand deposit and a small part of the east flank is located in the Monument. The remainder is within Capitol Reef National Park. Although there has been little recent commercial interest in extracting oil from the tar-sand deposits of the Circle Cliffs, researchers have estimated that as many as 550 million barrels of oil might be contained within tar sands of the Monument (Ritzma, 1980).

Non-Fuel Minerals. Metallic mineral occurrences in the Monument include gold, copper, manganese, titanium, zirconium, uranium, and vanadium. Most occurrences are small, low grade, and have little development potential. Minerals such as titanium, zirconium, and vanadium, however, are considered "strategic and critical" (Cammarota, 1984; U.S. Department of Defense, various) and may have development potential within the Monument. Uranium with associated copper plus trace amounts of cobalt occurs in the Shinarump Member of the Triassic Chinle Formation in the Circle Cliffs area of the northeastern section of the Monument. About 75,000 pounds of U_3O_8 was reportedly produced from these deposits during the 1950s and 1960s. Vanadium associated with the uranium was produced as a by-product. Anomalously radioactive outcrops of the Jurassic Morrison Formation have been noted on the east side of the Straight Cliffs, suggesting the possibility that uranium minerals extend beneath the Kaiparowits Plateau.

Fossil, placer titanium-zirconium deposits occur in the Straight Cliffs Formation in a forty- to 50-mile-long belt along the east side of the Kaiparowits Plateau. The deposits were never developed commercially because they are remote and because of problems associated with mining and processing. However, the deposits are reportedly rich in rutile (titanium) and zircon (zirconium). Dow and Batty (1961) estimate that the aggregate size of fourteen individual deposits is from 1 to 3 million tons of raw material.

Records obtained from the Utah Division of Oil, Gas and Mining indicate that five small mining operations are currently under permit in the Monument. About 300 tons of alabaster, a fine-grained form of gypsum used for ornamental carvings, is quarried annually in four of these operations. The fifth is a suspended operation that mined petrified wood.

Resource Recovery in Parks and Monuments

One of the more controversial issues the Monument's planning team will have to address is whether, and to what extent mineral resource development will be allowed in the Monument. Fortunately there are hundreds of precedents and decades of experience that can help guide them.

Mining and oil and gas drilling and production have been going on in national parks and monuments almost as long as the park system has existed. Most everyone is aware of the famous "twenty mule team" associated with borax mining in what is now Death Valley National Park. The boundaries of the Grand Staircase–Escalante National Monument were established to include part of the Upper Valley oil field, the ninth largest in Utah.

NPS Region	Number of Active Operations[1]		Number of Mining Claims		Number of Abandoned Sites[2]			Administrative Mineral Material Sites		Number of Park Units Affected
	Mining[3]	Oil & Gas	Unpatented	Patented	Mine Sites	Mine Openings	Oil & Gas Wells	Abandoned & Unidentified Status	Active & Inactive	
Alaska	3	0	529	542	459	461	0	73	32	14
Intermountain	6	222	7	15	517	517	4	205	75	46
Midwest	7	94	0	0	126	241	10	74	5	26
National Capital	0	0	0	0	9	24	0	0	0	3
Northeast	7	13	0	0	223	1201	0	27	4	15
Pacific West	7	0	4318[4]	186[5]	762	5098	1	153	47	27
Southeast	1	255	0	0	458	146	18	293	0	15
TOTAL	31	584	4854	743	2554	7688	33	825	163	146

[1] Active sites include shut-in and any other type of temporarily halted operations, as well as wells that need to be plugged.

[2] The California Desert Protection Act significantly increased the number of abandoned mineral land sites in the Pacific West Region. Information is still being gathered and the data have not been incorporated in this chart.

[3] Includes operations on mining claims and nonfederal operations other than oil and gas.

[4] The California Desert Protection Act of 1994 significantly modified the number of mining claims in the Pacific West Region. The unpatented mining claim data reported are undergoing refinement.

[5] The California Desert Protection Act of 1994 modified the number of patented mining claims in the Pacific West Region; changes in patented claim data have not been incorporated.

Table 1.1. Mining and mineral development in the national parks. (Source: National Park Service, April 1997).

The National Park Service (NPS) reports that there are 31 mining operations and 584 oil and gas operations active in 146 different park units around the country (Table 1.1). In many cases, these operations were grandfathered, that is, they were in place prior to the designation of the park or monument and allowed to continue. However, there is at least one prominent example where resource development had no historical basis and was initiated to satisfy national needs. Uranium was mined in Grand Canyon National Park starting in the 1950s. President Kennedy signed a law in 1962 authorizing continued mining until 1987, at which time the mined areas would revert to NPS control.

The NPS also undertook a drilling program in the late 1980s on the south rim of the Grand Canyon, using a full-size oil and gas drill rig. The purpose was to drill a hole to the bottom of the canyon for a pipeline to carry water to the top for visitor use. The NPS reportedly received no complaints from the public about this drilling operation, even though it was adjacent to the visitor center during the height of the tourism season.

Given the presence of an active oil field, a number of active quarries, and scores of inactive or abandoned mines and wells, it does not seem unreasonable that the Bureau of Land Management allow continued responsible and prudent energy and mineral resource development in the Grand Staircase–Escalante National Monument. Indeed, given the widespread presence of wells and mines throughout the national park system, it would not be unusual for such development to take place.

Acknowledgments

Some passages in this paper were excerpted from UGS Circular 93, compiled by the author (Allison, 1997). A number of UGS staff geologists contributed sections to that circular. Kimm Harty provided a thorough and much appreciated review of this paper, which greatly helped clarify it.

References

Allison, M. L., compiler. 1997. *A preliminary assessment of energy and mineral resources within the Grand Staircase–Escalante National Monument.* UTAH GEOLOGICAL SURVEY CIRCULAR 93.

Blackett, R. E. 1995. *Coal in the Straight Cliffs Formation of the southern Kaiparowits Plateau Region, Kane County, Utah.* UTAH GEOLOGICAL SURVEY OPEN-FILE REPORT 314.

Cammarota, V. A., Jr. 1984. *America's dependence on strategic minerals.* Pages 29-58, in Mangone, G. J., editor. AMERICA'S STRATEGIC MINERALS. New York, Crane Russak.

Davidson, E. S. 1967. *Geology of the Circle Cliffs area, Garfield and Kane Counties, Utah.* U.S. GEOLOGICAL SURVEY BULLETIN 1229.

Doelling, H. H. 1975. *Geology and mineral resources of Garfield County, Utah.* UTAH GEOLOGICAL AND MINERAL SURVEY BULLETIN 107.

Doelling, H. H., and F. D. Davis. 1989. *The geology of Kane County, Utah.* UTAH GEOLOGICAL AND MINERAL SURVEY BULLETIN 124.

Doelling, H. H., and R. L. Graham. 1972. *Southwestern Utah coal fields—Alton, Kaiparowits, and Kolob-Harmony.* UTAH GEOLOGICAL AND MINERALOGICAL SURVEY MONOGRAPH SERIES, NO. 1.

Dow, V. T., and J. V. Batty. 1961. *Reconnaissance of titaniferous sandstone deposits of Utah, Wyoming, New Mexico and Colorado.* U.S. BUREAU OF MINES REPORT OF INVESTIGATION 5860.

Gregory, H. E., and R. C. Moore. 1931. *The Kaiparowits region, a geographic and geologic reconnaissance of parts of Utah and Arizona.* U.S. GEOLOGICAL SURVEY PROFESSIONAL PAPER 164.

Hettinger, R. D., L. N. R. Roberts, L. R. H. Biewick, and M. A. Kirschbaum. 1996. *Preliminary investigations of the distribution and resources of coal in the Kaiparowits Plateau, southern Utah.* U.S. GEOLOGICAL SURVEY OPEN-FILE REPORT 96-539.

Montgomery, S. L. 1984. *Kaiparowits Basin-an old frontier with new potential.* PETROLEUM FRONTIERS 1:4-25.

Peterson, P. R. 1973. *Upper Valley field.* UTAH GEOLOGICAL AND MINERALOGICAL SURVEY OIL AND GAS FIELD STUDIES 7.

Rauzi, S. L. 1990. *Distribution of Proterozoic hydrocarbon source rock in northern Arizona and southern Utah.* ARIZONA OIL AND GAS CONSERVATION COMMISSION SPECIAL PUBLICATION 5.

Ritzma, H. R. 1980. *Oil-impregnated sandstone deposits, Circle Cliffs Uplift, Utah.* Pages 343-351, in M. D. Picard, editor. HENRY MOUNTAINS SYMPOSIUM GUIDEBOOK. Volume VIII. Utah Geological Association.

Sargent, K. A. 1984. *Environmental geologic studies of the Kaiparowits coal-basin area, Utah.* U.S. GEOLOGICAL SURVEY BULLETIN 1601.

Sargent, K. A., and D. E. Hansen. 1980. *Landform map of the Kaiparowits coal-basin area, Utah.* U.S. GEOLOGICAL SURVEY MISCELLANEOUS INVESTIGATIONS SERIES MAP I-1033-G, SCALE 1:125,000.

Uphoff, T. L. 1997. *Precambrian Chuar source rock play-an exploration case history in southern Utah.* AMERICAN ASSOCIATION OF PETROLEUM GEOLOGISTS BULLETIN 81:1-15.

U.S. Department of Defense. STRATEGIC AND CRITICAL MINERALS REPORT TO THE CONGRESS (issued bi-annually). Government Printing Office. Washington, D.C.

CHAPTER TWO

Paleontological Resources

David D. Gillette

President Clinton cited outstanding paleontological resources in his proclamation that established the Grand Staircase–Escalante National Monument. Paleontology has been important in this region of Kane and Garfield Counties in southern Utah, particularly in the past two decades. Geological formations that crop out at the surface in the Monument, and are therefore accessible for paleontological research, range in age from the mid-Permian to Quaternary (the past 256 million years). The formations found to be the most productive for fossils are from the Cretaceous period, during the time of dinosaurs.

This paper is a shortened and modified version of the more comprehensive assessment of paleontological resources in the Grand Staircase–Escalante National Monument published earlier this year by the Utah Geological Survey (Gillette and Hayden, 1997). Geological terminology follows that of Doelling (1975), Doelling and Davis (1989), and Allison (1997). Sources of paleontological information used to compile this report are given in Gillette and Hayden (1997).

Stratigraphy

Sedimentary rocks, deposited over the past 256 million years, dominate the surficial geology of the Monument (Figure 2.1; Doelling and Davis, 1989). Following is a description of the most prominent geological formations and the environments in which they were deposited for each of the three geological eras: the Paleozoic, Mesozoic, and Cenozoic.

Permian System (286 to 245 million years ago; Late Paleozoic era). The oldest exposed rocks in the region are Permian in age and include the Hermit Shale, Coconino Sandstone, Toroweap Formation, White Rim Sandstone, and Kaibab Limestone. The sediments that comprise these formations were deposited in marine and shallow marine environments.

Triassic System (245 to 208 million years ago; early Mesozoic era). Triassic rocks in the Monument include the Moenkopi Formation (deposited in intertidal or shallow marine environments) and the Chinle Formation (stream deposits).

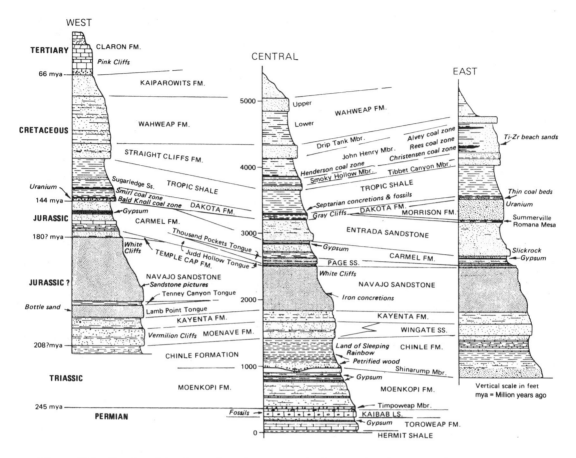

Figure 2.1. Stratigraphic relationships (west to east) of exposed rock units in the Grand Staircase–Escalante National Monument (from Doelling and Davis, 1989).

Jurassic System *(208 to 145 million years ago; Middle Mesozoic era).* The Lower Jurassic Wingate Sandstone (massive dunes), Moenave Formation (stream and lake deposits), Kayenta Formation (stream and lake deposits), and the Navajo Sandstone (massive dunes), are the oldest of the Jurassic formations in the Monument.

The Middle Jurassic formations are the Page Sandstone and Carmel Formation (marine limestones, mudstones, and evaporites); and the Entrada Sandstone and Romana Sandstone, which are marginal marine sediments, evaporites, and massive dune fields.

The Morrison Formation represents the Upper Jurassic series, deposited as lake sediments, floodplain sediments, evaporites, dunes, mudflats, and stream sediments. Elsewhere the Morrison has yielded some of the most spectacular dinosaur fossils in the world.

Cretaceous System *(145 to 65 million years ago; Late Mesozoic era).* As much as 7,500 feet of Upper Cretaceous strata and 3,000 feet of Tertiary strata underlie the Kaiparowits Plateau. Upper Cretaceous strata include, in stratigraphic order (oldest to youngest), the Dakota, Tropic Shale, Straight Cliffs, Wahweap, and Kaiparowits Formations, and the lower part of the Canaan Peak Formation. The Dakota Formation, Tropic Shale, and Straight Cliffs Formation are exposed along the margins of the Kaiparowits Plateau but are buried by younger strata in the central region. These sedimentary units were deposited under conditions ranging from shallow marine to terrestrial. The fossils found in the Cretaceous formations in the Monument reflect fluctuations in sea level during the time that inland oceans were retracting from this part of the North American continent. They contain some of the most outstanding records of Mesozoic fossil mammals in the world.

Tertiary System (65 to 1.8 million years ago; Cenozoic era). By early Tertiary time, regional tectonic activity and sea level changes had caused the final withdrawal of the shallow marine seaways. Volcanic activity in the region produced volcanic deposits that blanketed the area periodically, while rivers and streams eroded upland areas and deposited sediments in lowlands. Tertiary strata in the Monument include the upper part of the Canaan Peak Formation, the Pine Hollow and Wasatch (Claron) Formations, and the overlying volcanic rocks of the Mount Dutton Formation and Osiris Tuff. Tertiary fossils have been found in the Claron Formation, but otherwise are not well known in the Monument.

Quaternary System (1.8 million years ago to the present; Late Cenozoic era). By the Quaternary period, the Colorado Plateau was elevated well above sea level, and tectonic activity in the Rocky Mountain region had produced massive mountain ranges in Utah and surrounding states. Fluctuating glacial conditions on a global scale included alpine glaciers as far south as central Utah, with attendant climate fluctuations that affected the entire continent. In the Monument, sediments that accumulated during this time include windblown sand, a variety of river and stream deposits including silt, sand, and gravel, and mass-wasting deposits such as landslides and talus debris. Basalts from nearby volcanic vents also accumulated in the Monument during the Quaternary, affecting drainage patterns and erosional conditions.

Paleontology

Most of the geological formations in the Monument contain fossils. Certain rock types, especially limestones and coal, are almost always richly fossiliferous. Because some formations crop out more extensively, or are more accessible, scientific surveys of the various formations in the Monument are uneven. Exposed surfaces are widespread, allowing access to most formations within the Monument. These exposures facilitate paleontological fieldwork. Paleontological studies have been conducted within the boundaries of the Monument and vicinity since the middle of the 19th century. The fossil record includes marine and terrestrial fossils that are critical to correlating the Monument's stratigraphy with other areas, reconstruction of ancient environments, and the study of the evolving faunas and floras.

Reports of fossils from the Monument used for stratigraphy date back to the early part of the 20th century. Most of those published records are imprecise at best, making it difficult to determine the exact locations of the discovered fossils. In the past decade, paleontological research in the area now included in the Grand Staircase–Escalante National Monument has expanded dramatically. To the extent that the locality information is accurate and available, it is possible to summarize the knowledge of the paleontology of the Monument with a measure of confidence. Nevertheless, knowledge of the paleontology for all geologic formations in the Monument remains meager at best. Despite long lists of animals and plants that constitute the known biotas for each formation, most fossils have not been thoroughly studied. However, paleontologists have recently contributed a considerable effort to improve that knowledge, especially for the Cretaceous formations.

Most of the formations that are exposed in the Monument are found elsewhere in Utah. Some extend throughout the Colorado Plateau and beyond. However, because of changing geographic conditions related to plate tectonics, the fossils in each formation in the Monument represent specific, ancient geographic conditions. For example, the Morrison Formation, famous for its Jurassic dinosaurs, extends from central New Mexico to northern Montana, and from western Oklahoma to central Utah. Exposures of the Morrison Formation in the Monument are at the westernmost occurrence of that formation; Morrison dinosaurs and other organisms found in the Monument are therefore the westernmost biota known for that formation. The Morrison biota in the Monument should reflect the influence of geography on habitat, a subject that has not yet reached maturity in paleontological research. Paleontologists suspect that animal and plant distributions were not uniform throughout the Morrison, but instead varied north to south, east to west, lowland to upland, and wet land to dry land. Geographic and climatic conditions during the depositional history of the Morrison within the Monument were therefore different from conditions elsewhere in the Morrison outside the Monument. Consequently, the group of fossil organisms (or biota) found in the Morrison Formation in the Monument is unique. Similar statements can be made for each formation in the Monument.

In contrast, several Cretaceous formations are known only from southern Utah, in particular the Straight Cliffs, Wahweap, and Kaiparowits Formations, all of which are exposed extensively within the Monument. Because of the extremely limited geographic extent of these formations, their biotas represent restricted and unique habitats and populations. Paleontologists have begun to study the fossils from these formations in earnest because of these unique conditions of limited geography and restricted populations.

Fossils from every formation in the Monument are important for a variety of reasons: (1) they represent the populations that lived in this area when the sediments in those formations were deposited; (2) they represent various habitats and geographic effects in the Monument that were influenced by tectonic activity and sea level changes; and (3) some represent highly restricted habitats and depositional conditions with unique biotas that are known only from southern Utah, especially from the Monument. The biotas in those formations are therefore unique and cannot be duplicated anywhere else.

Several of the geologic formations in the Monument are virtually barren of fossils, and in several others the fossil record is sparse. In some formations, however, the fossil record is expanding rapidly, owing to considerable research that has been conducted in the area since the mid-1980s. Recently, several of the Cretaceous formations have been studied intensely for their record of vertebrate life. Mammals and dinosaurs are particularly important targets for this ongoing research, which has produced thousands of specimens that are housed in several major institutions.

Fossils occur broadly throughout the formations within the Monument. Most technical publications do not provide exact locality information. Most records in the Utah Geological Survey (UGS) database are specific only to the level of township and range (roughly thirty-six square miles).

The list of fossil localities is incomplete for primarily two reasons: Paleontologists and their museums are generally reluctant to divulge exact locality information in print in order to protect the sites; and fossils occur broadly throughout the formations, rather than only at isolated sites. Fossils found in one location may be expected elsewhere at the same stratigraphic horizon. Therefore, a specific fossil locality is an indication of the fossil content of a formation at a certain stratigraphic position.

Selected Paleontological Resources by Geologic Formation

Gillette and Hayden (1997) presented a comprehensive overview of the fossil record for each formation in the Monument, including extensive faunal and floral lists. Knowledge of the paleontology of these formations is uneven, as is illustrated by the following three examples. Cretaceous formations have been studied with great intensity in the Monument and surrounding area, while formations of all other ages have been examined only cursorily.

Example 1: Chinle Formation (Late Triassic). Geologists working in the Monument and immediate vicinity have reported abundant carbon-based material, logs of petrified wood, a palynological (pollen) assemblage of twenty taxa, and extensive occurrences of as yet unexamined fossil bones and plants. Very little of this record has been studied systematically. The floral and faunal list spans a broad spectrum of fossils, including plants, petrified wood, snails, clams, fish, insects, horseshoe crabs, ostracodes, reptiles, and tracks.

The plants and animals of the Chinle Formation represent terrestrial and freshwater habitats. Elsewhere (for example, the Petrified Forest National Monument, Arizona, and the Ghost Ranch area, New Mexico) the Chinle Formation has produced hundreds of species, including the oldest dinosaurs in North America, and perhaps the world. Exposures of the Chinle Formation hold great promise for discovery of important plants and animals that constituted the biota that existed with the earliest dinosaurs. This formation deserves systematic fieldwork in the Monument for its potential fossil content, especially dinosaurs and their relatives.

Example 2: *Morrison Formation (Late Jurassic)*. The list of confirmed fossils in the Morrison Formation in the Monument and its vicinity includes plants, dinosaurs, and other reptiles. None of these have been identified to even the genus level of classification. In essence, almost nothing is known about the fossils of this formation in the Monument.

Elsewhere, the Morrison Formation has produced the classic dinosaurs of the Jurassic period (for example, *Allosaurus, Apatosaurus, Barosaurus, Brachiosaurus, Camptosaurus, Ceratosaurus, Diplodocus, Seismosaurus, Stegosaurus, Supersaurus*, and many others). Dinosaurs and associated animals and plants from the Morrison Formation have become the world standard for Late Jurassic faunas and floras.

Faunal and floral lists from important sites such as Dinosaur National Monument typically include several hundred taxa of fish, amphibians, reptiles (including dinosaurs), mammals, invertebrates, plants, pollen, and spores. Many of the most important sites in the Morrison Formation are in Utah and Colorado, but none are close to the Monument. Unpublished records of dinosaur sites in this formation within the Monument indicate that it holds considerable promise for productive and important sites. Discovery of dinosaurs and associated fossils in the Monument will be critical to understanding the geographic and temporal variation of the Late Jurassic dinosaurs because of its geographic setting as the westernmost occurrence of the Morrison Formation in North America.

Example 3: *Kaiparowits Formation (Late Cretaceous)*. This formation is the youngest of the Cretaceous formations in the Monument. Pollen and spores, turtle shell fragments, dinosaur bones, molluscs, and plant fossils had been recognized in the Kaiparowits Formation prior to the 1980s. Until the past decade, little concentrated paleontological research in this formation was undertaken in the Monument.

The Kaiparowits Formation in the Monument has been the focus of considerable attention by paleontologists since the mid-1980s. With 155 taxa known from the Kaiparowits, its fauna and flora is the most extensive Late Cretaceous biota in Utah, and one of the most important in North America. The biota includes a long list of pollen and spores, plants, clams, snails, sharks, skates, rays, bony fish, amphibians, turtles, lizards, crocodiles, dinosaurs, birds, and mammals.

The stratigraphic position of the Kaiparowits Formation, immediately preceding the major extinction episode at the end of the Cretaceous period, is especially critical for the mammals in this formation. The fauna includes roughly thirty taxa of mammals, all of them small and ranging in size from that of shrews to squirrels. The list includes some of the earliest marsupial mammals and true placental mammals in the world. These mammals existed immediately before the great expansion of mammals following the extinction of the dinosaurs. Research on the habitats and paleobiological setting of the terrestrial animals and plants of the Late Cretaceous is presently the object of considerable effort within the Monument.

Conclusion

Fossils occur throughout the Grand Staircase–Escalante National Monument. The paleontological record for several formations has been recognized in recent years as worthy of considerable research for purposes of stratigraphic correlation, understanding changing paleobiological conditions on the land and in the sea, and understanding the evolution of plants and animals during the waning stages of the reign of dinosaurs in North America in the Cretaceous period. Additional research should be directed toward Triassic and Jurassic formations, which have high potential for critical discoveries relating to the origin and radiation of dinosaurs, and Quaternary sediments, which probably contain mammoths and their associated floras and faunas.

Knowledge of the paleontology of all the formations in the Monument is still rudimentary, as indicated by the recent intensified interest in the fossils of the Monument and vicinity. For all formations, fieldwork, museum curation, and laboratory analysis are essential.

A comprehensive plan to identify and study fossils in the Monument should be organized to amplify knowledge of the prehistoric life of all formations that have fossils. Execution of the plan must extend beyond simple inventory of sites, to include three principal features. First, the plan should provide for a preliminary analysis, including literature research, database review, and communications with active researchers; on-the-ground prospecting and sampling; specimen preparation and curation of samples in appropriate museums; and evaluation of the samples and prospecting results. Second, the plan should address excavation, including excavation of selected important localities; laboratory preparation on excavated specimens; curation in accredited museums; and research and publication by specialists as appropriate. Third, provisions must be made for final evaluation of sites and formations for their fossils, including assessment of long-term potential for additional production of important specimens; assessment of scientific and educational values; and recommendations for mitigation.

The state-supported natural history museums in Utah are understaffed and underfunded for paleontological research and collection management. These are the Utah Museum of Natural History, University of Utah; the Prehistoric Museum, College of Eastern Utah; and the Utah Fieldhouse of Natural History State Park in Vernal. With sufficient support to carry out the mandate to conduct excavations, study, and curate Utah's paleontological resources, the knowledge concerning the past life of the Monument, and indeed all of Utah, would be greatly expanded.

References

Allison, M. L., compiler. 1997. *A preliminary assessment of energy and mineral resources within the Grand Staircase–Escalante National Monument.* UTAH GEOLOGICAL SURVEY CIRCULAR 93.

Doelling, H. H. 1975. *Geology and mineral resources of Garfield County, Utah.* UTAH GEOLOGICAL AND MINERAL SURVEY BULLETIN 107.

Doelling, H. H., and F. D. Davis. 1989. *The geology of Kane County, Utah—geology, mineral resources, geologic hazards.* UTAH GEOLOGICAL AND MINERAL SURVEY BULLETIN 124.

Gillette, D. D., and M. C. Hayden. 1997. *A preliminary inventory of paleontological resources within the Grand Staircase–Escalante National Monument, Utah.* UTAH GEOLOGICAL SURVEY CIRCULAR 96.

CHAPTER THREE

The Biota and Ecology

Jayne Belnap

The Antiquities Act of 1906 gives the president of the United States the power to set aside areas of outstanding scientific interest, with the caveat that these areas be the minimum necessary to protect the identified objects of interest. This chapter will survey the objects of biological interest that are found in the Grand Staircase–Escalante National Monument, discuss why they are unique or of interest to scientists and the public, and determine whether the Monument is the minimum area required to protect their scientific value.

What Is of Biological Interest in This Area?

Wildlife. The Monument is home to approximately 300 species of amphibians, birds, mammals, and reptiles. This diverse set of wildlife species includes more than 20 species of birds of prey such as the bald eagle and the peregrine falcon. It is within the historical range of the California condor. This region contains two of the seven recognized centers of endemism for fishes of the western United States (Davidson et al., 1996). Successful reintroductions of bighorn sheep, Rocky Mountain elk, and Merriam and Grand turkeys have added to the biodiversity found here. More than 360 km of streams in the Monument add greatly to the value of this area as wildlife habitat (F. C. Jensen pers. commun.; Utah Wilderness Coalition, 1990).

Vascular Plants. Among the most outstanding biological resources in the Monument are the diverse and unusual vascular plant populations. Although deserts in general have lower plant diversity than more mesic areas, the Monument has more species than would be predicted for this type of landscape. In addition, many of the plants found in this region are unique. The Canyonlands vegetation province, much of which is within the Monument boundaries, is considered the richest floristic region in the Intermountain West. It contains 50 percent of Utah's rare flora, with 90 percent of these rare and endemic species found on substrates typical of the Monument (Cronquist et al., 1972). In the United States, Utah has one of the highest rates of endemism (percentage of the flora considered for listing as threatened or endangered, and percentage of flora considered as rare species; Davidson et al., 1996). Kane and Garfield Counties have the highest rates of endemism in the state. As a result, the Monument contains an astounding 125 species of plants that occur only in Utah or on the Colorado Plateau. Eleven species of plants found in the Monument are found nowhere else (Albee et al., 1988; Atwood et al., 1991; Shultz, 1993; Utah Natural Heritage Program unpublished; Welsh, 1978). Consequently, this area has one of the highest rates of plant endemism in the United States (Cronquist et al., 1972).

High floral diversity and high rates of endemism occur for several reasons. First, four major floras are represented in the Monument. Plants from the Great Basin to the northwest and the Arizona deserts to the south dominate the flora, and are mixed with a smaller number of plants from the Mojave Desert to the southwest and the Great Plains to the east. With such a large pool of plant species to draw from, there is an unusually high number of species for a desert region.

Second, the area contains a large number of ancient plant species. Many areas of the Monument have been uplifted over geologic time with little deformation. Subsequent erosion has thus exposed large expanses of more or less "pure," unmixed substrates. In addition, the area was not directly affected by ice sheets in the Pleistocene, and thus it offered refuge to many plants during times of climatic and geological instability in other regions. As a result, the area contains many components of the past Arcto-Tertiary flora, which have both enriched the present flora as well as provided material for the evolution of new plant species.

Third, this area contains a rich concentration of diverse substrates occurring in proximity to each other. Different substrates are a result of different environments present during deposition. Within the Monument are sediments that were laid down under a range of sea depths and under different oxygen concentrations. Freshwater and aeolian (windblown sand) deposits are represented as well. Each resultant layer of rock, and soils derived from that rock, has different chemical and textural characteristics, and therefore supports different plant communities. Thus, a high diversity of substrates contributes directly to high diversity in plants.

Fourth, the Monument contains lands that stretch from low deserts to high plateaus. These elevational gradients provide many varied environments and niches for plants to occupy, resulting in high numbers of plant species.

Speciation is generally favored by a combination of isolation and stressful environments, occurring in this area on several scales. The entire Colorado Plateau is isolated by large mountains that act as barriers to the dispersal of plants adapted to arid and semiarid environments. On an intermediate scale, large expanses of substrates that differ in chemistry may act as a barrier to plants not adapted to those conditions. Many soils in the Monument have high levels of shrink/swell clays and/or salt levels that limit the establishment and growth of many plants. Therefore, plants on these substrates tend to be highly specialized, and these soils can act as effective barriers to the dispersal of non-adapted species. On a still smaller scale, many small pockets of specialized environments occur throughout the Monument including habitats such as hanging gardens, dunal pockets, tinajas, highly saline soils, and year-round springs. Plants adapted to these conditions are isolated by large expanses of unsuitable habitat. Barriers can be fairly small, but highly effective. An example of this is the Waterpocket Fold. Even though this geologic feature is only 5 km wide in some places, it is an effective barrier to many species of vascular plants. The subsequent isolation has resulted in differential plant speciation. As a consequence, the same formation, Mancos shale, supports different floras on each side of the fold.

Organisms have difficulty in adapting to extreme and/or unpredictable environments. Low precipitation and large temperature ranges result in deserts being extreme environments. Because areas with lower rainfall also experience high variability in the timing and amounts of rain, deserts are unpredictable environments as well. Certain soil types may exacerbate these extreme or unpredictable conditions. For example, whereas sandy soils provide plants with fairly constant, though low, levels of water and nutrients, clay or shale soils often experience wide fluctuations in the availability of these resources. Sandy soils generally support a wide variety of plant species with more generalist characteristics, whereas clay soils generally have a more restricted, specialized flora. Because of this, many of the fine-textured soils in the Monument are highly stressful, and have provided strong selective forces for plant evolution.

Limited geologic deformation, combined with an erosional rather than a depositional environment, has exposed many substrates with minimal mixing. Lack of mixing has resulted in large exposures of "pure" parent material, with little or no gradation between vastly different soil chemistries and textures. The resulting sharp contrasts between soils has isolated many plant species, providing opportunity for speciation (Axelrod, 1960; Cronquist et al., 1972; Davidson et al., 1996; K. Harper pers. commun.; Shultz, 1993; Stebbins, 1985).

Invertebrates. Few studies on invertebrates have been conducted in desert environments, and even fewer in remote regions such as those in the Monument. However, given the number of unique and isolated environments in this area, many new and unusual species undoubtedly await discovery.

Many plant species have specialized pollinators. Since many plants in this region have highly restricted distributions, we can also expect to find associated invertebrate species with similarly restricted distributions. For example, a recent survey of ground-dwelling bees in the San Rafael Swell, Utah, a nearby area with similarly high rates of plant endemism, found an astonishing 316 species of these bees, with 42 of these species new to science (Davidson et al., 1996; T. Griswold pers. commun.). Since the Monument contains a wider variety of substrates and a greater number of unique plant species than the Swell, invertebrate surveys would be expected to turn up a similar, if not greater, number of unique invertebrates.

Other uncommon or unique invertebrates are to be expected in the isolated and/or specialized environments in the Monument. For instance, the limited dispersal capabilities of soil-dwelling organisms such as nematodes and microarthropods may have resulted in the isolation necessary for new species to evolve (Michener, 1979; Neff and Simpson, 1993).

Riparian Areas-Movement Corridors. Perennial streams are a highly limited resource in deserts. The Utah Division of Wildlife Resources estimates that over 80 percent of desert wildlife rely on these areas for food and cover, making them critical habitat for many animals (M. Moretti pers. commun.). These areas also act as migration corridors for many species, including deer, neotropical migrants, mountain lions, and bears. The Monument contains several perennial streams that connect the high plateaus to the low desert, preserving these migration corridors and increasing the Monument's ability to conserve genetic and population diversity of plants and animals (IUCN, 1978; Kushlan, 1979; Meffe and Carroll, 1994; Newmark, 1985; Pickett and Thompson, 1978; Primack, 1993; Soule, 1987; Soule and Wilcox, 1980).

Adaptation to Disturbance. Plants and soil organisms are generally adapted to the disturbance regimes under which they evolved. Consequently, changing the type, quantity, or timing of disturbance can have profound, ecosystem-wide effects. On the Colorado Plateau, where prehistoric soil disturbance was restricted to a few large mammals (J. Mead pers. commun.), current populations of invertebrates and small mammals are limited compared with other deserts (Belnap, 1995; D. Davidson pers. commun.), and decomposition rates (and therefore nutrient availability) are very slow (Webb and Wilshire, 1996). The introduction of livestock and recreation has resulted in widespread changes in ecosystem functions.

The Monument offers many opportunities to explore the effects of such changes in land use. Within the boundaries are grasslands, blackbrush and piñon-juniper communities that have never been grazed by domestic livestock, and that are seldom visited by people. There are waterfall-blocked canyons that offer a rare opportunity to study relatively undisturbed riparian areas (Utah Wilderness Coalition, 1990).

Cryptobiotic Soils. Cryptobiotic soil crusts, consisting of soil cyanobacteria, lichens, and mosses, play an important ecological role in the Monument. Most soils in the Monument have varying degrees of cryptobiotic crusts, which increase soil stability of otherwise easily eroded soils, increase water infiltration in a region that receives limited precipitation, and increase fertility in soils often limited in essential nutrients such as nitrogen and carbon (Belnap et al., 1994; Belnap and Gardner, 1993; Harper and Marble, 1988; Johansen, 1993; Metting, 1991; Williams et al., 1995a,b).

Cyanobacteria and cyanolichen components of these soil crusts are important contributors of fixed nitrogen (Mayland and McIntosh, 1966; Rychert and Skujins, 1974). These crusts appear to be the dominant source of nitrogen in cold-desert piñon-juniper and grassland ecosystems in southern Utah (Evans and Ehleringer, 1993; Evans and Belnap, in press). Biological soil crusts are also important sources of fixed carbon on sparsely vegetated areas common throughout the West (Beymer and Klopatek, 1991). Plants growing on crusted soil often show higher concentrations and/or greater total accumulation of various essential nutrients when compared with plants growing in adjacent, uncrusted soils (Belnap and Harper, 1995; Harper and Pendleton, 1993).

Cryptobiotic soil crusts are highly susceptible to soil surface disturbances such as trampling by hooves or feet, or driving of off-road vehicles, especially in soils with low aggregate stability such as the sands found throughout the Monument (Belnap and Gardner, 1993; Gillette et al., 1980; Webb and Wilshire, 1983). Cyanobacterial filaments, lichens, and mosses are brittle when dry, and crush easily when subjected to compressional or shear forces by trampling or vehicular traffic. Because crustal organisms are only metabolically active when wet, reestablishment time is slow in arid systems. While cyanobacteria are mobile, and can often move up through disturbed sediments to reach needed light levels for photosynthesis, lichens and mosses are incapable of such movement and often die as a result of burial. On newly disturbed surfaces, mosses and lichens in desert environments generally have extremely slow colonization and growth rates. Assuming adjoining soils are stable and rainfall is average, recovery rates for lichen cover in southern Utah have been most recently estimated at a minimum of 45 years, while recovery of moss cover was estimated at 250 years (Belnap, 1993). Due to this slow recolonization underlying soils are left vulnerable to both wind and water erosion for at least 20 years after disturbance (Belnap and Gillette, 1997). Because soils take 5,000 to 10,000 years to form in arid areas such as the Monument (Webb, 1983), accelerated soil loss may be an irreversible loss. Loss of soil also means loss of site fertility through loss of organic matter, fine soil particles, nutrients, and microbial populations in soils (Harper and Marble, 1988; Schimel et al., 1985). Moving sediments further destabilize adjoining areas by burying adjacent crusts, leading to their death, or by providing material for "sandblasting" nearby surfaces, thus increasing wind erosion rates (Belnap, 1995; McKenna-Neuman et al., 1996)

Soil erosion in arid lands is a major threat worldwide. Beasley et al. (1984) estimated that in rangeland of the United States alone, 3.6 million hectares have some degree of accelerated wind erosion. Relatively undisturbed biological soil crusts can contribute a great deal of stability to otherwise highly erodible soils. Unlike vascular plant cover, crustal cover is not reduced in drought, and unlike rain crusts, these organic crusts are present year-round. Consequently, they offer stability over time and in adverse conditions that is often lacking in other soil surface protectors. Unfortunately disturbed crusts now cover vast areas in the western United States as a result of ever-increasing recreational and commercial uses of these semiarid and arid areas. Based on the results of several studies (Belnap and Gillette, 1997; McKenna-Neuman et al., 1996; Williams et al., 1996) the tremendous land area currently being impacted may lead to significant increases in regional and global wind erosion rates.

Within the Monument, grazing, offroad vehicles, and other forms of recreation have greatly impacted crustal integrity. On one hand, it can be expected that soil erosion has been increased and nitrogen inputs in these areas have been greatly reduced. On the other hand, the Monument contains many areas that have not been extensively grazed, where crusts and other soil processes are relatively undisturbed.

Lack of Well-Traveled Roads. Many animal species are affected by habitat fragmentation, which can be a result of radical land use changes such as the construction of houses, or more subtle developments such as roads or trails. Roads provide increased human access. Increased access can result in direct impacts, such as trampling of soil resources and soil erosion, and indirect impacts, such as disruption of wildlife at critical places or times. Depending on the species of concern, severe disruption of migration movements, foraging patterns, and/or reproductive success can result. The Monument is an important resource because roadless areas occur within its boundaries; of the roads that do exist, most are seldom traveled, thus reducing their fragmentation impact (Bolger et al., 1991; Davidson et al., 1996; Harris, 1984; Oxley et al., 1974; Rost and Bailey, 1979; Saunders et al., 1991).

Roads also pose problems because they act as corridors for exotic plant and animal invasions. Because roadsides are disturbed habitats, they generally favor those species evolved to succeed in such environments. Car tires, clothing, and pets can rapidly spread exotic plant propagules over large areas. Animals often hitchhike in cars. Few roads and limited traffic are essential to keeping exotics to a minimum.

More than 50 percent of the western United States is dominated by exotic plant species, threatening the population viability of many native plants and animals. More than 300,000 acres are irreplaceably converted to exotic annual grasses a year, increasing fire frequency that results in loss of forage and habitat for both wildlife and livestock. Once an ecosystem is dominated by exotic plant species, it is generally difficult or impossible to reestablish native species (Bergelson et al., 1993; Billings, 1990, 1994; EPA-EMAP unpublished).

What Scientific Opportunities Does the Monument Offer?

The biological resources found within the Monument have extraordinary scientific value. The Monument provides an unparalleled opportunity to study speciation and evolution, independent of climate, given its close juxtaposition of diverse substrates. Having ancient plant species alongside new species lets us examine how plant species adapt to different conditions. The presence of steep elevational gradients allows scientists to sort out the differential roles of temperature and precipitation in the structuring of plant and animal communities. The elevational gradients with substrates of diverse depositional environments help scientists determine the respective roles of soil chemistry, soil physical characteristics, rainfall, and temperature factors in controlling community structure and functioning. And of great importance, these substrates and elevational gradients are replicated within the Monument, giving scientists the ability to speak much more confidently of their findings, as well as to extrapolate their results to a much larger area.

Relatively undisturbed habitats can provide information on the natural variation of ecosystems, supplying a baseline against which to measure the effects of different land uses on the major vegetative communities. Undisturbed habitats also provide goals for restoration and management. Replicated perennial streams offer the ability to study animal migrations and the importance of riparian areas to desert species. Given limited temporal and spatial disturbance on the Colorado Plateau, ecologists can use this area for comparison with other deserts and ecosystems that have evolved with much greater and more frequent disturbance.

The ability to apply insights gained from areas of one size to areas of a different size is important, and the Monument contains many different, discrete, and relatively simple ecosystems that occur on several scales. Effects of isolation on different scales and in different habitats can be addressed here, using communities such as hanging gardens, salty soils, tinajas, shallow soils, and dunal pockets.

The Monument is well suited to answering questions about global climate change. Because it is dry, and located on the boundary between ecosystems dependent on summer precipitation and those dependent on winter precipitation, vegetative communities in this area should be especially sensitive to changes in precipitation. The presence of elevational gradients makes this area even more interesting for such studies. Through packrat middens in the area we can reconstruct past floras, and therefore past climates. This in turn helps us understand the effect climate change has had on plants and animals in the past so we can predict what might happen with climate change.

Relatively few systems have as low spatial and temporal disturbance as are found in the Monument. And even fewer systems, especially in the western United States, have areas ungrazed by livestock. As a result, the Monument offers a unique opportunity to study the effects of disturbance on a landscape not evolutionarily adapted to such disturbance and how such disturbance structures plant and animal communities.

Is the Monument the Minimum Size Necessary to Protect the Listed Objects of Interest?

Several characteristics make an area especially valuable for science. One of the most important is the ability to replicate studies across a large area. Through replication, scientists can make much stronger statements about the results of their studies. Validating results found in one area using additional areas enables scientists to justify extrapolating their results to much larger areas. By containing replicates of the different major substrates, vegetation communities, elevations, and perennial streams, the Monument is of far more value to science than if it were so small as to have only one or two examples of each.

As pressures increase on natural resources and some are lost inadvertently, protecting multiple examples of different resources will become increasing important to ensure their preservation. For example, multiple corridors for animal movement between high plateau and low desert regions provides replication for scientists as well as insurance that some migration corridors will be protected, in spite of wildfire, development, or other events that may compromise other corridors.

It is well accepted in conservation biology that the connection of protected areas increases the value of those protected areas. Consequently, the connection the Monument provides between Glen Canyon, Canyonlands, Grand Canyon, Capitol Reef, and Bryce Canyon National Park units increases the value of all these areas for protection of viability of plant and animal populations. It is, indeed, the minimum size necessary to achieve its purposes.

Sheer size and vastness of the Monument is essential to protect the objects listed in the proclamation. Great diversity of habitats is critical to protection of natural resources, especially wildlife. Protection of the "plant speciation laboratory" that the Monument provides is dependent on large expanses of substrates as well (IUCN, 1978; Kushlan, 1979; Loope et al., 1988; Meffe and Carroll, 1994; Newmark, 1985; Pickett and Thompson, 1978; Primack, 1993; Soule, 1987; Soule and Wilcox, 1980).

References

Albee, B. J., M. Schultz, and S. Goodrich. 1988. ATLAS OF THE VASCULAR PLANTS OF UTAH. Utah Museum of Natural History, Occasional Publications No. 7. University of Utah, Salt Lake City, UT.

Atwood, D., J. Holland, R. Bolander, B. Franklin, D. E. House, L. Armstrong, K. Thorne, and L. England. 1991. UTAH THREATENED, ENDANGERED, AND SENSITIVE PLANT FIELD GUIDE. BLM, Utah State Office, Salt Lake City, UT.

Axlerod, D. I. 1960. *The evolution of flowering plants.* Pages 227-305 in S. Tax, editor. EVOLUTION AFTER DARWIN. Volume I, The evolution of life. University of Chicago Press, Chicago, IL.

Beasley, R. P., M. Gregory, and T. R. McCarty. 1984. EROSION AND SEDIMENT POLLUTION CONTROL. 2nd edition. Iowa State University Press, Ames, IA.

Belnap, J. 1993. *Recovery rates of cryptobiotic crusts: Inoculant use and assessment methods.* GREAT BASIN NATURALIST 53: 89-95.

Belnap, J. 1994. *Potential value of cyanobacterial inoculation in revegetation efforts.* Pages 179-85 in S. B. Monsen and S. G. Kitchen, editors. PROCEEDINGS-ECOLOGY AND MANAGEMENT OF ANNUAL RANGELANDS. U.S.D.A. Forest Service, Technical Report INT-GTR-313, Ogden, UT.

Belnap, J. 1995. *Surface disturbances: Their role in accelerating desertification.* ENVIRONMENTAL MONITORING AND ASSESSMENT 37: 39-57.

Belnap, J., and J. S. Gardner. 1993. *Soils microstructure in soils of the Colorado Plateau: The role of the cyanobacterium* Microcoleus vaginatus. GREAT BASIN NATURALIST 53: 40-47.

Belnap, J., and D. A. Gillette. 1997. *Disturbance of biological soil crusts: Impacts on potential wind erodibility of sandy desert soils in SE Utah, USA.* LAND DEGRADATION AND DEVELOPMENT. In Press.

Belnap, J., and K. T. Harper. 1995. *The influence of cryptobiotic soil crusts on elemental content of tissue of two desert seed plants.* ARID SOIL RESEARCH AND REHABILITATION 9: 107-15.

Bergelson, J., J. A. Newman, and E. M. Floresroux. 1993. *Rates of weed spread in spatially heterogeneous environments.* ECOLOGY 74: 999-1011.

Beymer, R. J., and J. M. Klopatek. 1991. *Potential contribution of carbon by microphytic crusts in pinyon-juniper woodlands.* ARID SOIL RESEARCH AND REHABILITATION 5: 187-98.

Billings, W.D. 1990. Bromus tectorum, *biotic cause of ecosystem impoverishment in the Great Basin.* Pages 301-322 in G. M. Woodell, editor. THE EARTH IN TRANSITION: PATTERNS AND PROCESSES OF BIOTIC IMPOVERISHMENT. Cambridge University Press, Cambridge, UK.

Billings, W.D. 1994. *Ecological impacts of cheatgrass and resultant fire on ecosystems in the western Great Basin*. Pages 22-30 in S. B. Monsen and S. G. Kitchen, editors. PROCEEDINGS, ECOLOGY AND MANAGEMENT OF ANNUAL RANGELANDS. U.S.D.A. Forest Service, technical report INT-GTR-313, Ogden, UT.

Bolger, D. T., A. C. Alberts, and M. E. Soule. 1991. *Occurrence patterns of bird species in habitat fragments: Sampling, extinction, and nested species subsets*. AMERICAN NATURALIST 137: 155-66.

Cronquist, A., A. H. Holmgren, N. H. Holmgren, and J. L. Reveal. 1972. INTERMOUNTAIN FLORA. Volume I. Hafner Publishers, NY.

Davidson, D. W., W. D. Newmark, J. W. Sites, D. K. Shiozawa, E. A. Rickart, K. T. Harper, and R. B. Keiter. 1996. *Selecting Utah wilderness areas to conserve Utah's biological diversity*. GREAT BASIN NATURALIST 56: 95-118.

Evans, R. D., and J. Belnap. *Long term consequences of disturbance on nitrogen cycling in an arid grassland*. ECOLOGY. In press.

Evans, R. D., and J. R. Ehleringer. 1993. *Broken nitrogen cycles in arid lands: Evidence from 15N of soils*. OECOLOGIA 94: 314-17.

Gillette, D. A., J. Adams, A., Endo, D., Smith, and R. Kihl. 1980. *Threshold velocities for input of soil particles into the air by desert soils*. JOURNAL OF GEOPHYSICAL RESEARCH 85: 5621-30.

Harper, K. T., and J. R. Marble. 1988. *A role for nonvascular plants in management of arid and semiarid rangelands*. Pages 135-69 in P. T. Tueller, editor. VEGETATION SCIENCE APPLICATIONS FOR RANGELAND ANALYSIS AND MANAGEMENT. Kluwer Academic Publisher, Dordrecht, Germany.

Harper, K. T., and R. L. Pendleton,. 1993. *Cyanobacteria and cyanolichens: Can they enhance availability of essential minerals for higher plants?* GREAT BASIN NATURALIST 53: 89-95.

Harris, L. D. 1984. THE FRAGMENTED FOREST: ISLAND BIOGEOGRAPHY THEORY AND THE PRESERVATION OF BIOTIC DIVERSITY. University of Chicago Press, Chicago, IL.

IUCN. 1978. CATEGORIES, OBJECTIVES AND CRITERIA FOR PROTECTED AREAS. Morges, Switzerland.

Johansen, J. R. 1993. *Cryptogamic crusts of semiarid and arid lands of North America*. JOURNAL OF PHYCOLOGY 29: 140-47.

Kushlan, J. A. 1979. *Design and management of continental wildlife reserves: Lessons from the Everglades*. BIOLOGICAL CONSERVATION 15: 281-90.

Loope, L. L., P. G. Sanchez, P. W. Tarr, W. L. Loope, and R. L. Anderson. 1988. *Biological invasions of arid land nature reserves*. BIOLOGICAL CONSERVATION 44: 95-118.

Mayland, H. F., and T. H. McIntosh. 1966. *Availability of biologically fixed atmosphere nitrogen-15 to higher plants*. NATURE 209: 421-22.

McKenna-Neuman, C., C. D. Maxwell, and J. W. Boulton. 1996. *Wind transport of sand surfaces crusted with photoautotrophic microorganisms*. CATENA 27: 229-47.

Meffe, G. K., and C. R. Carrol. 1994. PRINCIPLES OF CONSERVATION BIOLOGY. Sinauer, Sunderland, MA.

Metting, B. 1991. *Biological surface features of semiarid lands and deserts*. Pages 257-93 in J. Skujins, editor. SEMIARID LANDS AND DESERTS: SOIL RESOURCE AND RECLAMATION. Marcel Dekker, Inc., NY.

Michener, C. D. 1979. *Biogeography of the bees*. ANNALS OF THE MISSOURI BOTANICAL GARDEN 66: 277-347.

Neff, J. L., and B. B. Simpson. 1993. *Bees, pollination systems and plant diversity*. Pages 143-67 in J. LaSalle and I. E. Gauld, editors. HYMENOPTERA AND BIODIVERSITY. C. A. B. International, Wallingford, UK.

Newmark, W. D. 1985. *Legal and biotic boundaries of western North American national parks: A problem of congruence*. BIOLOGICAL CONSERVATION 33: 197-208.

Oxley, D. J., M. B. Penton, and G. B. Carmody. 1974. *The effects of roads on populations of small mammals*. JOURNAL OF APPLIED ECOLOGY 11: 51-59.

Pickett, S. T. A., and J. N. Thompson. 1978. *Patch dynamics and the design of nature reserves*. BIOLOGICAL CONSERVATION 13: 27-37.

Primack, R. B. 1993. ESSENTIALS OF CONSERVATION BIOLOGY. Sinauer, Sunderland, MA.

Rost, G. R., and J. A. Bailey. 1979. *Distribution of mule deer and elk in relation to roads*. JOURNAL OF WILDLIFE MANAGEMENT 43: 634-41.

Rychert, R. C., and J. Skujins. 1974. *Nitrogen fixation by blue-green algae-lichens crusts in the Great Basin desert*. SOIL SCIENCE SOCIETY OF AMERICA PROCEEDINGS 38: 768-71.

Saunders, D. A., R. J. Hobbs, and C. B. Margules. 1991. *Biological consequences of ecosystem fragmentation: A review*. CONSERVATION BIOLOGY 5: 18-32.

Schimel, D. S., E. F. Kelly, C. Yonker, R. Aguilar, and R. D. Heil. 1985. *Effects of erosional processes on nutrient cycling in semiarid landscapes*. Pages 571-80 in D.E. Caldwell, J. A. Brierley, and C. L. Brierley, editors. PLANETARY ECOLOGY. Van Nostrand Reinhold, NY.

Shultz, L. M. 1993. *Patterns of endemism in the Utah flora*. Pages 249-63 in R. Sivinski and K. Lightfoot, editors. SOUTHWESTERN RARE AND ENDANGERED PLANTS. New Mexico Department of Forestry and Resources Conservation Division, Miscellaneous Publication No. 2., Santa Fe, NM.

Soule, M. E. 1987. VIABLE POPULATIONS FOR CONSERVATION. Cambridge University Press, Cambridge, UK.

Soule, M. E., and B. A. Wilcox. 1980. CONSERVATION BIOLOGY: AN EVOLUTIONARY-ECOLOGICAL PERSPECTIVE. Sinauer, Sunderland, MA.

Stebbins, L. C. 1985. A FIELD GUIDE TO WESTERN REPTILES AND AMPHIBIANS. Houghton Mifflin Co., Boston, MA.

Utah Wilderness Coalition. 1990. WILDERNESS AT THE EDGE. Peregrine Smith Books, Layton, UT.

Webb, R. H. 1983. *Compaction of desert soils by off-road vehicles*. Pages 31-80 in R.H. Webb, and H. G. Wilshire, editors. ENVIRONMENTAL EFFECTS OF OFF-ROAD VEHICLES: IMPACTS AND MANAGEMENT IN ARID REGIONS. Springer-Verlag, NY.

Webb, R. H., and H. G. Wilshire. 1983. ENVIRONMENTAL EFFECTS OF OFF-ROAD VEHICLES: IMPACTS AND MANAGEMENT IN ARID REGIONS. Springer-Verlag, NY.

Welsh, S. L. 1978. *Endangered and threatened plants of Utah, a reevaluation*. GREAT BASIN NATURALIST 38: 1-18.

Williams, J. D., J. P. Dobrowolski, N. E. West, and D. A. Gillette. 1995a. *Microphytic crust influences on wind erosion*. TRANSACTIONS OF THE AMERICAN SOCIETY OF AGRICULTURAL ENGINEERS 38: 131-37.

Williams, J. D., J. P. Dobrowolski, and N. E. West. 1995b. *Microphytic crust influences on runoff and sediment production*. TRANSACTIONS OF THE AMERICAN SOCIETY OF AGRICULTURAL ENGINEERS 38: 128-31.

CHAPTER FOUR

An Archaeological Assessment

Duncan Metcalfe

At the beginning of the 20th century, five bills were introduced in the U.S. Congress to protect important historic and prehistoric sites (Rosenberg, 1980). The bills reflected a growing recognition of the magnificent archaeological sites throughout the United States (especially the Southwest), the importance of those sites as national resources, and the fact that sites were being damaged or destroyed at an alarming rate. All the bills failed. One bill was sponsored by Rep. John Lacey of Iowa, who later sponsored another piece of legislation known today as the Antiquities Act, which was signed into law by Theodore Roosevelt in 1906.

The Antiquities Act provides for punishments—fines and/or imprisonment—for unauthorized disturbance of archaeological sites located on lands managed by federal agencies. In addition, the Antiquities Act provides the president of the United States with broad (some critics say essentially unlimited) powers to create national monuments in order to protect historic and prehistoric sites and objects. Since 1906 the Antiquities Act has been used to create at least eighty-five national monuments, the most recent one being the 1.7-million-acre (2,700-square-mile) Grand Staircase–Escalante National Monument in south-central Utah.

As a formal discipline, archaeology was in its infancy in 1906. More than twenty years would pass before the exciting discovery at Folsom, New Mexico, would push the date of the earliest Americans back from about 3,000 to more than 10,000 years ago. Another 25 years or so would elapse before the invention of radiocarbon dating, which allowed archaeologists for the first time to compare prehistoric developments in Utah with those in New Hampshire, or southern France. The Antiquities Act was passed more than sixty years before American archaeologists began transforming their discipline into a truly scientific study of prehistoric lifeways.

Laws dealing with specific issues, such as the preservation of archaeological resources, often become outdated due to social, political, economic, and technological changes. Edgar Lee Hewitt, the archaeologist who drafted the legislation that became the 1906 Antiquities Act, could never have anticipated the breadth of the technologies, methods, and theories available to archaeologists today. Nor was Hewitt likely to have anticipated the magnitude of current trends related to urbanization, transportation, population growth, recreation, and tourism—factors that all contribute to the disturbance and complete destruction of a large, but largely unknown, number of archaeological sites each year. What Hewitt and his contemporaries clearly did recognize was that unless archaeological sites were protected the time would come when all the significant sites had been plundered or otherwise destroyed. The two-pronged approach incorporated in the Antiquities Act, prohibiting unauthorized disturbance of individual sites and allowing areas containing important archaeological sites to be designated national monuments, was the principal archaeological preservation legislation in the United States for sixty years.

It has become clear in the years since the establishment of the Antiquities Act that limiting development on large tracts of land is an important key to protecting sites. A number of studies, many completed in southern Utah, have demonstrated that there is a strong relationship between ease of access and the amount of damage archaeological sites have sustained (Ahlstrom et al., 1992; Honeycutt and Fetterman, 1985; Kvamme, 1990; Nickens et al., 1981; Simms, 1986a; Wylie and Nagel, 1989). Although such a strategy does not affect the amount of damage to sites by natural processes or commercial looting, it does minimize the adverse effects of "weekend" looting, vandalism, and overvisitation, now perhaps the major sources of damage to archaeological sites in this state.

Another significant advantage to setting aside large areas of land relates to archaeology as a developing science. In the past, archaeologists often focused on the excavation and analysis of individual sites and the artifacts they yielded. However, only a relatively small fraction of the range of activities conducted by prehistoric peoples is likely to be represented in any single site. Today our interest is in patterns of prehistoric land use and how those changed through time and across space (Binford, 1978, 1983). Catherine Fowler's (1982) synthesis of Isabel Kelly's (1964) ethnography of the Southern Paiute illustrates the challenge involved in ascertaining these patterns (Figure 4.1).

The Southern Paiute interviewed by Kelly provided information about their use of the environment. The most detailed data are for the Southern Paiute on the Kaibab Plateau. Kaibab settlements and camps were tightly tethered to springs, each of which was said to have had an owner. Households camping at particular springs tended to form economic units that moved across the landscape as a group, albeit a group whose membership was fairly fluid and one that might divide and fuse several times during the year.

Figure 4.1 is reflective of the reconstructed annual movements of a group of about thirty-five people from the 1870s whose winter camp was a cave in Lower Houserock Valley (#59). Their usual summer camp was located about 30 km to the north near some rock shelters south of the Paria Plateau and Vermilion Cliffs (#56; Kelly, 1964:18-19; Fowler, 1982:127,130). During the summer, they gathered Indian ricegrass and goosefoot and cached the seeds in the nearby rock shelters. They sometimes moved 50 kilometers to the south also to gather seeds (#67). In some years, during the late summer and fall, they would move to the Kaibab Plateau near Jacob Lake to hunt for deer and to gather

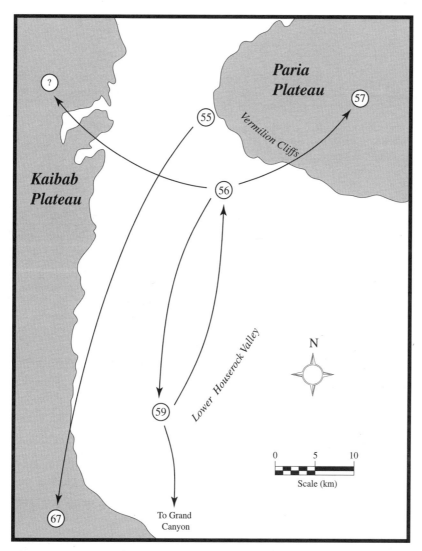

Figure 4.1. Seasonal movements of Kaibab Southern Paiute economic cluster VII (modified from Fowler 1982). Numbered locations are identified in the text.

pine nuts; in other years they moved to a spring on Paria Plateau to collect pine nuts and sagebrush seeds. When the pine nut harvest was meager, they moved to the rim of the Grand Canyon to collect agave. Each winter they returned to the cave in Lower Houserock Valley (#59) and made frequent trips to their summer camp to obtain supplies of the seeds cached there.

A few points in this ethnographic example are worth emphasizing. First, the general settlement pattern varied from year to year due to local factors influencing the availability of wild resources. Second, the settlement pattern includes both residential moves (changing the location of their camps) and logistical strategies (traveling to the summer camp during the winter to bring cached seeds back to the winter camp). Last, and without including the trips to the rim of Grand Canyon when the pine nut harvest was poor, the map covers an area of approximately 2,000 square kilometers. In other words, for an archaeologist to reconstruct the annual round of this group would require investigating a very large area.

This is not to suggest that the Southern Paiute provide a perfect analogy for how prehistoric peoples structured their movements across the landscape. It does, however, provide archaeologists with a ballpark estimate of the likely scale at which prehistoric settlement patterns will need to be investigated.

The Grand Staircase–Escalante National Monument

The area within the Monument consists of a series of plateaus, mesas, and deep canyons. Elevations range from about 2,250 meters in the northeastern section of the Monument to below 1,400 meters in the south-central portion. The highest elevations are dominated by ponderosa pine and the lowest areas are sagebrush flats. Areas intermediate in elevation support piñon-juniper woodlands. Drainages are characterized by cottonwoods, willows, and various annual plants. Caves and alcoves are frequently located in the walls of canyons and were commonly used by the prehistoric inhabitants of the region.

Archaeological investigations have been conducted sporadically within and around the Monument for about the past eighty years. The first serious work was conducted by Neil Judd, Bureau of American Ethnology, beginning in 1915. Judd focused on the sites located in the many canyons around the town of Kanab, but also visited House Rock Valley and the Paria Plateau (Judd, 1926). Jesse Nusbaum excavated the now famous early Anasazi site known as Cave Du Pont located just outside of Kanab in 1920 (Nusbaum, 1922). Julian Steward completed an archaeological reconnaissance of a number of the north-south trending canyons that bisect the Vermilion Cliffs between Kanab and the Paria River, recording a total of 142 prehistoric sites (Steward, 1941). At about the same time two brief excursions onto the Kaiparowits Plateau revealed the presence of a substantial number of prehistoric sites (Kluckhohn, 1933; Beals et al., 1945).

The largest archaeological project conducted in the area of the Monument was the Glen Canyon Salvage Project, conducted in the late 1950s and early 1960s by the University of Utah and Northern Arizona University in anticipation of the creation of Lake Powell (Jennings, 1966). While most of the effort of Jesse Jennings and his students was devoted to exploring areas inside what is now the Glen Canyon Recreation Area, substantial investigations were also undertaken in the southeastern portion of the Kaiparowits Plateau, near the center of the Monument, and along Johnson Creek, which traverses the western boundary of the Monument.

The survey on the Kaiparowits Plateau east of Basin Canyon recorded over 250 prehistoric sites (Gunnerson, 1959). Three years later, the University of Utah excavated 11 of those sites, as well as adding to the inventory of recorded prehistoric sites (Fowler and Aikens, 1963). These investigations were followed by the excavation of Bonanza Dune and Sand Hill Dune located in Johnson Canyon (Aikens, 1965). Since the mid-1960s, a few additional excavations have been conducted in or near the Monument (e.g., Moffitt et al., 1978, Nickens and Kvamme, 1981, Metcalfe, 1982, Tipps, 1992). Results of substantial surveys in and around the Monument are provided by Hauck (1979), Tipps (1988), and McFadden (1996). Tipps (1988) provides an excellent and recent summary of previous work.

In reviewing this work, two points quickly come to the fore. First, although investigations in other parts of the state clearly put humans on the scene by about 10,000 years ago, evidence for Archaic use of the region within the Monument is relatively scarce. Archaic peoples, who lived in western North America from 10,000 to 2,000 years ago, relied entirely on hunting wild animals and collecting plants to feed themselves; farming did not begin until about 2,000 years ago. Most of our understanding of Archaic lifeways is the result of excavating caves where people took shelter overnight or where they lived for part of a season. In all but the richest areas, these people appear to have been extremely mobile, moving from one area to another in pursuit of wild foods. Their tool kit was simple but diverse and suitable to their mobile lifestyle.

Evidence of Archaic people in the Monument proper consists primarily of scatters of flaked stone tools and debitage, the latter referring to the stone flakes resulting from tool making and maintenance. Affiliation is generally based on finding projectile points that are temporally diagnostic of this early time. While numerous caves are common in some of the geological strata exposed in the Monument, there is only limited evidence that they contain deposits related to Archaic occupations. Tipps (1992) reports the results of the excavation of several sites along the Burr Trail. One site, Horse Canyon Rock Shelter, had stratified deposits dating to the Late Archaic. Another site proved to be transitional between Late Archaic and Fremont. So while the evidence for significant Archaic sites on the Monument is rather scant, this may be a poor sample due to the historical emphasis of archaeologists on studying the later Anasazi and Fremont complexes.

Unlike the case for the Archaic, it is clear that the Monument contains numerous significant Anasazi and Fremont sites that range from the inception of these traditions to their demise. These local farming complexes, part of the Great Southwest Formative, which extends from northern Mexico as far north as southern Idaho, began around A.D.1 and lasted until around 1300. Characterized by variable reliance on the farming of corn, beans, and squash, these groups lived in small homesteads, villages, and towns. Sometimes producing exquisite pottery, tools of stone, bone, wood, and fiber, these groups managed to survive in the environmentally diverse and often harsh areas incorporated in the new Monument.

A number of research questions have crystallized that justify investigating the Monument. One set of questions relates to the adoption of farming by local populations.

These are fundamental questions in anthropology, since they relate to an economic transition that occurred many times in many different areas of the world after the end of the last ice age. Many of these transitions are clearly independent; people began domesticating indigenous varieties of plants and, primarily outside of the Americas, animals. In the Americas, people began cultivating and domesticating corn, beans, and squash; in Southeast Asia, rice and tubers; in the Near East, wheat and barley.

On an evolutionary time scale, these independent transitions are nearly synchronous, suggesting that a process, rather than an individual with a new idea, is responsible. Understanding that process of adaptation is the core of anthropology, and obviously has tremendous implications for understanding ourselves and our relationship with the environment today.

The prehistoric farmers in the American Southwest provide an ideal venue for investigating the advent and demise of farming as an important way of life. In Utah corn was available hundreds of years before there was a widescale shift to farming, which brought with it the production of ceramics, construction of substantial architecture, and the creation of extensive refuse areas (Wilde and Newman, 1989, Talbot and Richens, 1996). The reason for this delay is unknown; it may be that the introduced corn was a strain that grew in only a few favored locations and the delay relates to the evolution of a new strain that could thrive in the arid regions of southern Utah. Perhaps the transition to wide-scale farming required a minor climatic change; perhaps both. Only research incorporating the rapidly evolving fields of DNA analysis and climatic reconstruction will resolve this question.

In the Southwest, the transition from hunting and gathering to farming was never complete; to varying degrees, farmers continued to hunt wild animals and gather wild plants (Simms, 1986b, Madsen, 1989, Barlow, 1997). Some prehistoric groups appear to have invested heavily, at least in some years, in farming; other groups appear to have invested far less effort in preparation, planting, and tending their fields. To fully understand this variability will require studying it among modern, technologically simple farmers (Barlow, 1997), but it can also be studied in environmentally diverse areas such as the Grand Staircase. For example, based on work within and around the Monument, McFadden (1996) has proposed that the prehistoric farmers employed planned moves between multiple residences to deal with the uncertainties of farming in southern Utah. He suggests that this pattern of land use is long-lived and substantially different than that found in other areas of the Colorado Plateau. Studies such as this, which focus on patterns of variability, are likely to provide better understanding of what life was like in the prehistoric past.

And of course there is the question of what became of these prehistoric farmers after about A.D. 1300. This period is often called the Late Prehistoric because archaeologists know so little about it. Most agree that a change in climate probably made farming unprofitable on the Colorado Plateau, but there is little consensus about how the early farmers reacted to that change. Did they migrate to areas such as the Hopi Mesas where farming was still profitable, did they revert to full-time hunting and gathering, or were they displaced by other hunter-gatherers who may have come into the area at this time (Madsen and Rhode, 1994)? The fate of these peoples is probably explained by some combination of these hypotheses, but what combination is still open to debate.

Planning for the Future

Any viable management scheme of the archaeological sites within the Grand Staircase–Escalante National Monument will require a detailed assessment of their number, location, and type. McFadden (1996) recorded 457 sites in a 12.3-square-mile area in the southwest portion of the Monument, or about 37 sites per square mile. Extending this ratio across the Monument as a whole yields an estimate of nearly 100,000 sites within the Monument's boundary. This figure is probably high, however, because much of the Monument has a less rich environment than the area included in McFadden's work. Tipps (1988) reports locating 54 sites in a survey of 7.5 square miles in the area of the Circle Cliffs, or about 7 sites per square mile. This figure provides an estimate of about 18,900 sites on Monument lands. These two estimates likely bracket the actual number of prehistoric sites in the Monument, and the true number will only be discovered with additional investigation. Locating, recording, and evaluating these sites will obviously require a sustained, long-term effort.

From the perspective of learning about human adaptation on the Colorado Plateau for the 12,000 or so years prior to European exploration and eventual settlement, the archaeological record (the sites and objects left behind by these people) is the only source of information. Naturally enough, archaeologists are committed to this quest. Archaeologists, both professional and avocational, tend to be strong advocates for the preservation of prehistoric and historic sites. There are several reasons for this persuasion, not the least of which is the recognition that these sites are basically fragile, nonrenewable resources. It may be trite to point out that no "new" 5,000-year-old sites are produced today, but the implications of this fact strongly favor preservation. In many respects, archaeological sites can be viewed as the ultimate "endangered species." In addition, investigation by archaeologists is often a destructive process: Excavated sites cannot be reexcavated. Archaeology is a rapidly evolving science; many of the tools used today for better interpreting the archaeological record were unavailable just a decade ago. Unless there is a clear, explicit research goal, or a site is in imminent danger of being destroyed, it is prudent to preserve the site for excavation by our students, or our students' students, who will have more robust methods and theories for learning about the past.

Modern cultural resource management, or the management of archaeological sites, is largely structured by the National Historic Preservation Act. The significance of a site is determined by its eligibility for listing on the National Register of Historic Places. Eligibility of prehistoric sites is nearly always evaluated using Criterion D as the standard—whether the site has yielded, or is likely to yield, information about the past. Not all sites should be, or are, assigned equal importance according to this standard.

A broader standard has been proposed because archaeology has many different constituents with different views of the value of archaeological sites. Originally developed in New Mexico, this scheme allocates sites for specific purposes (Green and Plog, 1983, Green, 1993). Structural sites near roads can be stabilized and developed for interpretation. Sites that are being damaged by slope erosion or trampling by cattle are reserved for studying the effect of these processes on the distribution of artifacts on their surfaces. Sites with integrity and buried cultural deposits are divided into two categories-a set that can be investigated at any time with an appropriate research design, and a set that is not to be excavated for at least 100 years. Certain sites can be set aside for training junior high and high school students in archaeological field techniques, others limited to field schools run by colleges and universities. Sites that have religious significance to modern Native Americans are set aside and not investigated without permission of the relevant tribes.

Such a plan should be flexible and allow, in fact encourage, reassessments of the value of sites as our understanding of the prehistory of the Monument improves and conditions change. If development requires that a site allocated to long-term preservation be excavated, then another can be allocated in its place. If increased visitation to the Monument results in some scientifically important sites being disturbed, then they should be reallocated for stabilization and interpretation.

The difficulty with implementing this plan is, of course, the cost associated with locating and recording the 19,000 to 100,000 or so sites within the new Monument. It is impossible to manage that which is not known. Initially, systematic sampling procedures could be employed to ascertain the type, age, and integrity of the sites within the Monument. Eventually, however, a significant portion of the Monument will have to be surveyed. This is one of the many challenges that President Clinton gave the Bureau of Land Management when he used the 1906 Antiquities Act to create the Monument.

Acknowledgments

I wish to thank Betsy Tipps, P-III Associates, for supplying me with a number of important references and qualifying my assessment of the evidence for the Archaic presence within the Monument.

References

Ahlstrom, R. V. N., M. Adair, R. T. Euler, and R. C. Euler. 1992. *Pothunting in central Arizona: The Perry Mesa archeological site vandalism study.* CULTURAL RESOURCES MANAGEMENT REPORT NO. 13. U.S.D.A. Forest Service, Southwestern Region and Bureau of Land Management, AZ.

Aikens, C. M. 1965. *Excavations in southwestern Utah.* UNIVERSITY OF UTAH ANTHROPOLOGICAL PAPERS 76.

Barlow, K. R. 1997. FORAGERS THAT FARM: FREMONT ECONOMICS. Ph.D. Dissertation, Department of Anthropology, University of Utah, Salt Lake City, UT.

Beals, R. L., G. W. Brainard, and W. Smith. 1945. *Archeological studies in northeast Arizona.* UNIVERISTY OF CALIFORNIA PUBLICATIONS IN AMERICAN ARCHEOLOGY AND ETHNOLOGY 44(1).

Binford, L. R. 1978. *Willow smoke and dogs' tails: Hunter-gatherer settlement systems and archaeological site formation.* AMERICAN ANTIQUITY 45:4-20.

————. 1983. IN PURSUIT OF THE PAST. Thames and Hudson, London, UK.

Fowler, D. D., and C. M. Aikens. 1963. *1961 Excavations, Kaiparowits Plateau, Utah.* UNIVERSITY OF UTAH ANTHROPOLOGICAL PAPERS 66.

Fowler, C. S. 1982. *Settlement patterns and subsistence systems in the Great Basin: The ethnographic record.* Pages 121-138 *in* D. B. Madsen and J. F. O'Connell, editors. MAN AND ENVIRONMENT IN THE GREAT BASIN SOCIETY FOR AMERICAN ARCHAEOLOGY PAPERS 2.

Green, D. F. 1993. ARCHEOLOGY OF THE BEAR CAMP ALLOTMENT: 1993 SUMMARY. U.S.D.A. Forest Service, Warner Mountain Ranger District, Modoc National Forest, Cedarville, CA.

Green, D. F., and F. Plog. 1983. *Problem orientation and allocation strategies for prehistoric cultural resources on the New Mexico National Forests.* CULTURAL RESOURCES MANAGEMENT REPORT NO. 3. U.S.D.A. Forest Service, Southwestern Region.

Gunnerson, J. H. 1959. *Archeological survey of the Kaiparowits Plateau.* UNIVERSITY OF UTAH ANTHROPOLOGICAL PAPERS 39.

Hauck, F. R. 1979. *Cultural resource evaluation in south central Utah 1977-1978.* BUREAU OF LAND MANAGEMENT CULTURAL RESOURCE SERIES 4. Bureau of Land Management, UT.

Honeycutt, L., and J. Fetterman. 1985. WOODS CANYON ARCHAEOLOGICAL CONSULTANTS, YELLOW JACKET, COLORADO. Submitted to Bureau of Land Management, Moab District Office, UT.

Jennings, J. D. 1966. *Glen Canyon: A summary.* UNIVERSITY OF UTAH ANTHROPOLOGICAL PAPERS 81.

Judd, N. M. 1926. *Archeological observations north of the Rio Colorado.* BUREAU OF AMERICAN ETHNOLOGY BULLETIN 82.

Kelly, I. T. 1964. *Southern Paiute ethnography.* UNIVERSITY OF UTAH ANTHROPOLOGICAL PAPERS 69.

Kluckhohn, C. 1933. BEYOND THE RAINBOW. Christopher Publishing House, Boston, MA.

Kvamme, K. L. 1990. SAN JUAN COUNTY, UTAH, ARCHAEOLOGICAL VANDALISM: AN ASSESSMENT OF A VANDALISM MODEL AND PRACTICES. Arizona State Museum, University of Arizona, Tucson, AZ.

McFadden, D. A. 1996. *Virgin Anasazi settlement and adaptation on the Grand Staircase.* UTAH ARCHAEOLOGY 1996 (in press).

Madsen, D. B. 1989. EXPLORING THE FREMONT. Utah Museum of Natural History, Salt Lake City, UT.

Madsen, D. B., and D. Rhode. 1994. ACROSS THE WEST: HUMAN POPULATION MOVEMENT AND THE EXPANSION OF THE NUMA. University of Utah Press, Salt Lake City, UT.

Metcalfe, D. 1982. *The Cockscomb project.* UNIVERSITY OF UTAH ARCHEOLOGICAL CENTER REPORTS OF INVESTIGATIONS 80-2.

Moffitt, K., S. Rayl, and M. Metcalf. 1978. *Archaeological investigations along the Navaho-McCullough transmission line, southern Utah and northern Arizona.* MUSEUM OF NORTHERN ARIZONA RESEARCH PAPER, NO. 10.

Nickens, P. R., S. L. Larralde, and G. C. Tucker. 1981. *A survey of vandalism to archaeological resources in southwestern Colorado.* BUREAU OF LAND MANAGEMENT CULTURAL RESOURCE SERIES 11. Bureau of Land Management, CO.

Nickens, P. R., and K. L. Kvamme. 1981. *Archaeological investigations at the Kanab site, Kane County, Utah.* BUREAU OF LAND MANAGEMENT CULTURAL RESOURCE SERIES 9. Bureau of Land Management, UT.

Nusbaum, J. L. 1922. *A basket-maker cave in Kane County, Utah*. INDIAN NOTES AND MONOGRAPHS, MISCELLANEOUS SERIES 29. Museum of the American Indian, Heye Foundation, New York, NY.

Rosenberg, R. H. 1980. *Federal protection for archaeological resources*. ARIZONA LAW REVIEW 22:701-35.

Simms, S. R. 1986a. CULTURAL RESOURCE INVESTIGATIONS IN SOUTHEASTERN UTAH TO AID IN THE ASSESSMENT OF ARCHAEOLOGICAL VANDALISM. Archaeological Technician Program, Weber State College, Logan, Utah. Submitted to U.S.D.A. Forest Service, Salt Lake City and Monticello, UT.

————. 1986b. *New evidence for Fremont adaptive diversity*. JOURNAL OF CALIFORNIA AND GREAT BASIN ANTHROPOLOGY 8(2):204-16.

Steward, J. H. 1941. *Archaeological reconnaissance in southern Utah*. BUREAU OF AMERICAN ETHNOLOGY BULLETIN 128:277-356.

Talbot, R. K., and L. D. Richens. 1996. *Steinaker Gap: An early Fremont farmstead*. MUSEUM OF PEOPLES AND CULTURES OCCASIONAL PAPERS NO. 2. Brigham Young University.

Tipps, B. L. 1988. *The Tar Sands project: An inventory and predictive model for central and southern Utah*. BUREAU OF LAND MANAGEMENT CULTURAL RESOURCE SERIES 22. Bureau of Land Management, UT.

Tipps, B. L. 1992. THE BURR TRAIL ARCHEOLOGICAL PROJECT: SMALL SITE ARCHEOLOGY ON THE ESCALANTE PLATEAU AND IN THE CIRCLE CLIFFS, GARFIELD COUNTY, UTAH. P-III Associates, Salt Lake City, UT

Wilde, J. D., and D. E. Newman. 1989. *Late Archaic corn in the eastern Great Basin*. AMERICAN ANTHROPOLOGIST 91(3):712-20.

Wylie, J., and B. Nagel. 1989. *Quantifying and modeling archeological looting: The interagency GIS project*. Paper presented at the Society of American Archaeology Anti-Looting Working Conference, Taos, NM.

PART TWO

Shaped by the Land

A Socioeconomic Profile

*"The Monument…is a place where one can see how nature
shapes human endeavors in the American West."*
—President William J. Clinton
Proclamation No. 6920

*"I love the land…it's…an abiding love. That kind
of love comes from making a living off the land."*
—Louise Liston
Garfield County Commissioner

KAIPAROWITS PLATEAU

Photograph courtesy of Manuscript Division, J. Williard Marriott Library, University of Utah.

Previous page: Sun Petroglyph from Calf Creek confluence, Site 4
*from Kenneth B. Castleton, **Petroglyphs and Pictographs of Utah**, Volume 2 (1979).*

CHAPTER FIVE

A Human History

Dean L. May

It might at first glance appear that reviewing the human history of the Grand Staircase–Escalante region is an easy task. This is, after all, a land so tortured and remote that it was the last in the American West to be systematically explored by European people. Wallace Stegner (1954) wrote that it contains the last river and the last mountains added to the map of the lower forty-eight states: the Escalante River and the Dirty Devil Mountains. Some claim that the town of Boulder was the last in the States to have automobile access, when the Escalante River was finally bridged in 1935. Electric power did not reach the town until 1948 (Daughters of the Utah Pioneers, 1949), so to most outside observers, there is not much there. It seems to be a land that, as Brigham Young reportedly said of the Uintah Basin, serves no other purpose than "to hold the other parts of the world together" (McCool, 1992).

But that is, of course, the perspective of people who visit or pass through the region, not of those who live there. It happens that my wife, Cheryll Lynn May, is descended from Grand Staircase–Escalante people on both sides. Her grandmother's family were the founders of Johnson, the second Anglo community within the present boundaries of the Monument, a settlement planted in the spring of 1871 by four Johnson brothers—Joel, Joseph, Benjamin, and William—together with their multiple wives and abundant families. The town of Johnson was, appropriately enough, in Johnson Canyon, some fourteen miles east of Kanab at the southeastern edge of what is now the Grand Staircase–Escalante National Monument. The village was abandoned temporarily in the fall of 1871, due to rumors of impending Navajo raids, but the settlers found the rumors unfounded and returned the next spring. The Johnsons farmed and ran cattle, providing the core of a sufficient population to form a Latter-Day Saints bishop's ward that continued, though just barely, into the 20th century, but is now defunct. From there they spread to virtually every settlement of the Grand Staircase–Escalante country and then to the rest of the West. They are considered among the most prolific of all the early Mormon families, and of course are intricately intermarried with other families of the region, including the Hatches, Gouldings, Asays, and Lynns.

But theirs is, of course, only the most recent human history of the region, and their tenure has been brief, not much over a hundred years. The human record that is most enduring and pervasive across the landscape is that of Native Americans. The Paleo-Indians go back some 10,000 years and the Desert Archaic people appeared about 8,500 years ago. By A.D. 1 they were succeeded by the Fremont and Anasazi, who were joined about A.D. 1000 by the Kayenta Pueblo people, who lived in parts of the Escalante River drainage. The entire span of these cultures was well over a millennium, until about A.D. 1300 (Jennings, 1978; Madsen, 1979, 1986). Some 1,450 sites indicating the presence of prehistoric peoples have been recorded or noted in the region, and clearly they are only a small portion of the whole (BLM website on Grand Staircase–Escalante Objects of Prehistoric Interest, 1996). Three aspects of their presence that are important to remember: their remarkable tenacity in an extraordinarily difficult landscape; the extensiveness of their presence, their artifacts covering large portions of the Grand Staircase–Escalante region; and the suddenness and apparent finality of their departure, around A.D. 1300.

Though debate continues, and we do not have final answers, it appears that the historic Indians arrived at about the same time that the Fremont and Anasazi disappeared: the Shoshonean-speaking people from the Southwest, and the Athapascan-speaking from the Northwest (Euler, 1966; Inter-Tribal Council of Nevada, 1976; Jennings, 1959; Papanikolas, 1976; Sapir, 1992; Stewart, 1942). The Shoshonean group includes present Shoshoni, Ute, Southern Paiute, Hopi, and Gosiute people; the Athapascan, the Navajo and Apache. Evidence suggests early Hopi incursions into the Grand Staircase–Escalante region, and that Ute, Southern Paiute and Navajo also have frequented the area since the 1300s. By the 1840s, Southern Paiutes commonly were found in most of the Monument area, while the Utes inhabited the northeast corner.

These people had traversed the area for 600 years before the Europeans arrived. They had explored its canyons, identified its springs and waterways, climbed its block mountains, hunted its upland forests, and fished its mountain lakes. They had evolved patterns of subsistence that gave them an enduring, though painfully maintained presence in the place. However, there are few, if any, reservations or tribal lands that served as principal habitats for historic Indians squarely in the Monument or even close to its borders. Moreover, the relatively sparse reference to these people by settlers of the Grand Staircase towns suggests that these people, more than the Fremont and Anasazi, found the landscape formidable. Although they journeyed through the area to exploit its resources, they preferred to spend most of their time in more verdant zones (Bitton, 1977).

Europeans did not approach the region until the mid-16th century when Francisco Coronado and his entourage were turned away by the Canyon of the Colorado in their search for the legendary cities of Cibola. They came about as close as President Clinton when he announced the creation of the new Monument. Franciscan Fathers Dominguez and Escalante and their small party skirted its western and southern edges during their epic journey in 1776, crossing south out of Utah near Hurricane to the Colorado, and then wandering north and east past the mouth of the Paria and on up the river until they found a crossing (Warner and Chavez, 1995). They did not see the river that John Wesley Powell later named in their honor.

Nearly a century later, a militia company from St. George, Utah, headed by James Andrus, traversed the area during the Black Hawk War, chanced upon the Escalante River near the present town, and while they noted oases that might be settled, seemed glad to retreat when their mission was over. In his explorations of 1869 and 1871, John Wesley Powell, his river boats deep within Glen Canyon, saw mainly sandstone cliffs, and hence did not encounter the Grand Staircase directly. But in the latter voyage he commissioned Mormon scout Jacob Hamblin to bring a cache of new supplies to the mouth of the Dirty Devil River to replenish his stock on his journey down river (Bailey, 1948). Even Hamblin, who knew the area better than any Anglo, and had the confidence of Indians who knew it better still, was confused by the terrain and followed the Escalante River to its mouth, thinking it was the Dirty Devil (Woolsey, 1964).

During the rest of the 1870s, several surveys were conducted by Powell's men, especially Almon Harris Thompson, Frederick S. Dellenbaugh, and photographer J. K. Hillers. The major work in Grand Staircase–Escalante, however, was by Clarence E. Dutton, who with artists William Henry Holmes and Thomas Moran, explored the entire region, named its canyons, mountains, and rivers, rendered evocative illustrations of the landscape, and evolved a new mode of geological understanding and description in the process (Dutton, 1880, 1882; Powell, 1895; Stegner, 1954). Their work was supported by Mormons, especially residents of the recently settled towns of Kanab and Johnson, whose villages served as a supply and rest station for the Powell expeditions. Even before Powell's first expedition, Peter Shurtz had planted in 1866 a lonely village on the Paria, about thirty-five miles north of the river's confluence with the Colorado. The settlement was threatened during the Black Hawk War, abandoned, and then resettled in 1870 by several families (Daughters of the Utah Pioneers, 1960). Then, as opportunities for the young in more settled areas began to diminish, Mormon villages, starting in the mid-1870s, began to sprout like mountain juniper, wherever roots could find a crevice.

The second settlement was that of the Johnson family, located up Johnson Canyon, in 1871. Escalante, now the metropolis of the region, was founded in 1875 and had reached 623 people by 1880, when Johnson had only 87, most of them Johnsons, of course. In that year, the famed Hole-in-the-Rock expedition set forth from Escalante on a mission to build a road down into southeastern Utah that resulted in the founding of Bluff (Woolsey, 1964). Paria, by 1880, had just barely surpassed Johnson with 94 residents. The same decade saw Anglo settlements established near the headwaters of the Paria River, on the northeastern reaches of the present Monument, and the early settlers of Clifton, Losee, and Georgetown eventually abandoning their hamlets to inhabit the present towns of Cannonville, Henrieville, and Tropic, now nestled between Bryce and the Grand Staircase–Escalante.

In the 1920s, Mormon historian Andrew Jensen laboriously surveyed virtually all Mormon settlements in the West. He described the last settled Anglo towns of the Grand Staircase–Escalante region by observing that "this valley is by no means easy of access, for in order to reach it, the traveler has to make his way over almost impassable

Town	County	Founded	80P	90P	00P	10P	20P	30P	40P	50P	60P	70P	80P	90P	TP
Paria	Kane	1865	94	0	31	0	474	0	0	558					1157
Johnson	Kane	1871	87	0	90	66	0	36	0	0					279
Escalante	Garfield*	1875	623	667	723	846	1032	1016	1161	850					6918
Clifton	Garfield	1876	0	0	0	0	0	0	0	0					0
Losee	Garfield	1876	0	0	0	0	0	0	0	0					0
Cannonville	Garfield*	1877	137	273	211	219	311	227	255	217					1850
Henrieville	Garfield	1883	0	0	181	158	170	207	241	180					1137
Georgetown	Garfield	1886	0	0	0	0	0	0	0	0					0
Boulder	Garfield	1889	0	0	104	91	177	192	216	197					977
Tropic	Garfield	1891	0	0	379	404	474	458	562	558					2,835
AREA TOTALS			941	940	1719	1784	2164	2163	2435	2002	1717	1515	1763	1910	21,053
Garfield County		1890	941	2457	3400	3660	4768	4624	5253	4151	3577	3157	3673	3980	43,641

* Originally Iron County.

Table 5.1. Grand Staircase–Escalante area population by town and decade. Data was gathered from printed population schedules for the appropriate years. After 1950, populations of minor civil divisions under 1,000 are not reported separately. Estimates of district populations after 1950 in the text and Figure 5.1 are projected from the proportion of the whole Garfield County population prior to that time.

mountain roads and dugways, almost perpendicular rocky heights and bad river crossings, but after once reaching the valley a miniature paradise opens to view." Settlement began in the "miniature paradise" of Boulder in 1889 and this, the last community planted in the 19th century, has survived to the present.

These were all Mormon settlements, which made them different in character from much of the old West. The local terrain made it difficult to replicate precisely the classic Mormon (village compact with farmlands on the outskirts), but that was still the model. And if the physical character of the towns was a variation on the Mormon theme, the social character followed squarely the leitmotif. Frederick S. Dellenbaugh (1908) offered his impressions of nearby Kanab during the second Powell expedition in 1871:

The village, which had been started only a year or two, was laid out in the characteristic Mormon style with wide streets and regular lots fenced by wattling willows between stakes. Irrigating ditches ran down each side of every street and from them the water, derived from a creek that came down the canyon back of the town, could be led to any of the lots, each of which was about one quarter of an acre.... Fruit trees, shade trees, and vines had been planted and were already beginning to promise near results, while corn, potatoes, etc., gave fine crops....

The entire settlement had a thrifty air, as is the case with the Mormons. Not a grog-shop, or gambling saloon, or dance-hall was to be seen; quite in contrast with the usual disgraceful accompaniments of the ordinary frontier towns.

The whole population of the ten Mormon towns founded in the Grand Staircase–Escalante district has never surpassed 3,000 and only in three decades—the 1920s, 1930s, and 1940s—of this century did it rise above 2,000 (See Table 5.1). The earliest decades of the 1870s, 1880s, and 1890s were a settling-in time, the population remaining stable from 1880 through 1890 at fewer than a thousand. The last decade of the 19th century, however, saw a dramatic 45 percent increase in population, as stock raising and more efficient dam and canal systems provided an economic base sufficient to support a larger portion of the numerous offspring. Yet for an entire century now, population has grown only minimally, and it indeed experienced continuous decline from 1950 through 1970, the 1970 count of 1,515 being fewer than at any time since 1890. The population through 1990 has still not recovered to its 1920 level (See Figure 5.1).

Nor are there great prospects for a boom in population growth. The distribution of ages suggests why. In 1990 the population was older, on average, than that of the state as a whole, with 14 percent being over 65, compared with a statewide average of 8.7 percent (See Figure 5.2). The proportion under 5 is only slightly smaller than that statewide, but in the 18 to 24 age group a major difference is evident, a difference that

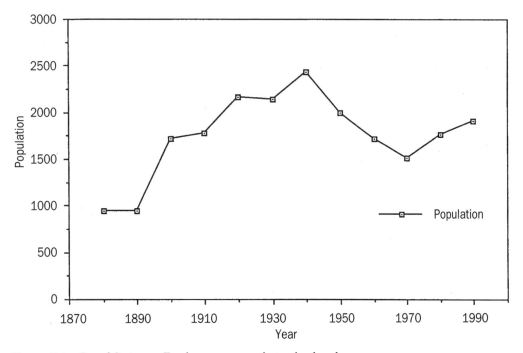

Figure 5.1. Grand Staircase–Escalante area population by decade.

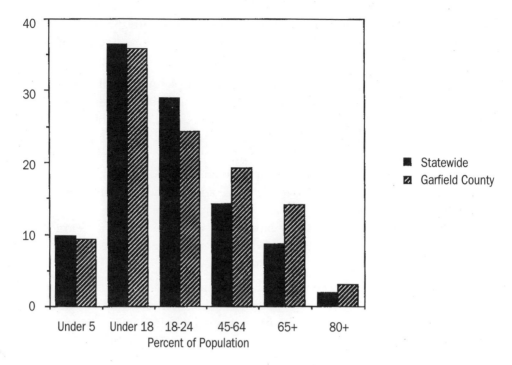

Figure 5.2. Age distribution of Garfield County, Utah 1990.

widens continuously up to the 80-and-above category, where the Grand-Staircase region has nearly twice the percentage as the rest of the state. Clearly, youth who reach their maturity move away to find a livelihood, with some perhaps returning to retire after rearing children and ending careers elsewhere.

And that's about it so far as Anglo populations are concerned; a few hundred people here and there, their villages clustered mostly around the edges of the Monument, the people laboring to farm whatever level land to which they can bring water (which isn't much) and relying heavily on grazing sheep and cattle in the badlands to make a living. It would be easy, I suspect, to dismiss the region as unpeopled, much as Anglos had done the rest of the West, as they steadily encroached upon lands peopled by Native Americans, oblivious to the power of their history and the uniqueness of their culture. Still, we could overromanticize the scene.

The Johnson family is a case in point. The combination of high fertility, limited arable land, and a paucity of water had from the beginning been the bugaboo of the Mormon wish for family coherence. The reason Johnson children spread out in all directions from their secluded canyon is obvious—it couldn't possibly hold them all. My wife's great-grandfather, George Washington Johnson, moved out by 1887 to help found the now defunct Georgetown. He stayed there eight years, until 1895, but then moved to nearby Tropic. In Tropic he established a successful sawmill, but already again, by

1901, the push of maturing youth was pressing on available land and water. Devastated by the loss from typhoid fever of two little girls, Clara and Elva, on April 7, 1903, the grieving family decided to join the flow of young neighbors to northern Wyoming's Big Horn Basin. So many Johnsons joined that migration that in Lovell, Wyoming, the folks gave them nicknames to distinguish them, Honeybee Johnson, being quite a different character from Sawmill Johnson. George and his wife, Henrietta, she pregnant for the tenth time, traveled most of the 700 miles from Tropic to Lovell by train. (They had already lost in infancy five of the nine children she had born. In Lovell her tenth child, Joel, would die the day after his birth, on December 5, 1903.)

Though the parents traveled by train, shipping draught animals and wagons by rail was prohibitive. The oldest child, sixteen-year old Lizzie, and her brother Alvin, fourteen, were given the task of driving a team and wagon laden with family possessions all the way to the Big Horn Basin. A few days out, the teamster hired by her father to accompany them appropriated the boy's lasso. Lizzie promptly fired him, and drove the rest of the way without his services. Her anger at the man for taking advantage of her brother was evident when she related the incident seventy years later. The family remained in Lovell. She, an expert seamstress, endowed her posterity with magnificent quilts, woven rag rugs, and other needlework, all exhibiting a keen sense of color and design. When temple burial clothes had to be made in a day or two, she was the person in the community assigned to make them. Her son, whom she named Juan (my wife's father) spent most of his working life in Marin County, California, but now has retired to the home Lizzie's husband built shortly after their wedding and in which she lived nearly her whole married life.

The Johnsons are fairly typical of these folk from Grand Staircase–Escalante. They are a tough, hardy breed, people of grit and with a character as solid and sometimes as eccentric as the rocks that surround them. They are a people of faith, but not above letting down their hair and having a good time. But are there implications in our brief consideration of their past for our time? I think so.

First, it is evident that these people, even with their relatively advanced technology, were no more successful at making enduring settlements in Grand Staircase–Escalante than any of the other human populations that preceded them; indeed, much less so than the Anasazi and Fremont peoples. The prehistoric Indians had a long tenure here, but eventually packed up and left, apparently not, as with the Anglos, because their population grew quickly to exceed the resources, but because climatological change (drought) drastically reduced the resources. The historic Indians are still here, but the Grand Staircase–Escalante was always somewhat marginal for them, its limited game, inaccessible rivers, and difficult terrain offering little temptation for regular habitation. Half of the ten settlements in the region made by Anglos were abandoned by the end of the 19th century, and while five settlements survive, their combined population is still not appreciably greater than it was in 1900. The fact is that the land is intractable, and the population will never be large.

Second, the hope of providing economic niches for children in order to maintain family coherence was never realized. It is a dream parents always have, to keep their children close, but in Grand Staircase–Escalante it was from the outset an impossible dream. As the life of Elizabeth Johnson Lynn illustrates, for every Johnson that remains, there are perhaps a hundred Johnsons living outside the region. To the extent that our policies are oriented toward finding a niche for every child born there, they will fail. Even the remarkably persistent Fremont and Anasazi eventually had to move.

We nonetheless need to remember that there is deep history that resides in the minds of the people. Two years ago my wife and I visited Johnson Canyon for the first time. It was a moving experience, the setting magnificent, but aside from a few summer homes and an occasional ranch house there is little left. The most notable structures are in fact an illusion, the storefront facades of a Wild West town, built by Hollywood outsiders as a set for movies made there in the 1940s and 1950s.

Pondering the meaning of that artifact, the fact that the most monumental human structure there was made to depict a stridently individualistic and violent culture, utterly alien to the gentle people who once had lived there, we made our way up to the Bryce Canyon area where I suggested we drive down to Tropic and find a motel for the night. My wife was inexplicably reluctant to do so. When I pressed her to explain, she said she could not bear the thought of staying in Tropic, where the two little girls, sisters of her grandmother, had died in 1903 and were buried in the same coffin. The human past, like the monuments of sandstone that surround us in Grand Staircase–Escalante are part of the setting. That past cannot be seen as alien and expendable, for it is alive in the remnant that has endured, and has, generation after generation, sent their children out into the broader world.

And finally, it is a mistake to imagine that these people have no regard for the majesty of the place and would despoil it if the government did not stop them. I think it is true that those whose lives are rooted in Grand Staircase–Escalante have a more practical perspective on its beauties. Ebenezer Bryce, for whom the canyon is named, reportedly said that it was "a hell of a place to loose a cow." But on the other hand, Franklin B. Wooley (Geary, 1992), who was part of the St. George militia that rode through the region in 1866, wrote stirringly of the view from Boulder Top, north of Escalante:

> We came suddenly out on to a high bold promontory of the S. Eastern face of the mountain overlooking the country. ... Down ... to the S.E. is the Colorado Plateau Stretching as far as the Eye can see a naked barren plain of red and white Sandstone crossed in all directions by innumerable gorges. ... [There are] Occasional high buttes rising above the "breakers" or rocky bluffs of the larger streams. The Sun shining down on this vast red plain almost dazzled our eyes by the reflection as it was thrown back from the firey [sic] surface.

In fact, Wooley's terms are almost precisely the same as those used later by Clarence Dutton, Powell's colleague and the arch-romantic geologist. According to Dutton (1880):

It is a sublime panorama. The heart of the inner Plateau Country is spread out before us in a bird's-eye view. It is a maze of cliffs and terraces lined off with stratification, of crumbling buttes, red and white domes, rock platforms gashed with profound canyons, burning plains barren even of sage-all glowing with bright colors and flooded with blazing sunlight. Everything visible tells of ruin and decay. It is the extreme of desolation, the blankest solitude, a superlative desert.

The Mormons gave the spectacular canyon to the east their highest compliment by calling it Zion, their name for spiritual perfection, a name that persisted in spite of the efforts of government officials to change it. I think the people who live in Grand Staircase–Escalante understand as well as most how magnificent is the setting of their lives-so much so, in fact, that their hope will never die that they and their children and their children's children will be able to stay. But the fundamental fact is that the lives of the people there are changing no less than the pillars, pediments, and plateaus of Grand Staircase–Escalante. Change, even in this land that seems so timeless, has always been the one constant, and will always be so. To try to stem that change is to fight against nature itself.

References

Bailey, P. D. 1948. JACOB HAMBLIN, BUCKSKIN APOSTLE. Westernlore Press, Los Angeles, CA.

Bitton, D. 1977. GUIDE TO MORMON DIARIES & AUTOBIOGRAPHIES. Brigham Young University Press, Provo, UT.

Daughters of the Utah Pioneers. 1949. GOLDEN NUGGETS OF PIONEER DAYS, A HISTORY OF GARFIELD COUNTY. Panguitch, UT.

————. 1960. HISTORY OF KANE COUNTY. The Utah Printing Co., Salt Lake City, UT.

Dellenbaugh, F. S. 1908. A CANYON VOYAGE: THE NARRATIVE OF THE SECOND POWELL EXPEDITION DOWN THE GREEN-COLORADO RIVER FROM WYOMING, AND THE EXPLORATIONS ON LAND, IN THE YEARS 1871 AND 1872. Yale University Press, New Haven, CT. Reprinted in 1926.

Dutton, C. E. 1880. REPORT OF THE GEOLOGY OF THE HIGH PLATEAUS OF UTAH. U.S. Government Printing Office, Washington, D.C.

Euler, R. C. 1966. SOUTHERN PAIUTE ETHNOHISTORY. University of Utah Press, Salt Lake City, UT.

Geary, E. 1992. THE PROPER EDGE OF THE SKY: THE HIGH PLATEAU COUNTRY OF UTAH. University of Utah Press, Salt Lake City, UT.

Inter-Tribal Council of Nevada. 1976. NUWUVI: A SOUTHERN PAIUTE HISTORY. Reno, NV.

Jennings, J. D. 1959. INDIANS OF UTAH: PAST AND PRESENT. University of Utah Extension Division, Salt Lake City, UT.

————. 1978. PREHISTORY OF UTAH AND THE EASTERN GREAT BASIN. University of Utah Press, Salt Lake City, UT.

Madsen, D. 1979. PREHISTORY OF THE EASTERN GREAT BASIN. VOLUME 1. Smithsonian Press, Washington, D.C.

————. 1986. PREHISTORY OF THE EASTERN GREAT BASIN. VOLUME 1. Smithsonian Press, Washington, D.C.

McCool, D. 1994. *Utah and the Ute Tribe are at war*. HIGH COUNTRY NEWS, JUNE 27:12.

Papanikolas, H. Z. 1976. THE PEOPLES OF UTAH. Utah Historical Society, Salt Lake City, UT.

Powell, J. W. 1895. CANYONS OF THE COLORADO. Dover Publications, New York, NY. Reprinted 1961.

Sapir, E. 1992. SOUTHERN PAIUTE AND UTE LINGUISTICS AND ETHNOGRAPHY. Mouton De Gruyter, New York, NY.

Stegner, W. 1954. BEYOND THE HUNDREDTH MERIDIAN: JOHN WESLEY POWELL AND THE SECOND OPENING OF THE WEST. Penguin Books, New York, NY. Reprinted 1992.

Stewart, O. C. 1942. UTE-SOUTHERN PAIUTE. University of California Press, Berkeley and Los Angeles, CA.

Warner, T. J., ed., and F. A. Chavez, trans. 1995. THE DOMINGUEZ-ESCALANTE JOURNAL: THEIR EXPEDITION THROUGH COLORADO, ARIZONA, AND NEW MEXICO IN 1776. University of Utah Press, Salt Lake City, UT.

Woolsey, N. G. 1964. THE ESCALANTE STORY: A HISTORY OF THE TOWN OF ESCALANTE, AND DESCRIPTION OF THE SURROUNDING TERRITORY, GARFIELD COUNTY, UTAH. Art City Publishing Company, Springville, UT.

CHAPTER SIX

Defining a Cultural Context

Ralph Becker

The rich traditions of the people in and around Grand Staircase–Escalante National Monument are integral to the successful future of the Monument. People are part of the Monument. As the proclamation creating the Monument states: "The [M]onument has a long and dignified human history: it is a place where one can see how nature shapes human endeavors in the American West, where distance and aridity have been pitted against our dreams and courage" (Proclamation, 1996). Any planning and management efforts should carefully consider the contributions and needs of past, present, and future residents of the Monument region.

I am not comfortable drawing conclusions about the peoples who have resided and still reside in the region of the Monument. Those people who live in the area are best able to define their needs. Perhaps the contributions of past residents will be recounted in the research and writings to be incorporated into the Monument's management scheme. Instead, I will offer some observations on the region and discuss how the socioeconomic setting may be incorporated into the management of this new jurisdictional entity.

A Personal Introduction

In preparing this paper, I have confronted my own relationship with this phenomenal region—one of the most truly magnificent landscapes I have seen.

I came west twenty-five years ago, an easterner enchanted with the landscapes of the Colorado Plateau and particularly the Grand Canyon. I could not get enough of the scenery and explored the land at every opportunity. While I enjoyed the people of the region, they were secondary in importance to me when I compared them to the geological wonders of the area.

I worked for the National Park Service and hiked at the Grand Canyon through my college years in the early 1970s. After moving to Utah in 1974, I adopted Capitol Reef National Park as my exploration ground—in part because of its striking beauty and geology, and in part because of the opportunities for solitude. I have never been disappointed in my more than 100 days hiking in the Waterpocket Fold. Likewise, I have enjoyed recreating in the Escalante region, part of the Monument.

Out of a love for the Colorado Plateau landscapes and a desire to make a career in the National Park Service, I studied law and planning (with an environmental emphasis). I believed that those fields would best permit me to pursue a career in park management.

For much of the past twenty years, I have tied my work to my recreational pursuits in the region of the Monument. In three years working on a proposal to consolidate Utah state lands in an exchange with the federal government (Project Bold), I worked closely with county commissioners and local public land users. For the past twelve years, I have worked as a consultant on planning and policy projects with communities throughout rural Utah, including the Monument region.

These experiences have given me the opportunity to get to know dozens of people who have carved out lives and built and sustained communities in this most unlikely environment. I have come to realize that the story of any region would be much poorer without fully including the stories of the people who live there.

My continuing education in environmental matters has also changed my thinking about management of a national monument. I have realized that "natural" landscape is a relative term—humans are part of the landscapes. To a limited extent, we have shaped all of the environments we live in, though the stark, arid region of the Monument has, by its nature, been less altered by human imprint.

Planning for and managing the Monument is a rare opportunity to develop an administrative scheme that incorporates the geologic, ecological, and human heritage of a region.

Prehistoric Native American Cultures

Humans occupied the Monument region during the Archaic, Basketmaker, and Pueblo periods, dating back several thousand years (Fowler and Madsen, 1986). In the period between 8000 B.C. and A.D. 1 to 500, small groups of people foraged on plant and animal resources in the region. However, little information is available on any settlements from that era. After A.D. 300 to 500, agricultural communities, which included small village sites, subterranean pit houses and masonry, and adobe surface structures were established in the area (Fowler and Madsen, 1986). Some larger villages with structures totaling forty to fifty rooms were also built during this period. The residents grew maize and beans, collected a variety of plant resources, and hunted deer, antelope, mountain sheep, rabbits, and other small rodents (Fowler and Madsen, 1986).

From A.D. 400 A.D. to 1300, a mix of Fremont and Anasazi cultures occupied the Monument area (Marwitt, 1986). Shoshonean peoples, predecessors to the modern day Southern Paiute bands, began occupying the area in A.D. 1000 (Fowler and Madsen, 1986).

Southern Paiutes

The Monument area is the tribal homeland of the Southern Paiutes. Other tribes, notably the Navajos and Utes, have traveled throughout the area and may have occupied parts of the region (Kelly and Fowler, 1986). Small Southern Paiute groups and bands in the Monument area survived by harvesting native plants, hunting, and growing irrigated crops (Kelly and Fowler, 1986).

This remote area may have been the last to be influenced by European culture. When the Dominguez-Escalante expedition passed through in 1776, aboriginal conditions appeared to be intact. Expedition members observed that Southern Paiutes lived in small groups, and were "notably pacific" (Kelly and Fowler, 1986). Unlike many western North American tribes, the Southern Paiutes did not adopt the horse as an integral part of their transportation or cultural patterns; the Monument region was too barren to sustain horses well (Malouf and Findlay, 1986). The region also did not contain beaver, which precipitated dramatic changes for other western Indian tribes through their contact with European trappers (Malouf and Findlay, 1986). Anglo-Americans traveling along the Old Spanish Trail grazed their livestock and hunted game in a manner that adversely affected the ability of the Southern Paiutes to survive north of the Monument area. However, Southern Paiutes in the Monument region do not appear to have been affected by this activity (Malouf and Findlay, 1986).

Prior to Mormon settlement, Southern Paiutes were the subject of slave trading by Spaniards and other tribes trading with Spaniards (Kelly and Fowler, 1986). The presence of permanent Mormon settlements ended slave trading practices, but also displaced Southern Paiutes from their best gathering and horticultural lands (Kelly and Fowler, 1986). While some conflicts occurred between Southern Paiutes and Mormon settlers, most were between Navajos and Mormons (Robinson, 1970). As they settled the Monument region, Mormons also provided the Southern Paiutes with food, clothes, and work (Malouf and Findlay, 1986).

The Kaibab Reservation, just south of Kanab in Arizona, was established in 1917. The Southern Paiutes in this area appear to have continued to lead a largely subsistence lifestyle independent of Mormon and governmental influence (Klemmer, 1986).

Incorporation of the cultural traditions and use of the landscape by the Southern Paiutes and prehistoric cultures should be an important part of the planning and management of the Monument.

Mormon Settlement and Relationships with the Federal Government

The Monument region was the last area discovered by European Americans in the continental United States. The Henry Mountains, just northeast of the Monument and east of Capitol Reef National Park, were the last mountain range discovered and were not identified until 1869. The mouth of the Escalante River, missed on the first Powell expedition down the Green and Colorado Rivers, was not discovered until 1871.

Settlement in the Monument region by Mormons is well documented. Wallace Stegner recognized some of the remarkable accomplishments and characteristics of Mormon settlers in this region in his writings. Other excellent sources of information are available that recount these settlers' efforts to establish their communities (Robinson, 1970; Woolsey, 1964; Chidester, 1949; May, 1985). In the 1860s, Mormon settlements in Kanab and along Kanab Creek focused on agriculture for subsistence. However, the limitations of water and arable land encouraged later settlers to convert to livestock operations to sustain themselves. Before the end of the century, stock raising was the most common industry (May, 1985). As more and more people discovered the scenic wonders of the Monument region, tourism and filmmaking became increasingly important as a source of employment and contributed significantly to the overall economy (May, 1985). This history and these traditions also add to the wealth of the Monument.

The Current Socioeconomic Setting

Demographics. The Monument is located in Garfield and Kane Counties. From 1960 to 1994, the population of Kane County more than doubled from 2,670 to 5,700, while Garfield County has grown at a much slower pace, from 3,580 to 4,200 (Governor's Office of Planning and Budget [GOPB] 1977). At the same time, Utah's population more than doubled, from 890,630 to 1,916,000 (GOPB, 1997). During this period, Garfield County has experienced a net out-migration, while Kane County has experienced net in-migration (GOPB, 1997). The state as a whole has experienced a period of net in-migration since 1960 (GOPB, 1997).

Economics. The economies of these counties were slower in 1960, and remained slower than the state average in 1994, with wages approximating 75 percent of state wages (GOPB, 1997). Unemployment in Garfield County is more than three times as high as Utah's average unemployment, and the unemployment rate in Kane County is more than twice that of the state's average (Utah Department of Employment Security, 1996). Recently the economic base and sources for local government revenues have shifted toward tourism (GOPB, 1997).

This shift is partly explained by the presence of Bryce Canyon National Park and Glen Canyon National Recreation Area. Other units of the National Park System are located nearby, as are numerous specially designated U.S. Forest Service and Bureau of Land Management lands. A decline in the traditional employment sectors of mining, agriculture, and logging, has also prompted changes in the source of family incomes and community character.

Cultural Setting and Relationship to Capitol Reef National Park History

How might Monument management incorporate local culture into the development and management of this new entity in the human landscape?

My search for a different perspective on incorporating local communities into a nationally protected site led me to an excellent ethnographic study of Fruita and its relationship to Capitol Reef National Park (White, 1994). The designation of Capitol Reef National Park was similar to that of the Grand Staircase–Escalante National Monument, and is therefore instructive. The park was originally created as a national monument in 1938, consisting of 37,000 acres that included the community of Fruita, the northern part of the Waterpocket Fold, and the Cathedral Valley (Proclamation, 1938). The original Capitol Reef National Monument was promoted by local community leaders including E. P. Pectol, a state legislator from Wayne County, who sponsored a resolution calling for Congress to set aside the area as a national park named Wayne Wonderland (White, 1994). The creation of Capitol Reef National Monument was celebrated by local residents with a program, barbecue, and melon feast (White, 1994).

Initially, National Park Service management of Capitol Reef was limited. Local communities continued to use and manage the orchards, and the Park Service allowed residents to remain in their homes within the new monument. However, conflicts arose over various community uses including grazing (especially in the campgrounds) and uranium mining proposals during the 1950s (White, 1994). These conflicts occurred even though Capitol Reef was quite isolated and undeveloped. Electricity first came to Fruita in 1948, and the road from nearby Torrey to Fruita was first paved in 1957 (White, 1994).

In 1968, as Lyndon Johnson was leaving office, he expanded Capitol Reef by proclamation to 250,000 acres, incorporating all of the Waterpocket Fold. No notice was given to state or local residents. The town of Boulder was so enraged that the town council adopted the resolution changing the town's name to Johnson's Folly. The townspeople believed that the expansion of Capitol Reef and resulting impacts on their winter grazing areas would lead to the demise of the town. (The Utah attorney general later ruled that the name change was illegal, and Boulder kept its name.)

The Park Service had a firm commitment to protect the dramatic and unique Waterpocket Fold, and often took an adversarial posture with the local communities (White, 1994). Over time, the Park Service purchased, and in many instances tore down, the homes that made up Fruita and reduced the size of traditional orchards. The Park Service did not consult residents of Wayne County and Fruita when it made decisions affecting the Fruita orchards. As a result, the residents of Wayne County resented the presence of the National Park Service (White, 1994).

Fruita was regarded by local residents as a Garden of Eden, with tremendous value to them as a fertile oasis where they could maintain orchards. It also held a value of "place" because it reflected the accomplishments of its settlers who scratched out a living there.

Conclusion

Relationships with the federal government have not always been adversarial in southern Utah. Certainly, the history of the Mormon exodus to the Great Basin (Stegner, 1992; Stegner, 1981), and the struggle for statehood created tension between Utahns and the federal government. But the local residents' hospitality toward the John Wesley Powell expeditions in southern Utah (Robinson, 1970) and their celebration of the creation of

Capitol Reef National Park (White, 1994) demonstrated their pride in the qualities of the region and an acceptance of a federal presence. Indeed, the local population began to resent the federal government only when they were prevented from participating fully in Park Service decisions and from continuing their relationship with the land.

This discussion of Capitol Reef National Park is not intended as a criticism of the National Park Service. My experience with the National Park Service is that it is fully committed to the National Park System and has superb, dedicated managers. But by seeing Capitol Reef National Park through the lenses of outsiders marveling at the geologic phenomenon of the Waterpocket Fold, the Park Service may have lost an opportunity to tell a remarkable story and to involve fully some of the "native" people in the park.

For the Grand Staircase–Escalante National Monument, there is a valuable lesson to be learned from the Capitol Reef experience. Truly, we have one of the most remarkable natural wonders in the world in the labyrinth of Escalante Canyons and remote Kaiparowits Plateau. But we also have a place where communities have made a living for at least 10,000 years. My research of the Indian traditions of the region suggests we have much to learn and interpret about the prehistorical residents and the Southern Paiutes. That story of subsistence, survival, and cultural adaptation continued with the Mormon settlers and remains today. Anyone who has traversed Phipps–Death Hollow along the horse mail trail from Escalante that served Boulder until 1935, must appreciate the people that inhabited and continue to inhabit this region.

To realize the opportunity of the Monument, the planners and managers of this new national treasure should open themselves to the community. It is difficult, under the circumstances of a mandate imposed from far away, to gain the trust and confidence of the communities in the region. But if Garfield and Kane county officials and residents can be included in the plans and designs for this Monument, it can serve as a new model for protecting an invaluable resource and for sharing a community's culture and changing relationship to this austere environment.

References

Clemmer, C., and O. Stewart. 1986. *Treaties, reservations, and claims.* Pps. 525-57 *in* W. D'Azevedo, editor, HANDBOOK OF NORTH AMERICAN INDIANS: GREAT BASIN. Volume XI. Smithsonian Institution, Washington, D.C.

Fowler, D., and D. Madsen. 1986. *Prehistory of the southeastern area.* Pps. 173-82 in W. D'Azevedo, editor, HANDBOOK OF NORTH AMERICAN INDIANS: GREAT BASIN. Volume XI. Smithsonian Institution, Washington, D.C.

Kelly, I., and C. Fowler. 1986. *Southern Paiute.* Pps. 369-97 in W. D'Azevedo, editor, HANDBOOK OF NORTH AMERICAN INDIANS: GREAT BASIN. Volume XI. Smithsonian Institution, Washington, D.C.

Malouf, C., and J. Findlay. 1986. *Euro-American impact before 1870.* Pps. 499-516 in W. D'Azevedo, editor, HANDBOOK OF NORTH AMERICAN INDIANS: GREAT BASIN. Volume XI. Smithsonian Institution, Washington, D.C.

Marwitt, J., 1986. *Fremont cultures.* Pps. 161-72 in W. D'Azevedo, editor, HANDBOOK OF NORTH AMERICAN INDIANS: GREAT BASIN. Volume XI. Smithsonian Institution, Washington, D.C.

May, D. 1985. *Utah writ small: Challenge and change in Kane County's past.* UTAH HISTORICAL QUARTERLY 53:170.

Proclamation Creating Capitol Reef National Monument. 1938. No. 2246, 50 Stat. 1856.

Proclamation—Establishment of the Grand Staircase–Escalante National Monument. September, 1996. 61 FEDERAL REGISTER 50223.

Robinson, A. 1970. A HISTORY OF KANE COUNTY. Kane County Daughters of Utah Pioneers. Salt Lake City, UT.

Stegner, W. 1964. THE GATHERING OF ZION: THE STORY OF THE MORMON TRAIL. McGraw-Hill, New York, NY.

Stegner, W. 1942. MORMON COUNTRY. Duell, Sloan & Pearce, New York, NY.

Utah Department of Employment Security. 1996. QUARTERLY NEWSLETTER. THIRD QUARTER. Utah Governor's Office of Planning and Budget.

White, D. 1994. BY THEIR FRUITS YE SHALL KNOW THEM: AN ETHNOGRAPHIC EVALUATION OF THE ORCHARD RESOURCES AT THE FRUITA RURAL HISTORIC DISTRICT, CAPITOL REEF NATIONAL PARK, UTAH. National Park Service. Torrey, UT.

Woolsey, N. 1964. THE ESCALANTE STORY. Springville, UT.

CHAPTER SEVEN

The Economy of the Rural West and the New Monument

Gail Blattenberger and David Kiefer

The Grand Staircase–Escalante National Monument is located in rural Garfield and Kane Counties in southwestern Utah. As with many rural communities, economic well-being is an issue. In both counties, per capita income is low compared with the national average (Figure 6.1). From 1969 to 1994, it has fluctuated between 60 and 70 percent with a few brief exceptions. This has been a persistent problem; it is not necessarily the result of increased environmental regulation. Nonetheless, the economic impact of the new Monument designation is an important issue.

We initially examine the role of extractive industries in Garfield and Kane Counties and the opportunity cost associated with the decision to create a national monument. In our view, the opportunity cost is small; extractive industries are not a viable solution to the economic situation prevailing in these counties. Next we explore the relationship between jobs and environmental protection, finding only a weak correlation. Finally, we turn to the role of the growing service industry in the economy, and show that services are more than tourism or associated menial jobs. The presence of the Monument, therefore, could substantially improve the economic prospects of Garfield and Kane Counties by attracting high-tech service enterprises, given a local investment in communications infrastructure. The Monument area's attraction is more the quality of life it represents than its role as a tourist magnet.

The Opportunity Cost of the National Monument

Opportunity cost is a fundamental concept in economics. It is the cost of excluding the most favorable alternative. In the case of the Monument, the opportunity cost is the cost of foreclosing the opportunity to mine and to explore for oil. In his announcement speech, President Clinton alluded to the opportunity cost issue when he said, "Mining is important to our national economy..., but we can't have mines everywhere, and we shouldn't have mines threaten our national treasures."

Mining. Before President Clinton declared the new Monument, it was reported that the designation would cost the schoolchildren of Utah "$640 million to $1.1 billion,"

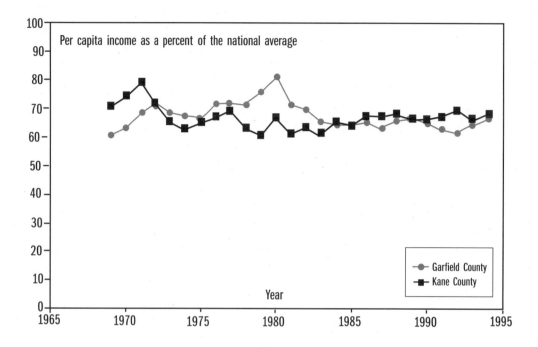

Figure 6.1. Per capita income in southern Utah has long been below average (Bureau of Economic Analysis, 1996).

which represents a substantial amount of money (Bird, 1996). The figures were derived by first estimating the number of tons of coal buried underground in lands dedicated to the Utah school trust fund within the new Monument's borders (about 500 million tons). This tonnage was then multiplied by the current market price of such coal (about $20/ton) and the state's royalty rate (about 10 percent).

The method used in making this calculation, however, illustrates how mistakes can be made in evaluating the opportunity cost of environmental protection when it involves forgoing some mutually exclusive land use. The estimate is based on the implicit assertion that schoolchildren (most of whom live along the Wasatch Front) are the only interested parties. But other people will gain or lose from the creation of the Monument. If the Kaiparowits remains open for mining, the stockholders of Andalex Resources and other mining companies might have earned a profit after incurring the costs associated with mining the proposed Sleepy Hollow Mine. Many residents of Garfield and Kane Counties, as well as Page, Arizona, might have earned greater incomes from working in the proposed mine. This is the part of opportunity cost emphasized in local reports concerning the Monument. Other residents of these locations, however, might earn higher incomes from services provided to an increased flow of tourists visiting the Monument. In fact, tourist interest in the Monument is reportedly high. Mining would be a loss for the potential recreationists who would have visited the Monument.

This $20/ton figure is the price of a ton of coal delivered to the consumer, not the price for a ton of coal in the ground. To move the Kaiparowits coal to market, the additional costs of mining (including mine site restoration) and trucking and rail transportation will be incurred. This includes not just the costs of trucks and drivers' wages, but also of constructing a road to the mining site and bypass roads around towns along the route to reduce the noise and danger associated with large-scale trucking operations. When these costs are subtracted from the market price of coal, the net benefits are reduced considerably for the Andalex shareholders, though not to schoolchildren for whom the royalty is figured on the market value. In fact, the stockholders may even incur a loss, because the proposed Sleepy Hollow project is so close to the break-even point.

Another common error involves the definition of the alternatives involved. The above calculation assumes that the alternative is mining all of the Kaiparowits coal versus complete loss of all royalty revenues. But these extreme alternatives are not realistic. It is unlikely that all of the coal could be profitably brought to market. Some of the 500 million tons will involve such high mining and transportation costs that it will not be worth the effort. The estimate should instead be based on the most likely mining total. The fact that the Kaiparowits has remained unmined for so long indicates a high assessment of its mining costs. A recent study indicates that "a vast deposit of coal found beneath the Kaiparowits Plateau of southern Utah has more sulfur and less energy than deposits being mined in central Utah.... This lower quality coal ... makes it 'unlikely' Kaiparowits coal could compete on the market before 2020" (Woolf, 1997).

Another error is the implicit assumption that, with the new Monument designation, Utah's schoolchildren will receive no financial benefits. The president, however, committed himself to a land exchange for the school trust lands. If Utah's School Trust fund is the beneficiary of federal land of equal value for its Kaiparowits lands, the cost to schoolchildren is zero. In that case, the opportunity cost rests entirely on the costs to others. If the eventual deal is less than an equal swap, then the appropriate estimate is the likely value of the differential between Kaiparowits land and the swapped land.

In the preceding paragraphs, we have dealt with uncertain contingencies by making guesses about the most likely outcome. A more sophisticated analysis of uncertainty can be done by explicitly including our assessments of the probabilities of the various outcomes. For example, if we believe that there is a 50 percent chance that the federal government will renege completely on its promise of a land swap, and that there is a 50 percent chance that the promise of an equal value land swap will be kept, then the "expectation" of the cost to the school fund would be $500 million (assuming the value of the coal is $1 billion). State educational planners will undoubtedly have their own assessment of the uncertainty and the risk involved. But in any event, their risk-adjusted expectations will probably be less than the reported $1 billion.

Any evaluation of the cost incurred by prohibiting a particular mine should be done in terms of opportunity costs, that is the lost opportunity between the lost mining opportunity and the next best mining opportunity. If the Kaiparowits coal were the only feasible mining opportunity, then the appraisal should be based on the mine's full market value. However, there are vast deposits of coal in the West and therefore numerous other potential coal mines. Thus, a more accurate way to measure the value lost by the new Monument designation is to estimate the cost differential between the Kaiparowits coal and its next best unmined alternative. Most likely the next best alternative would entail only a slight decrease in profit. Regardless, the opportunity cost of not mining the Kaiparowits coal will be smaller than the $20/ton figure.

Timber. Both Garfield and Kane Counties have experienced timber production losses in recent years. The Kaibab Industries sawmill in Fredonia, Arizona, which is nine miles south of Kanab in Kane County, closed in 1995; the Forest Products sawmill in Escalante, Garfield County, closed in 1991. These closures have meant hard economic times for local residents in both counties. The mills provided steady employment at good wages. The possibility of employment in Kaiparowits coal mines presented an attractive opportunity.

For opportunity cost purposes, these sawmill closures must be examined in terms of the timber industry generally and the western timber industry in particular. Western mills have been consolidating and expanding their "working circles," the area from which the mills draw their timber. The larger mills can handle a larger variation in log diameter, which responds to the declining trend in the size of harvested trees. When the Fredonia mill closed, 40 workers in its 200-person workforce were transferred to the company's mill in Panguitch, Garfield County, which is capable of handling smaller trees (Duffy-Deno and Brill, 1995). These 40 workers, therefore, do not represent an overall loss to Garfield and Kane Counties. In addition, there have been substantial improvements in milling technology. The Escalante mill laid off half its workers a year before the shut-down, because new milling equipment required fewer mill operators. In 1991 the Fredonia mill also laid off 73 of its mill workers due to modernization.

Local residents, however, argue that smaller trees were being milled because of environmental limitations on where trees could be cut. Although third parties have begun to appeal U.S. Forest Service timber sales in Utah, no appeals have yet been sustained. The appeals may cause delay time, but not a loss of timber volume (Duffy-Deno and Brill, 1995:18). Moreover, environmentalists respond that the smaller tree sizes are a result of overcutting.

Most western mills rely on national forests for their timber. However, timber restrictions and productivity have resulted in a major shift in lumber production to the Southeast, where timber companies can take advantage of faster growing timber and private forests. Even in western locations other than Utah, production margins for public timber have been steadily declining. We conclude, therefore, that the closing of the Kane and Garfield county timber mills is largely the result of technical change in the timber industry and local inefficiency as compared with other operations elsewhere in the West.

Nonetheless, local residents view the Monument designation as another environmental blow to the traditional western lifestyle. Many former lumbermill workers moved away from Garfield and Kane Counties; those who remained have tried to adapt, but many are openly hostile to the Clinton administration. They believe their lifestyle is threatened by a national policy that is forcing them into low-paying jobs. They have made unflattering comparisons between lost timber jobs and future jobs flipping hamburgers.

At one time, community stability was a primary objective of Forest Service policy. The policy was designed to keep a constant level of federal timber available locally for marketing each year, and it largely accounts for the timber industry in Kane and Garfield Counties. The policy, however, has been brought into question, and the Forest Service has changed its policies in response to inefficiency concerns. Nationwide, the timber industry is heavily subsidized by the Forest Service from tax funds. From a national perspective, keeping the mills open would have been a cost to the federal taxpayer. The nation would incur a net social loss (local profits and income minus the taxpayer subsidy) to keep the mills open.

Jobs and the Environment

It is commonly believed that mining proposals bring high-wage jobs and prosperity to the local economy. That belief is no doubt derived from the history of the West and mining's important role in that history. Although mining was certainly important for the American frontier economy, it is unlikely that it will play such a role in the future development of the West. This raises questions concerning the economic well-being of rural western counties and the relation of rural jobs to the environment.

The *economic base model* underlies the theory of economic geography. This model observes that local economies export goods to the rest of the nation and to the world, while also importing other goods back. Without export sales, local economies would not be able to finance their imports. This idea is clearly illustrated by economist Thomas Michael Power, who observes:

> Most of us remember the maps in our geography books that associated regions with particular types of economic activity. On the map of the United States there would be an icon of a blast furnace at Pittsburgh, an automobile at Detroit, corn in Iowa, beer in Milwaukee and cotton in the Deep South. Geographically specialized economic activities presumably explained why people settled and lived where they did (Power, 1996:7).

Local export industries are labeled the local *economic base;* these are represented by the icons on the map. The rest of the economy is called *nonbasic;* it is derivative because it provides services to the export base, either to industry directly or to the basic workers as consumers. Mines export coal, iron ore, and such to the rest of the world, while tourism exports services to visitors from the rest of the world. Both are therefore basic industries. This theory explains why local planners are constantly searching for export-oriented firms and projects. It has also been invoked as a reason for rejecting environmental regulation that impinges on export-oriented industries. Its fundamental lesson is that local prosperity is intimately linked to the basic sector of the local economy.

While there is some truth to this lesson, it is also often invalid. The decline of extractive industries in the West has been said to imply economic doom. There are, however, many recent cases where the export industries have declined while the local economy has actually prospered. One well-known case involves the sharp decline in timber production in the Pacific Northwest to protect the spotted owl, which was allegedly responsible for lost jobs and community instability. But technological change offers an alternative explanation for the timber job losses in the Northwest and else-where. In any case, the loss of timber jobs did not doom the local economy: "Since the late 1980's, the Northwest has successfully moved from dependence on extractive indus-tries to a modern widely diversified economy that is based on technology, tourism, and professional services and draws heavily on a spirit of entrepreneurial self-reliance" (Seidman, 1996:67). Further, "in Oregon's high-tech industries the average annual wage is almost $40,000, compared with $28,000 in the timber products industries," and "salaries for full-time workers in the tourism industry average $21,000—and are edging closer to the wood products wage" (Seidman, 1996:68, 71). Another clear illustration of this involves the rise and fall of mining in Salmon, Idaho. A new mine added 500 jobs to the local economy, but it was open only for a few years. When the mine closed, the rest of the economy did not fall; instead, it responded with increased employment, not the expected depression. The connection between jobs in the export sector and the rest of the Salmon economy was neither strong nor obvious (Power, 1996:90).

When and why does the economic base hypothesis apply? And when does it fail? It did not apply in Oregon because the decline of extractive industries coincided with the rise of other industries. Any adverse multiplier effects associated with the decline of tim-bering went largely unnoticed, because of the rise of tourism and software companies. The economic base multiplier should be less important in localities where few of the ser-vices that extractive industries purchase are offered locally. Then the export industry is forced to look outside the region for the business services it needs, which was probably the case in Salmon. Economic base theory predictions also may fail when other sources of income rise to compensate for a decline in extractive income. This can occur when nationwide welfare programs (e.g., unemployment compensation) or retirement income fills the gap. Resort and retirement communities generate some service jobs, because they have an income source that is entirely independent of the tourist industry.

How do these observations relate to Garfield and Kane Counties? Figures 6.2 and 6.3 show earnings and employment for Garfield and Kane Counties together, broken down into extractive industries, tourism, and other industries.[1] Figure 6.2 shows the percentage distribution of earnings among industries; Figure 6.3 gives employment in number of workers. Extractive industries represented over 20 percent of earnings in Kane and Garfield Counties in 1969. By 1994, this had fallen below 10 percent. Tourism was 10 percent in 1969 and rose to almost 30 percent by 1994. The "other" residual per-centage rose slightly. In 1994, earnings were 64.8 percent of total personal income in Garfield County; it was 64.2 percent in Kane County (Bureau of Economic Analysis,

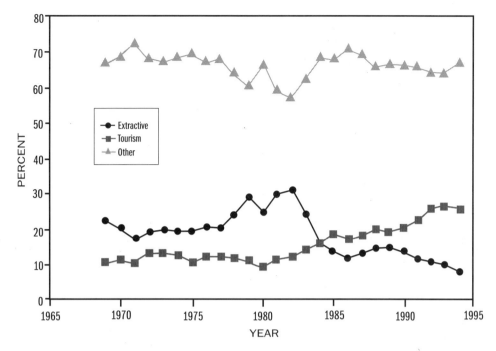

Figure 6.2. Earnings distribution for Kane and Garfield Counties.

1996). (Total personal income includes transfer payments such as social security and interest payments as well as earnings.) In 1980, total earnings increased substantially due mostly to the "other" category. This brief rise can be primarily attributed to a failed uranium mine project in Ticaboo. This mining project involved establishing a new town, which rose and fell within one year. Even in rural Garfield County, Ticaboo is off the beaten track and did not interact with the county as a whole. This confirms that export industries are often forced to look outside the region (or even the state) for needed business services. In addition, the 1980 increase in earnings was reinforced by a state highway construction project. Total earnings continued to rise through the 1991 mill closure, which produced a small decline in the extractive category.

Similar conclusions are derived from the employment statistics. Although employment in the extractive industries has declined, there has been continued growth in total employment. This pattern of decline mirrors a pattern that is widespread in the West (Power, 1995). The 1980 surge in total employment occurred in the "other" industries category: Employment was 2050 in 1979, rose to 2499 in 1980, and fell to 2112 in 1981. This mostly represents the workers brought in to work on the failed Ticaboo uranium project.

Thus, having a local economy based on mining can be a very risky option, and one with severe environmental costs. The West is dotted with mining ghost towns such as

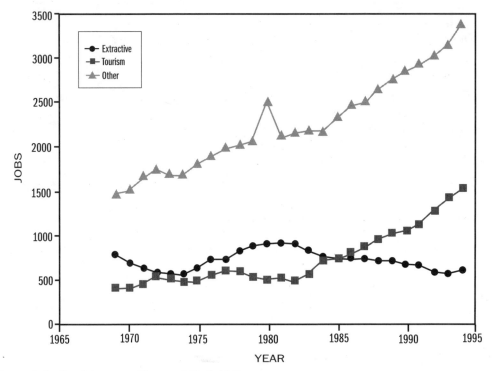

Figure 6.3. Employment in Kane and Garfield Counties.

Ticaboo. Many of these sites leave unsightly mine tailings and degraded environments, which can limit future economic options.

Economic Prospects for Garfield and Kane Counties

In the 19th century, the myth that "rain follows the plow" encouraged the migration of countless pioneer farmers. This generated many environmental scars on the western landscape, from which we are still recovering. A more recent version of this motto, with a much sturdier foundation, is that "jobs follow the people." This motto has empirical support:

> During the 1960's counties containing federally designated wilderness areas had population increases three times greater than other nonmetropolitan counties. In the 1970's they grew at a rate twice that of nonmetropolitan areas, and in the 1980's their population increased 24 percent—six times faster than the national average of 4 percent for nonmetropolitan areas and almost twice as much as counties in the rural West (Rasker, 1995:30).

One explanation is that people are drawn to these localities for the quality of life. For example, Joe Judd, who is county commissioner for Kane County and initially an opponent of the new Monument, relocated to southern Utah from Los Angeles for the quality of life (Larmer 1997:1). Business firms also look for quality of life in making relocation decisions. Given the quality of life available in Kane and Garfield Counties, it is clear that they will grow with the new Monument. The question is how they will grow, and whether they maintain their quality of life.

In both counties, tourism has been a growing component of earnings, and it undoubtedly will expand more with the Monument designation. Garfield County is currently the most tourism-dependent county in Utah (SUWA, 1994). Local residents, however, are justifiably wary of further expansion in tourism, which is a major concern with the new Monument.

Several lessons—both positive and negative—can be learned from the experience elsewhere: Not all tourism jobs involve menial labor. In Oregon the average incomes of full-time, tourism industry workers are approaching those in the wood products industry. New tourism industries need managers as well as maids, and they will need stability in management positions, which local residents can provide. Many workers in the tourism industry, however, are seasonal rather than full-time, and there are many low-skill jobs. When "outsiders" buy second homes in tourist locations, they can drive up real estate prices, making it hard for local residents to maintain affordable housing. In Moab, for example, real estate taxes have risen 350 percent since 1988.[2] Although tourism is a nonextractive industry, it too can impact the environment, sometimes quite adversely, although usually less than extractive industries. Moreover, a large influx of temporary visitors can substantially alter community structure.

Kane and Garfield Counties are taking steps to prepare for the coming changes. Both counties have asked Congress for funds to assist in preparing for the Monument. Kane County has established a community organization, the Coalition of Resources and Economics, to examine county economic planning (Larmer, 1997:8). Zoning ordinances and local tax structures should be examined with an eye toward the kind of community development that current residents desire. Tourism, like mining, can be a boom and bust industry. However, infrastructure improvements can be used to diversify the economy and to attract alternative industries besides tourism.

Service industries are an alternative to tourism. Infrastructure, quality of life, and a reliable skilled workforce are reasons for relocation in these counties. The service category is broad, including technical services, business services, health services, and education services. The service category can include retirement services, too. People choose retirement locations for the quality of life. Although retirement income is nonemployment income, it is still an infusion into the welfare of the community. It has similar economic properties to export industry income. Retirement services, however, may be demanding on the community and the environment. Advanced community planning can establish the structure to meet these demands.

Although residents of Garfield and Kane Counties often cite the Moab tourism experience as something to avoid, one of Moab's largest and highest paying employers is actually a nontourism, service industry. Will Petty, a computer specialist from Denver with experience in Japan, has located his firm, Tellica Pacifica, in Moab and employs workers correcting Japanese correspondence business exams (KUERa, 1997). Petty relocated for quality of life reasons, mainly to leave the city environment. His firm now provides high paid employment for Grand County residents.

In another case, a bicycle rack manufacturer from Los Angeles employing twenty people relocated to Parowan, Utah (KUERb, 1997). Kanab in Kane County also has its own example of a small industry relocation. Stamp 'Em Up, a company manufacturing rubber impressions was started in Las Vegas by two women from Kanab, who then moved back to Kanab with their company (Larmer, 1997:9). It employs 200 people and is the largest employer in Kanab. Bryce Canyon Mist, a bottled water company, is yet another example of a new local industry; it is the product of local entrepreneurship in Tropic, which is in Garfield County.

Industry relocations, however, are dependent on available infrastructure. Infrastructure is a widely used generic term that refers to the underlying or supporting structure for economic activity. It ordinarily includes roads, water, sewer and power systems, and some hotel and restaurant services. Communications network availability is increasingly important. The Bureau of Land Management, for example, chose Cedar City for its monument planning office partly because it has an interstate, an airport, and conference facilities. Infrastructure problems are mitigated by the onset of the information age, but can still present problems in remote locations. For example, Kanab failed to attract an outdoor equipment manufacturer last year due to lack of infrastructure (Larmer, 1997:9). If planning for the new Monument is managed wisely, the region could significantly improve its infrastructure.

New small industries can also improve county employment stability. The state of Utah has encouraged small industry relocations through the Industrial Assistance Fund, and it has supported local entrepreneurship through the Local Economic Development Initiative Program. Although industry relocations are not the complete answer to the economic situation in Garfield and Kane Counties, the diversification that such relocations provide can assist in stabilizing these rural economies.

Conclusion

Our overall evaluation of the Monument designation's economic impact is still tentative. We have not done a detailed estimation of its benefits and costs. However, based on the known facts and the experiences of other regions in the West, we believe that the benefits of the Monument exceed its costs. Many factors obviously need to be taken into account. Any accounting must include all of people who stand to gain from preservation of the Kaiparowits, including some who have never visited this land and who never will. Some people may obtain a benefit merely from the satisfaction of knowing that these lands are being preserved in case they decide to visit someday. However, there are people who will surely suffer losses from the creation of the Monument. Potential miners and mill workers may never find better—or even equal—jobs in Boulder, Escalante, and Kanab as they develop into tourist towns, retirement communities, or diversify into a variety of nonextractive industries.

Change will certainly come to these local economies, and it will entail more than adjusting to different jobs and careers. It will require coordinated planning and recognition of the forces of change. One knowledgeable observer has suggested that resistance to change is based on the desire for a land-based economy (Marston, 1996:14–15). Many people view such an economy as crucial to the quality of life in the rural West; they fear the present quality of life will be lost in the coming urbanization of the communities surrounding the Monument. Some locations have attempted to maintain the old land-based economy by creating land trusts to preserve working farms. Planning can help to reconcile the conflicts that will develop between established residents and newcomers who come to work or to marvel at the landscape. Moreover, serious efforts must be made to find ways of compensating the "losers" that are financed by the "winners." And similar efforts are required to find ways of preserving the land-based western lifestyle along with the natural treasures of the countryside.

End Notes

[1] The aggregation was performed courtesy of the Utah State Governor's Office of Planning and Budget. Aggregation of both counties was necessary for confidentiality reasons. In this aggregation, extractive industries include agriculture, mining, and lumber and wood products. Tourism includes eating and drinking establishments, hotels, lodging, amusement, and recreation. The "other" category contains the residual economic activities. Earnings represents wages and salaries, other labor income, and proprietors' income.

[2] This number originally came from Luther Propst of the Sonoran Institute at the Wallace Stegner Center Conference titled "To Cherish and Renew" on April 18-19, 1997, in Salt Lake City, Utah. Subsequently, the number was verified by the Grand County Clerk's Office in a phone conversation on April 28, 1997. According to Grand County tax data, the tax rate has fallen slightly but property valuation has risen from $66,831,039 in 1987 to $141,691,000 in 1995, representing an increase of 212 percent. These numbers are affected by the geographical limits considered and new construction.

References

Bird, M. 1996. Utah State Office of Education, as reported in the SALT LAKE TRIBUNE, September 6, 1996.

Bureau of Economic Analysis. 1996. *Regional economic information system*. U.S. Department of Commerce, Economics and Statistics Administration, Washington, D.C.

Duffy-Deno, K., and T. Brill. 1995. THE WESTERN SAWMILL IN TRANSITION. Office of Energy and Resource Planning, Utah Department of Natural Resources, Salt Lake City, UT.

Governor's Office of Planning and the Budget. 1995. KAIBAB INDUSTRIES RESTRUCTURING: ECONOMIC, DEMOGRAPHIC, AND FISCAL IMPACT ANALYSIS. Salt Lake City, UT.

KUERa. April 4, 1997. *Poverty in rural Utah*. FRIDAY EDITION. Salt Lake City, UT.

KUERb. March 28, 1997. *Poverty in rural Utah*. FRIDAY EDITION. Salt Lake City, UT.

Larmer, P. April 14, 1997. *Beauty and the beast.* HIGH COUNTRY NEWS. Paonia, CO.

Marston, Ed. December 23, 1996. *Denying the warts on the West's service economy.* HIGH COUNTRY NEWS. Paonia, CO.

Power, T. M. 1995. *The economics of wilderness preservation in Utah.* SOUTHERN WILDERNESS ALLIANCE NEWSLETTER (Winter). Salt Lake City, UT.

Power, T. M. 1996. LOST LANDSCAPES AND FAILED ECONOMIES. Island Press, Washington, D.C.; Covelo, CA.

Rasker, R. 1995. A NEW HOME ON THE RANGE. The Wilderness Society, Washington, D.C.

Rudzitis, G. 1993. *Nonmetropolitan geography: Migration, sense of place, and the American West.* URBAN GEOGRAPHY. 14(6): 574-85.

Seideman, D. July-August 1996. *Out of the woods.* AUDUBON MAGAZINE. Washington, D.C.

Southern Utah Wilderness Alliance (SUWA). 1994. *The economics of land protection in southern Utah* (mimeographed). Salt Lake City, UT.

Utah Foundation. 1996. STATISTICAL REVIEW OF GOVERNMENT IN UTAH, 1996. Salt Lake City, UT.

Woolf, J. 1997. *Kaiparowits coal is poor quality, BLM report says.* SALT LAKE TRIBUNE, MAY 14, 1997. Salt Lake City, UT.

CHAPTER EIGHT

An Outdoor Recreation Assessment

Edward J. Ruddell

On September 18, 1996, President Clinton signed a proclamation under the authority of the Antiquities Act to establish 1.7 million acres of southern Utah as the Grand Staircase–Escalante National Monument. Although both the Antiquities Act and the president's proclamation indicate that the designation of a national monument is for scientific and historic purposes, the designation also affords many outdoor recreation opportunities compatible with those uses. The purpose of this chapter is to describe the recreation opportunities, experience outcomes, and benefits that may flow from the Monument's use as a recreational resource. This chapter will also discuss planning, management, and research needs associated with recreation in the Monument.

The Physical and Social Setting

The Monument is divided into three distinct geographical areas. These are the canyons of the Escalante, the Grand Staircase, and the Kaiparowits Plateau. Because of year-round water availability, reputation for scenic beauty, and outdoor challenges offered, the canyons of the Escalante area experience a steady flow of recreation use as does the Grand Staircase. Much of this is concentrated along Cottonwood Canyon Road, the scenic backway that crosses the area. The last of the regions, the Kaiparowits Plateau, consists of dry and rugged terrain, with little water and limited access. The Smokey Mountain Road, which traverses the plateau, offers pleasure driving and related opportunities.

The attitudes and values of residents of southern Utah's Kane and Garfield Counties are rooted in an economy based on resource extraction. Historically, ranchers and miners are important claimants of the resources of nearby public lands. However, as extractive industries have declined in southern Utah and as the popularity of southern Utah has increased as a recreation resource, visitors ranging from backcountry users to sightseeing tourists have emerged as another important claimant of the area's resources. To date, the most significant recreational activity in the Monument area has been backcountry use.

A Conceptual Framework for Analyzing Recreation

Recreation as a Psychological Experience. In the parks, recreation, and tourism fields, recreation is seen as a set of psychological experiences associated with recreational activity. Under this model, hiking in the Escalante backcountry is identified as a vastly different experience than hiking along State Street in Salt Lake City. One important consequence of this thinking is that management of recreation opportunities is essentially facilitating psychological experiences. Yet managers cannot directly create experiences; experiences are the sole possession of the recreation participant. A framework for integrating circumstances that managers can control with the psychological outcomes visitors seek is needed. One such framework is the Recreation Demand Hierarchy.

Recreation Demand Hierarchy. The Recreation Demand Hierarchy is a conceptual framework for integrating recreation resource management with the psychology of the recreation experience (Figure 8.1). The Recreation Demand Hierarchy assumes that demand for recreation occurs at four levels simultaneously (Driver and Brown, 1978; Haas, Driver, and Brown, 1980). Level 1 is demand for activities, for example, swimming and hiking. Level 2 is demand for participation within specific kinds of settings such as developed campgrounds, tourist destinations, and desert wilderness. Level 3 is demand for satisfying desired psychological outcomes, for example, solitude, skill improvement, self-reliance, and recapitulation (reliving an earlier lifestyle or experience). Level 4 is the accomplishment of personal or social benefits, such as enhanced self-esteem, increased work productivity, and improved health.

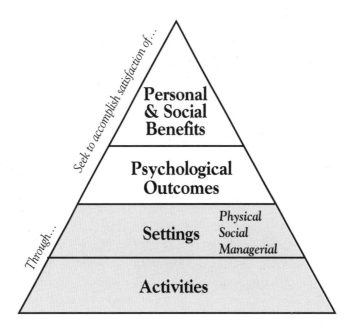

Figure 8.1. Recreation Demand Hierarchy schematic.

Levels 3 and 4 of the Recreation Demand Hierarchy (psychological outcomes and personal and social benefits) are experiences and outcomes managers cannot directly control. They are possessions of the individual visitor alone. Also, managers rarely have direct involvement with level 1 of the Recreation Demand Hierarchy, except perhaps to prohibit certain activities deemed incompatible with select settings or management goals. Visitors usually select and manage their own activities, especially in wildland settings. Therefore, outdoor recreation resource managers spend much of their energy managing level 2 of the Recreation Demand Hierarchy —the setting.

The Recreation Opportunity. In this context, the setting is a three-dimensional concept composed of physical, social, and managerial settings. The physical setting includes all of the physical attributes of a site including soil, vegetation, water, and wildlife. The social setting includes behaviors and other social characteristics associated with a site. The managerial setting comprises restrictions placed on visitor freedoms by management. The combination of physical, social, and managerial settings comprise a recreation opportunity. Thus, management creates the recreation opportunity; visitors create the recreation experience. In this context, the manager's role is to maximize the probability that desired psychological outcomes and personal and social benefits will accrue through wise and informed setting management.

Analyzing Opportunities, Experience Outcomes, Benefits, and Costs

A Continuum of Opportunity, Experience Outcomes, and Benefits. Combinations of physical, social, and managerial settings can be arranged along a continuum from undeveloped to highly developed. These varying arrangements are associated with varying psychological outcomes or experience opportunities and consequent benefits. Land management agencies such as the Bureau of Land Management (BLM) have institutionalized this idea in the Recreation Opportunity Spectrum (ROS). The ROS is anchored at one end by the "primitive" opportunity class. Setting characteristics of the primitive opportunity class are arranged as follows:

Physical Setting: The area is characterized by essentially unmodified natural environment of a fairly large size. Only essential facilities for resource protection are used and are constructed of on-site materials. No facilities for comfort or convenience of the user are provided.

Social Setting: Concentration of users is very low and evidence of other users is minimal. Spacing of groups is informal and dispersed to minimize contacts with other groups or individuals.

Managerial Setting: The area is managed to be essentially free from evidence of human-induced restrictions and controls. Motorized use within the area is not permitted (adapted from Brown, Driver, and McConnell, 1978).

At the other end of the ROS is the "modern urbanized" opportunity class.

Physical Setting: The area is characterized by a substantially urbanized environment, although the background may have natural elements. Vegetative cover is often exotic and manicured. Soil protection is usually accomplished with hard surfacing and terracing. A considerable number of facilities are designed for the convenience of large numbers of people. Facilities for highly intensified motor uses and parking are available, with mass transit often provided to carry people through the site.

Social Setting: Sights and sounds of people on-site are predominant. Large numbers of users can be expected both on-site and in nearby areas.

Managerial Setting: Controls and regimentation are obvious and numerous (adapted from Brown, Driver, and McConnell, 1978).

These markedly different settings are associated with different experience outcomes. In the primitive opportunity class there is "opportunity for isolation [from the sights and sounds of others], to feel a part of the natural environment, to have a high degree of challenge and risk, and to use outdoor skills" (Brown, Driver, and McConnell, 1978; cited in Manning, 1986:103). In the modern urban opportunity class, "opportunities to experience affiliation with individuals and groups are prevalent as is the convenience of sites and opportunities. These factors are more important than the setting of the physical environment" (Brown, Driver, and McConnell, 1978; cited in Manning, 1986).

Examples of different opportunity classes, ranging from pristine to highly developed, can be found in and near the Monument. For example, much of the Kaiparowits Plateau is an example of a primitive setting, as are many side canyons of the Escalante River. Places like these provide experience opportunities for solitude, reliving earlier traditions, aesthetic appreciation, and rest and relaxation. Primitive settings provide solitude where low densities and backcountry norms allow parties to remain out of sight and sound of each other and minimize self-disclosure except, perhaps, to members of one's own party. A primitive setting, free from conveniences and roads, also provides a good opportunity for challenge and self-reliance.

The opportunities for solitude, found in the primitive setting of the Monument, provide important personal and social benefits such as self-esteem as difficult accomplishments are achieved. Recapitulation opportunities, such as a tour of Hole-in-the-Rock Road, convey knowledge about pioneer history. Rest, relaxation, and physical exertion lead to stress reduction and improved health. Experiencing the dramatic and scenic environment of the Monument provides spiritual benefits such as a sense of connectedness with the environment and fellow humans. The Monument's abundant opportunities for solitude, as well as being alone with significant others, yields increased intimacy, bonding, and self-esteem.

At the other end of the ROS is the "modern urbanized" opportunity class as in some state parks, such as Kodachrome Basin, and other places found along the periphery of the Monument. Developed settings provide opportunities to experience nature safely and conveniently, and allow sightseeing and aesthetic appreciation, socializing, rest and relaxation, and escape from the sights and sounds of home or work. A state park with developed campsites, places for group camping, RV hook-ups, restrooms, and showers is an excellent place to experience nature without coping with the rigors and challenges of backcountry travel. Front-country norms encourage socializing. Many outdoor social experiences such as family reunions or large party get-togethers are nearly impossible (and environmentally damaging) without the water, sanitation, and other facilities offered here.

Recreation Costs. Designating an area as a national monument, national park, or wilderness area frequently generates increased knowledge of its existence, increased interest, and increased visitation. Increased use has costs for the experience opportunities previous users had been seeking as well as costs associated with environmental impacts.

Crowding can be viewed as a form of goal interference when the presence of too many others interferes with the experience. Backcountry solitude and enjoying pristine nature are easily infringed upon by too many people. Even behavioral traces, such as the sound of passing vehicles or tracks left by off-road vehicles, can interfere with the satisfaction of experience outcomes. Tourism-related development projects such as road improvements to increase access, site hardening for convenience, or resource protection and facilities development, can also be distracting.

Another set of costs associated with increased recreational use is environmental impact, which can occur from nearly all forms of outdoor recreational use including backpacking, camping, mountain biking, off-road vehicle use, and horse packing. Recreation impacts include impacts to water, soil, vegetation, and wildlife. Visitors use more water than they should (especially in potholes) and pollute what is left. Nutrient inputs such as phosphates from detergents and soaps result in algal blooms, a reduction in dissolved oxygen, and alteration of aquatic communities. Visitors can trample stream banks, increasing erosion and siltation, decreasing light penetration, altering water temperatures, and thereby impacting aquatic communities. Visitors can make too many trails, scarring the landscape and contributing to erosion. They can trample fragile, nutrient-rich cryptobiotic crusts that hold blowing desert sands in place. In addition to impacts to the resource base, recreation impacts can diminish values associated with historic, prehistoric, scientific, paleontological, or archaeological sites. Although recreation use always causes impact, many of these impacts can be mitigated with careful planning and wise management.

Planning, Management, and Research Implications

Multiple-Use Management. Multiple-use management has been the overriding practice of the BLM and will remain in the new Monument. Interim guidelines for the Monument have been established to dictate management until the master plan is completed in 1999. These guidelines state that management should "maintain existing management policies, designations, and allocations except where changes are necessary to protect the objects of scientific and historic interest within the Monument ... and to maintain the non-impairment standards for wilderness study areas ..." (director, Bureau of Land Management, memorandum to Utah State director, Nov. 8, 1996).

Approximately 60 percent of the area within the Monument is designated as Wilderness Study Areas (Maggie Kelsey, pers. commun., April 17, 1997). Wilderness Study Areas are those possessing wilderness qualities as specified under the Wilderness Act (P.L. 88-577; 16 U.S.C. 1131 et seq.). Many types of recreation can be prohibited in Wilderness Study Areas, such as motorized activity, bike use, and large outings. Presently, the more developed forms of recreation are located along the periphery of the Monument or along the scenic backways that cross the Monument and not in these Wilderness Study Areas.

Recreation Management. Although there are enough difficult planning and management implications associated with the Monument to support several careers, two recreation-related implications stand out. The first of these concerns experience zoning; the second is public relations.

Experience zoning is a planning and management strategy in which uses and levels of development are segregated on the basis of psychological outcomes to be produced. Allocation of ROS opportunity classes to specific tracts of land is an application of the experience zoning concept. As yet, no opportunity class zones have been established for recreational use of the Monument. Allocation of opportunity class zones should be completed within the framework of the Monument's overall multiple-use policy. For example, areas intended for recreational use and grazing might be zoned semiprimitive motorized; scenic backways such as Hole-in-the-Rock Road might be zoned as semiprimitive motorized or rustic under the ROS classification scheme.

A second pressing management implication concerns public relations and information dissemination. Many visitors will not know the difference between a national park and a national monument. Visitors to lesser-known areas such as national monuments often base their images and expectations of facilities, services, and management of sites on well-formed images such as national parks (Ruddell and Westphal, 1989). Further confusion can arise because, although most national monuments are managed by the National Park Service, the Monument will be managed by the BLM. The BLM operates under a multiple-use mandate; the National Park Service does not. Without knowledge of these distinctions, many visitors may encounter settings that differ from the nearby national parks. This may be especially true for foreign tourists who are encouraged to "come and see America's newest national park." Aggressive planning of information campaigns can help alleviate these potential image problems.

Research Implications. At least five research needs are associated with planning and management of the new Monument. The first concerns an underlying assumption behind many of the discussions regarding the Monument's use. It is assumed that designation of the area as a national monument will dramatically increase its use. Whether use actually increases and how long that increase will be sustained is an empirical question. Visitor counts will be useful in verifying this assumption. A second research need is an inventory of visitor motives. Motive inventories are necessary for matching settings to desired psychological outcomes. A third and related research need is an inventory of sites to assess whether they possess qualities that will satisfy the experience expectations of varying user groups. A fourth research need is an inventory of site resistance and resilience. Resistance is a site's ability to withstand impact associated with recreational use. Resilience is a site's ability to recover after recreational use. These are two key elements of a site's durability. Decisions regarding location of facilities and places for concentrated visitor use should correspond to site durability. Finally, policy research is needed to anticipate consequences associated with differing management alternatives. Building systems models and running policy simulations is a good way to balance public benefits among differing claimants. Integration of this research into management decisions will best enhance the recreational use of the Monument while preventing undue impact on other monument values.

References

Antiquities Act of 1906. 16 U.S.C. 431, 34 Stat. 225.

Altman, I. 1975. THE ENVIRONMENT AND SOCIAL BEHAVIOR: PRIVACY, PERSONAL SPACE, TERRITORY, CROWDING. Brooks/Cole Publishing Company, Monterey, CA.

Atkinson, J. W., and D. Birch. 1972. MOTIVATION: THE DYNAMICS OF ACTION. John Wiley and Sons, NY.

Brown, P. J., B. L. Driver, and C. McConnell. 1978. *The opportunity spectrum concept in outdoor recreation supply inventories: Background and application.* Pages 73-84 in PROCEEDINGS OF THE INTEGRATED RENEWABLE RESOURCE INVENTORIES WORKSHOP. U.S.D.A. Forest Service, General Technical Report RM-55.

Cates, K. April 29, 1997. *Change seeps slowly but ever so surely into S. Utah.* DESERET NEWS WEB EDITION, http://www.desnews.com/cgi-in/libstory?dn97&9704290201.

Driver, B. L., and P. J. Brown. 1978. *The opportunity spectrum concept in outdoor recreation supply inventories: A rationale.* Pages 24-31 in PROCEEDINGS OF THE INTEGRATED RENEWABLE RESOURCE INVENTORIES WORKSHOP. U.S.D.A. Forest Service, General Technical Report RM-55.

Driver, B. L., P. J. Brown, and G. L. Peterson. 1991. *Research on leisure benefits: An introduction to this volume.* Pages 3-11 in B. L. Driver, P. J. Brown, and G. L. Peterson, editors. BENEFITS OF LEISURE. Venture Publishing, State College, PA.

Federal Land Policy and Management Act of 1976. 43 U.S.C 1701, 90 Stat. 2743.

Haas, G. E., B. L. Driver, and P. J. Brown. 1980. *Measuring wilderness recreation experiences.* Pages 20-40 in PROCEEDINGS OF THE WILDERNESS PSYCHOLOGY GROUP. Durham, NH.

Interim Management Policy for Lands Under Wilderness Review. 1995. U.S. Department of the Interior, Bureau of Land Management, H-8550-1.

Lawler, E. E. 1973. MOTIVATIONS IN WORK ORGANIZATIONS. Brooks/Cole Publishing Company, Monterey, CA.

Manning, R. E. 1986. STUDIES IN OUTDOOR RECREATION. Oregon State University Press, Corvallis, OR.

Marshall, N. J. 1972. *Privacy and environment.* HUMAN ECOLOGY 1: 93-110.

Marshall, N. J. 1974. *Dimensions of privacy preferences.* MULTIVARIATE BEHAVIORAL RESEARCH 9: 255-72.

Proclamation—Establishment of the Grand Staircase–Escalante National Monument. September 1996. No. 6920, 61 FEDERAL REGISTER 50223.

Ruddell, E. J., and J. Westphal. 1989. *Images relating to park titles and ambient qualities at select National Park Service areas*. LANDSCAPE JOURNAL 8: 122-27.

Twight, B. W., K. L. Smith, and G. H. Wassinger. 1981. *Privacy and camping: Closeness to the self vs. closeness to others*. LEISURE SCIENCES 4: 427-41.

Westin, A. F. 1967. PRIVACY AND FREEDOM. Atheneum Books, NY.

Wilderness Act of 1964. 16 U.S.C. 1131 et seq.

PART THREE

Monument Planning

Legal Standards and Public Involvement

"The natural world is a screen onto which we project our own images."
—*Wallace Stegner*
The Marks of Human Passage

"Local government, and certainly the people…have a lot to offer
in the way of information about the lands being considered.
No one knows the monument lands better than we do."
—*Joe Judd*
Kane County Commissioner

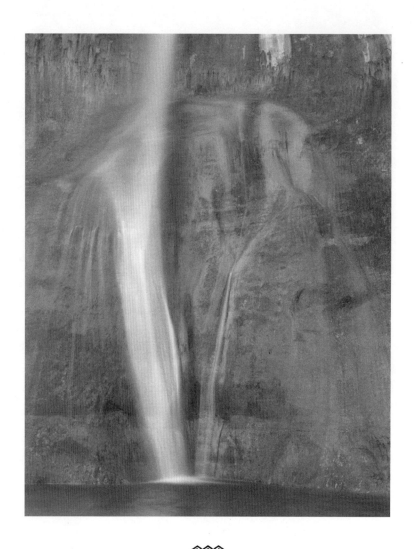

❧❧❧

LOWER CALF CREEK FALLS

Photograph by Dr. Laurel Casjens.

Previous page: Human Petroglyph from Deer Canyon, Site 1
from Kenneth B. Castleton, **Petroglyphs and Pictographs of Utah, Volume 2** *(1979).*

CHAPTER NINE

Putting the Antiquities Act in Perspective

John D. Leshy

When the definitive history of America's efforts to protect its natural and cultural resources is written, the Antiquities Act will loom very large and properly so. This is the law that gave President Clinton the authority he exercised in September 1996 to create the Grand Staircase–Escalante National Monument. Whenever any president has exercised his authority under this law, it has generally been an unqualified success and a tremendous boon to the quality of life in America.

The bare statistics do not tell the whole story, but they are quite impressive. Since the Antiquities Act was adopted by Congress in 1906, fourteen of the seventeen presidents who have occupied the White House have proclaimed 100 different national monuments. A number of these monuments have since been turned into national parks. Individually, they range in size from less than 10 acres to nearly 12 million acres. Although national monuments are found in twenty-four different states and the Virgin Islands, they have a distinctly western focus. In total, monument designations have protected about 70 million acres, or about 10 percent of the nation's federal land base.

What these statistics do not convey is the outstanding character of the resources protected by national monument designations, the magic and poetry of these places. They can, intellectually and spiritually, reach even the most hard-bitten and thick-skinned observer—the majesties of the Grand Canyon; the glories of Glacier Bay, Alaska; the mountains and rainforests of the Olympic Peninsula; the stark terrain of Death Valley; the spectacular formations of the Carlsbad Caverns; and the marine gardens of Buck Island Reef in the Virgin Islands. Blessed with some of the most spectacular country on the planet, it is not surprising that Utah holds some of the finest examples of Antiquities Act policymaking—Zion, Bryce, Capitol Reef, Arches, Natural Bridges, Cedar Breaks, and Dinosaur.

Protecting these wonders through the Antiquities Act has been a bipartisan undertaking. Interestingly, Democratic and Republican presidents have used it about an equal number of times. The first protectors of Zion, Bryce Canyon, and Death Valley were Republicans (Presidents Taft, Coolidge, and Hoover, respectively), while Acadia, Cedar Breaks, and Wrangell-St. Elias had Democratic parentage (Presidents Wilson, Franklin Roosevelt, and Carter, respectively). Regardless of their parentage, these are places for all Americans, indeed for all the world—as evidenced by the recent flood of Germans, Japanese, French, Australians, and others to the Southwest.

* * * * * *

The Antiquities Act is a somewhat unusual statute. By its terms, Congress has vested in the president a broad power to act, unilaterally, unencumbered by process or any legal duty to consult. It is the kind of power that appeals to presidents, which is why most presidents have exercised it.

The Antiquities Act also contains the kind of power, some diehards say, that ought to be curbed because it is too susceptible of misuse or abuse. Objectors note that presidents have sometimes acted under this act without much advance consultation, as President Clinton did with the Grand Staircase–Escalante. In fact, some proclamations were complete surprises.

Some national monuments were "parting shots" by lame duck presidents, sprung on unsuspecting Congresses, states, and localities. Teddy Roosevelt created the Olympic Peninsula, now Olympic National Park, with a few hours left in his presidency. President Hoover was particularly busy in the days just before he handed over the reins of power to Franklin D. Roosevelt; as a lame duck, he protected Saguaro, Black Canyon of the Gunnison, Death Valley, and set aside another 275,000 acres adjacent to Grand Canyon National Park. President Eisenhower created the C&O Canal National Monument in Washington, D. C., just two days before John F. Kennedy was sworn into office. President Lyndon B. Johnson proclaimed Marble Canyon (now part of Grand Canyon National Park) on January 20, 1969. For good measure, he added 360,000 acres to Katmai, Arches, and Capitol Reef the same day.

Sometimes monument proclamations have created controversy and local outrage. Franklin Roosevelt's creation of Jackson Hole National Monument in 1943 provoked Rep. Frank Barrett of Wyoming to call his action "contrary to every principle of freedom and democracy," and a "usurpation of power and the prerogatives of Congress." Sen. Edward Robinson called the action a "foul sneaking Pearl Harbor blow"—particularly strong language since this was in the middle of World War II, barely fifteen months after Pearl Harbor. Some in Congress, notably Rep. Gracie Pfost of Idaho and the ever-curmudgeonly Wayne Aspinall of Colorado, were so upset by President Eisenhower's decision to create the C&O Canal National Monument that they persuaded Congress to deny it funding for nine years. (It is now one of Washington's most used and best loved features.) Utah senator Wallace Bennett expressed shock and surprise at Lyndon Johnson's last minute enlargement of Arches and Capitol Reef, calling it an unwarranted "land grab," and promptly introduced a bill to overturn it.

The historical record soundly refutes the charge of abuse. To the contrary, the record reveals that—no matter how controversial the initial proclamation—Congress has usually come to embrace these areas as its own within a relatively few years. Generally, Congress has ratified monument proclamations and cemented them even more firmly into place.

And the affected states and localities have likewise come successfully and fully to terms with the designations, often becoming their fiercest defenders.

It is useful to think about national monument designations this way: Imagine the firestorm of protest that would ensue if a politician today proposed to remove the protections from the C&O Canal, Zion, Arches, Bryce Canyon, or Jackson Hole. Even former Wyoming governor and senator Cliff Hansen, who was a county commissioner in Jackson Hole when President Roosevelt designated the Grand Tetons a national monument in 1943, was recently quoted as saying that his condemnation of the president's action was a mistake.

A related charge sometimes leveled at the act is that it is antidemocratic. But the act is, after all, an act of the Congress—a deliberate decision, by the body that the Constitution vests with broad authority over the public lands, to hand over to the president a potentially sweeping power. At any time during the past ninety-one years, Congress could have repealed the act, or rescinded any or all presidential proclamations under it. With only two exceptions, however, Congress has chosen not to restrict the president's power in any way since 1906.

Nor has Congress, again with a few minor exceptions, chosen to rescind any proclamation created by the president under this act. The exceptions have been small areas of marginal value, and the names do not mean anything anymore. The areas total less than 5,000 acres out of the 70 million acres that have been proclaimed national monuments since 1906.

Far from being antidemocratic, the Antiquities Act furnishes a classic case study in presidential leadership. It gives the president a platform on which, acting on his own, he can take risks and be statesmanlike. It is noteworthy that, taking the long view, presidents have used the act's power more often to end controversies about the future management of these prize areas, than to ignite controversy. If the president's judgment and action are sound, they will eventually bring the country, the Congress, and the affected states and localities, along with him. That has almost always been the case, and will most likely be the case with the Grand Staircase–Escalante.

With the Antiquities Act, as in so much else with natural resource and public land policy, Teddy Roosevelt set the pattern. The act gave him the opportunity to practice what he preached from his bully pulpit, and he did not hesitate. The ink was barely dry on the Antiquities Act bill when, a few weeks later, he exercised this new power to create Devils Tower National Monument in Wyoming.

More relevant to the Grand Staircase–Escalante, however, is Teddy Roosevelt's action at the Grand Canyon. Roosevelt used the Antiquities Act to preserve parts of the Grand Canyon, which had been proposed—unsuccessfully—for national park status. The national park effort had always failed because of local opposition. In the early years of this century, a recalcitrant local politician and profiteer named Ralph Cameron was mining gold from tourists' pockets—via an access fee—through fraudulent mining claims that he had located on the south rim and on the Bright Angel Trail. When Roosevelt learned of this, he acted under the Antiquities Act to set it aside.

Although Cameron and some other local interests were outraged, who today would have the temerity to question the fundamental validity and wisdom of Roosevelt's action? Would anyone, except perhaps those few who believe any federal ownership is a sin? Certainly not Coconino County, Arizona, which reaps enormous economic benefits from visitors to the Grand Canyon. This fact alone must surely cause Ralph Cameron, former Coconino County sheriff, some discomfort in his grave. With President Roosevelt's action, fundamental debate about whether the Grand Canyon would be protected in public ownership and managed for future generations was over.

But President Roosevelt's proclamation had another consequence. Cameron sued to block the designation and contested its validity all the way to the U. S. Supreme Court. Cameron pointed out that the act speaks of "objects of historic or scientific interest," and that it explicitly cautions against proclaiming more than the "smallest area compatible with the proper care and management of the objects to be protected." Cameron argued with some plausibility, "How can a 270,000-acre reservation be squared with that language?"

The arguments were to no avail. On April 19, 1920, in a classic case of great facts making good law, the unanimous Supreme Court gave the act and the president's action a ringing endorsement. The opinion was written by Justice Willis Van Devanter of Wyoming, a former chief legal officer of the Department of the Interior. The decision came a little more than a year after Congress made Grand Canyon a national park, and a few months after Cameron took office as a senator (Arizona voters having not yet gained enlightenment). The decision set presidents and the country firmly on a course that would result in protection of many magnificent features of natural bounty, including the Grand Staircase–Escalante National Monument.

Other outstanding examples of presidential leadership under the Antiquities Act included President Eisenhower' s protection of the C&O Canal. Through the 1950s, bills to designate the canal as a national park enjoyed widespread support in Congress, but could not make it past Chairman Wayne Aspinall's House Interior Committee. Similar circumstances drove President Franklin Roosevelt's actions with the Jackson Hole designation and President Carter's monumental use of the act's authority in Alaska. In the case of Alaska, after Congress stalled over a nine-year effort to determine how the crown jewels of that state would be managed, Carter set aside 56 million acres in 1978.

*   *   *   *   *   *

Not surprisingly, President Clinton's proclamation of September 18, 1996, creating the Grand Staircase–Escalante National Monument has provoked considerable controversy. Perhaps the sharpest criticism of the president's action was that it was taken without any consideration of or consultation with local interests. Admittedly, while the Monument was being considered, a curtain of confidentiality was maintained around the proclamation. Reasonable people can differ about whether this initial confidentiality was appropriate, but several facts bear directly on the answer to that question.

First, the long-term management of this area of southern Utah—more precisely, whether it should be open to full scale industrialization—has been hotly, steadily, and widely debated for more than twenty years. There is perhaps no place on the federal lands that has had its future management so prominently thrust into the public arena. Citizens concerned about this area have probably been "consulted" on this issue more than any other public land constituency. In the year leading up to the proclamation, wilderness bills sponsored by the Utah congressional delegation had received a thorough airing in both houses of Congress. In short, the president did not act in a vacuum; he was keenly aware of that debate.

Second, the president did not make his decision to move forward without talking to the governor, the congressional delegation, and other local interests. In fact, the president and his senior advisers, including Secretary of the Interior Babbitt, had a number of direct conversations with Utah officials during the days immediately preceding his decision. These conversations addressed both whether to go forward with the proclamation and its terms. They continued until very shortly—just hours—before the president made his decision.

Third, the substance of the proclamation reveals that most state and local concerns were addressed. In conversations with the president, Utah officials expressed a number of legitimate specific concerns regarding grazing, water rights, hunting, fishing, mineral development, and interspersed state lands. They also asked what federal agency would be managing this area, and how management decisions would be made.

It is an obscure but important historical fact that most Antiquities Act proclamations are surprisingly terse. Typically, the proclamations are absolutely silent on many questions, leaving future management issues open to a wide range of uncertainty and ambiguity. They almost never speak to any of the questions that the Utah interests were raising.

In this case, by sharp contrast, the administration decided to break new ground and to address these concerns in the proclamation itself. Indeed, the Grand Staircase–Escalante National Monument proclamation is, by a wide margin, the most complete, exhaustive, and detailed Antiquities Act proclamation that has ever been signed by any president. It extensively described, with considerable care, the natural and historic objects being protected, and it directly addressed the management concerns.

The president knew that part of the audience for this proclamation was skeptical of his Monument designation decision. The proclamation was therefore written to describe clearly the value (in some cases the world-class value) of the resources being protected, seeking to persuade people that the Antiquities Act was an appropriate tool for that protection. And most important, the proclamation was written to inform people, as much as possible, about what its effects would be on future management of the area. These are laudable objectives, and the proclamation comes closer to reaching them than just about any of the 100 preceding national monument proclamations. Remarkably, for all the vigor with which objections about the process leading up to the proclamation have been voiced, there have been far fewer complaints about the substance and the *details* of the proclamation.

The proclamation is also unusual by explicitly mandating a closely consultative, open, and thoroughly public planning process. That process will produce, over the next three years, the details of how the area will actually be managed. In the meantime, interim management guidelines are in place that generally allow traditional uses to continue.

A final unique aspect of this proclamation was the president's decision to adopt Secretary Babbitt's strong recommendation that the Bureau of Land Management (BLM) be entrusted with managing the new Monument. The BLM already has under its stewardship some magnificent natural resources that approach in quality the crown jewels of our federal land base. The secretary viewed the new Monument as a great opportunity to show the nation that the BLM was well qualified to manage national monument resources. And Babbitt saw other opportunities: to show the affected local areas that their good, long-term working relationships with the BLM would be maintained; to give the local interests a greater sense of continuity and participation; and to challenge the BLM to undertake important new management responsibilities.

Having taken what history may regard as one of the outstanding acts in national conservation history, the president and Secretary Babbitt strongly believe that now is the time to move forward from conflict and tension to healing and cooperation. Indeed, there are tangible signs that this has already begun, as reflected in the state's involvement in the planning process and Governor Leavitt's determination to make that process work. As other interests step forward and engage themselves in the planning process, the future of the new Grand Staircase–Escalante National Monument will begin to take firm shape, and that can only bode well for the nation and the citizens of Utah.

CHAPTER TEN

Defining a Legal Framework
for BLM Management

Robert B. Keiter

Creation of the Grand Staircase–Escalante National Monument under the administration of the Bureau of Land Management (BLM) establishes a new and unprecedented public land management arrangement. When presidents have relied upon the Antiquities Act of 1906 (16 U.S.C. §§ 431-33) to establish national monuments, they have traditionally vested the preservation-oriented National Park Service with jurisdiction over these monuments. However, the proclamation creating the new Monument designation defies this precedent, giving the BLM unique protectionist planning and management responsibilities.

Several critical legal issues confront the BLM as it begins implementing these new management responsibilities. Chief among these issues are: (1) identifying the legal standards that govern Monument management; (2) establishing appropriate planning processes and procedures; (3) determining the scope, extent, and impact of valid existing rights, particularly those involving mineral resources; (4) addressing state and private inholdings in the planning process; and (5) determining whether additional regulations or legislation are necessary. How the BLM resolves these issues will affect, among other things, state school trust lands, private inholdings, wilderness study areas, mineral development opportunities, livestock grazing levels, access roads, and water rights. Sufficient direction can be gleaned from the establishing proclamation, existing judicial precedent, and related statutes to venture preliminary answers to the primary legal concerns.

Management Standards

The legal standards governing federal management authority for the new Monument are derived primarily from the Antiquities Act (16 U.S.C. §§ 431–33) and the proclamation establishing it. Additional legal guidance can be derived from the Federal Land Policy Management Act (FLPMA) (43 U.S.C. §§ 1701–82) and the National Environmental Policy Act (NEPA) (42 U.S.C. §§ 4231–61), as well as other related laws governing the public lands. These related laws include the General Mining Law of

1872 (30 U.S.C. §§ 21-42), the Mineral Leasing Act of 1920 (30 U.S.C. §§ 181–277), the Endangered Species Act (16 U.S.C. §§ 1531–43), the Wilderness Act (16 U.S.C. §§ 1131–36), and the Taylor Grazing Act (43 U.S.C. §§ 315–315r). Because the National Parks Organic Act addresses national monument management (16 U.S.C. § 1), the BLM might look to the Park Service's monument management plans and regulations for guidance. The BLM may also secure further guidance from proposed regulations developed by the U.S. Fish & Wildlife Service to govern national wildlife monuments in Alaska (44 Fed. Reg. 33754, June 28, 1979), another rare instance when an agency other than the Park Service was vested with jurisdiction over a national monument.

The Antiquities Act provides general guidance for managing national monuments. Besides vesting the President with discretionary authority to create national monuments for historic or scientific purposes, the Antiquities Act provides for the "proper care and management of the objects to be protected" (16 U.S.C. § 431). The act also authorizes the Secretary of the Interior to make uniform rules for implementing the legislation (16 U.S.C. § 432). In addition, the act requires permits for archeological excavations or the removal of "objects of antiquity" (16 U.S.C. § 432), and it imposes criminal penalties for the unauthorized excavation or removal of monument objects (16 U.S.C. § 433). In *Cappaert v. United States* (426 U.S. 129 [1976]), the Supreme Court interpreted the protective goals of the act broadly, rejecting the argument that it was limited only to archeological sites (426 U.S. at 141–42). In sum, the Antiquities Act establishes a clear protective management standard and obligates the BLM to give priority to safeguarding those resources that prompted the Monument designation.

The proclamation establishing the new Monument provides critical details identifying protected resources. In *Cappaert*, which is the principal judicial decision addressing national monument management authority, the Supreme Court carefully examined the proclamation establishing Devil's Hole as an addition to Death Valley National Monument in determining that federal reserved water rights attached to the monument designation. Recognizing that federal reserved water rights were necessary to protect the monument's scientific and historical fish resources, the Court sustained a lower court decision enjoining groundwater pumping on adjacent private lands that threatened these resources. For the Grand Staircase–Escalante, the proclamation expressly details numerous geologic, paleontological, archeological, historical, and biological features that justified its designation as a national monument. The proclamation also provides that "the Secretary of the Interior shall manage the monument through the BLM, pursuant to applicable legal authorities, to implement the purposes of this proclamation." Although the proclamation acknowledges "valid existing rights," continues state authority for fish and wildlife management, and authorizes continued livestock grazing, the guiding management principle is the protection of the Monument's historical and scientific objects.

The FLPMA (43 U.S.C. §§ 1701–84), the organic legislation governing BLM public lands, also may apply to national monument management. The FLPMA contemplates both multiple-use and protective management of BLM lands (43 U.S.C. § 1732[a]), and it establishes an interdisciplinary resource management planning process (43 U.S.C. §1712) to implement these purposes. Under FLPMA, the concept of multiple-use provides for "a combination of balanced and diverse resource uses that takes into account the long-term needs of future generations," including "recreation, ... wildlife and fish, and natural, scenic, scientific and historical values" (43 U.S.C. § 1702[c]). Those multiple-use activities allowed to continue under the proclamation's valid existing rights and livestock grazing provisions are therefore subject to reasonable regulation to accomplish the national monument's protective purposes. Moreover, these activities are subject to the FLPMA provision prohibiting "unnecessary or undue degradation of the lands" (43 U.S.C. § 1732[b]; Mansfield, 1991). In short, the FLPMA multiple-use mandate does not conflict with the protective national monument management obligations established under the Antiquities Act and the proclamation.

Various public lands located within the Monument boundaries are already subject to restrictive management obligations, either because of previous withdrawal orders or other reservations. The proclamation expressly does not revoke any prior withdrawals or reservations, but it does provide that "the national monument shall be the dominant reservation." In effect, this provision superimposes the protective national monument management goals over other management goals, thus superseding any contrary or less protective management standards. This provision should not, however, affect the 900,000 acres of designated wilderness study areas (WSAs) located within the Monument boundaries. Because the proclamation does not revoke the WSA designation, WSA lands should continue to be subject to the FLPMA nonimpairment management standard, which requires maintaining their suitability for wilderness preservation pending a final congressional wilderness designation decision (43 U.S.C. § 1782[c]). There is no apparent inconsistency between the protective management standards that attach to national monument lands and the similarly restrictive management standards that govern WSA lands. In fact, Congress has regularly designated wilderness areas within national monuments following initial creation of the monument (*e.g.*, 90 Stat. 2693 [Badlands], 90 Stat. 2692 [Bandelier]).

Other laws with potential application to management of the new Monument include the Endangered Species Act, General Mining Law of 1872, Mineral Leasing Act of 1920, and Taylor Grazing Act of 1935. The Endangered Species Act applies whenever "listed" endangered or threatened species are present; it prohibits anyone from "taking" an endangered species (16 U.S.C. § 1539[a]) and establishes an interagency consultation process that gives the U.S. Fish & Wildlife Service a potential veto over any proposed activity that could jeopardize "listed" species (16 U.S.C. § 1536[a][2]). Because several listed species have been found or sighted within the Monument (P. Wilkins, pers. commun.), the Endangered Species Act could limit activities that might take or jeopardize these species. The mining and grazing laws establish important statutory rights that are either acknowledged under the proclamation's valid existing rights provision or the separate grazing provision. These statutory rights are, however, subject to reasonable regulation to accomplish the Monument's protective purposes, so long as the regulation does not prohibit sanctioned activities and thus raise constitutional takings concerns.

Planning Processes

Neither the Antiquities Act nor the proclamation designating the new Monument establishes a management planning process. The proclamation directs the Secretary of the Interior to undertake a three-year planning process and authorizes him to promulgate management regulations, but it is otherwise silent concerning planning procedures. As a result, the BLM has decided to use its own FLPMA planning procedures for the Monument rather than attempt to devise new ones (J. Meredith, pers. commun.).

Because the BLM's FLPMA planning requirements contain several rigorous resource protection provisions consistent with the Monument designation (43 U.S.C. §§ 1711, 1712; 43 C.F.R. § 1600), it should prove suitable for national monument planning purposes. First, the breadth of the FLPMA multiple-use definition, which includes recreation, watershed, wildlife and fish, natural scenic, scientific, and historical values, provides a clear basis for protecting the Monument's resources (43 U.S.C. § 1702[c]). Second, the FLPMA expressly recognizes that plans must adhere to any standards established for specifically dedicated tracts of land (43 U.S.C. § 1732[a]), which would clearly include the new Monument designation. Third, the BLM's planning processes require that priority be given to management of "areas of critical environmental concern," which is defined in a manner that embraces the same resource values that underlie the Monument designation (43 U.S.C. §§ 1702[a], 1712[c][3]). Although the planning process also must address traditional multiple-use activities under the proclamation's valid existing rights provision, it is equally clear that the process should not be driven by these activities. Thus, the FLPMA planning procedures should prove adaptable to the more protective national monument setting.

The planning process will clearly require adherence to NEPA environmental analysis procedures. Under NEPA, federal agencies must prepare an Environmental Impact Statement (EIS) whenever a proposed action may significantly affect the human environment (42 U.S.C. § 4332[2][C]). Given the radical shift in management emphasis dictated by the new Monument designation as well as the public controversy accompanying it, the BLM plainly should employ the full EIS process in preparing its management plan. Under the FLPMA planning regulations, NEPA compliance is also required at the planning stage (43 C.F.R. § 1601.0–6). Moreover, the protective management standards governing Monument planning will require an analysis of cumulative environmental impacts from both a spatial and temporal perspective (40 C.F.R. §§ 1508.7, 1508.25), including analysis of impacts linked to state and private inholdings and adjacent lands. Because neither the Kanab nor Escalante resource management plans have been completed, there is no opportunity for tiering from existing resource management plans.

The planning process should ensure opportunities for state, local, and public involvement. Under NEPA, the EIS process contemplates public comment on draft EISs

(40 C.F.R. § 1503). Under FLPMA, the BLM land use planning process also provides for public involvement (43 U.S.C. §§ 1712[a] and [f]). In addition, the FLPMA planning procedures require coordination with the planning processes of adjacent federal, state, and local governmental entities (43 U.S.C. § 1712[c][9]), and calls for consistency between BLM resource management plans and state and local plans "to the maximum extent [the Secretary] finds consistent with Federal law and the purposes of this Act (43 U.S.C. § 1712[c][9])." Given the purposes of the new Monument designation, consistency will essentially require that state and local land use plans acknowledge the protective management standards governing the Monument. But recognizing the state and local sensitivities associated with the new Monument designation, the BLM should be prepared to explain any inconsistencies between Monument management goals and resource priorities on adjacent state and private lands during the planning process. Moreover, under the proclamation, the planning process must acknowledge and address the state's role in regulating wildlife and fish within the Monument.

According to the proclamation, the contentious issue of water for the new Monument is deferred to the planning process. The proclamation expressly "does not reserve water as a matter of Federal law"; rather, it directs the Secretary of the Interior to determine "in the management plan the extent to which water is necessary for the proper care and management of the objects of this monument and the extent to which further action may be necessary pursuant to Federal or State law to assure the availability of water." Thus, if BLM planners determine that instream water flows are necessary to meet the Monument's purposes, then they must examine the options for asserting a water rights claim. Since Utah water law provides that only designated state agencies can assert an instream flow claim (Utah Code Ann. § 73-3-3[11]), Monument managers may be forced to pursue a water claim under federal law and possibly in a federal forum.

Valid Existing Rights, Takings, and Related Concerns

The proclamation establishing the new Monument indicates that the designation "is subject to valid existing rights." Even though valid existing rights provisions have become standard language in public land legislation, the provision is subject to varying interpretations, has stirred considerable controversy, and cannot be divorced from related constitutional takings principles. Key questions that arise concerning this provision are: (1) whether a valid existing right is present; (2) the scope and duration of the right; and (3) the extent to which the right is subject to additional regulatory limitations to accomplish national monument management goals. These issues are particularly relevant to mining claims, mineral leases, and rights-of-way located within the Monument, as well as livestock grazing activities.

Several legal principles help to define the valid existing rights concept. First, under traditional administrative law doctrine, the agency charged with implementing a valid existing rights provision should enjoy considerable judicial deference in interpreting the provision (*Rocky Mountain Oil & Gas Ass'n [RMOGA] v. Watt*, 696 F.2d 734 [10th Cir.

1982]; *Sierra Club v. Hodel,* 848 F.2d 1068 [10th Cir. 1988]). Second, determination of whether valid existing rights have attached ordinarily requires a case-by-case examination of the law, legal instruments, or expectations that originally created the claimed right or property interest (88 I.D. 909, 912). Third, valid existing rights are not absolute (88 I.D. 909, 912); land management agencies may regulate (but not prohibit) preexisting uses or activities to accomplish new objectives, even if the regulation may result in some diminution in value (Laitos, 1989–90). Fourth, if a property interest has been created and if it is impacted by a new designation, the valid existing rights provision generally protects that interest to the same extent as constitutional takings doctrine (Bratt, 1989–90). In sum, the valid existing rights provision in the proclamation should not preclude the BLM from further regulating current activities to protect Monument resources, so long as the regulation does not unreasonably interfere with existing rights and thus cross the takings threshold.

The proclamation's valid existing rights provision could affect mining activities in the new Monument. In general, unless a valid mining claim has been established and recognized, the valid existing rights provision should not have any application. Under the General Mining Law of 1872, which governs precious metals and other hardrock minerals, different types of property interests or expectations are created at different stages in the mining process. Before location of a valid mining claim, the miner enjoys only a *pedis possessio* right that does not extend to the federal government (*United States v. Carlile,* 67 I.D. 417 [1960]) or constitute a valid existing right. After location of a valid unpatented mining claim, the miner obtains a less than full ownership property right, which is subject to federal regulation that does not unreasonably interfere with mining operations (*United States v. Doremus,* 888 F.2d 630, 633 [9th Cir. 1989]). In cases where the claim's validity has not yet been established, the cost of compliance with reasonable regulatory constraints, including requirements designed to protect Monument resources, should be a legitimate consideration in determining whether a valuable mineral discovery has occurred (*United States v. Kosanke Sand Corp.,* 80 I.D. 538, 546 [1973]; *In re Pacific Coast Molybdenum Co.,* 90 I.D. 352, 361 [1983]). For pending patent applications, a vested right does not arise until the validity of the mining claim has been established, which means contested claims are not covered by the valid existing rights provision (*Swanson v. Babbitt,* 3 F.3d 1348 [9th Cir. 1993]). However, for patent applications approved before the Monument designation, these mining claims are converted to private property and would no longer be subject to federal mining regulations.

The proclamation's valid existing rights language also could affect mineral leasing and exploration activities in the new Monument. Under the proclamation's withdrawal language, no new mineral leases may be issued. But oil and gas leases are already outstanding on Monument lands, and one leaseholder has applied for an exploratory drilling permit subsequent to the Monument designation. Although the Secretary of the Interior enjoys discretion under the amended Mineral Leasing Act of 1920 to determine whether to lease public lands (Coggins and Glicksman, 1997:§23.02)), once a lease is issued the lessee acquires a property interest that is defined by the terms of the lease.

Absent a nonsurface occupancy or other restrictive stipulation, the lessee ordinarily can expect to be able to conduct exploration activities on the leased lands, subject to compliance with NEPA environmental analysis requirements (*Colorado Environmental Coalition v. BLM*, 932 F.Supp. 1247; D. Colo. 1996; Coggins and Glicksman, 1997:§23.04[3]). In the BLM wilderness study area context, however, the courts have deferred to and affirmed the Secretary's interpretation that a statutory grandfather provision only protects those activities actually occurring on the date of the enactment (*RMOGA v. Watt, supra*). Under the *RMOGA* interpretation, exploratory drilling and other development activity proposed after the Monument designation would be subject to reasonable regulation to accomplish Monument purposes. But were that regulation to prohibit any exploration or development opportunity, then the valid existing rights provision may be violated and a takings claim might arise.

The valid existing rights provision also affects right-of-way claims across the new Monument. For some pre-1976 right-of-way claims, the governing law is R.S. 2477, which was grandfathered under FLPMA (43 U.S.C. §§ 1701[h], 1769[a]). The R.S. 2477 right-of-way issue has provoked considerable controversy over the relationship between federal and state law in defining the existence and scope of rights-of-way across public lands and the extent of federal regulatory authority (Hjelle, 1994; Lockhart, 1994). Legitimate R.S. 2477 rights-of-way are plainly covered under the proclamation's valid existing rights provision, but are also subject to reasonable federal regulation to protect Monument resources. This same principle applies to other pre-1976 right-of-way claims that are not based upon R.S. 2477 authority. For post-1976 right-of-way claims, the FLPMA governs (43 U.S.C. §§ 1761–70) and grants the Secretary of the Interior discretionary authority to grant or renew rights-of-way (43 U.S.C. §§ 1764[c], 1765). Under the FLPMA, the Secretary may regulate post-1976 rights-of-way to protect Monument resources, and he may attach protective terms and conditions to new right-of-way grants.

Under the proclamation, livestock grazing is addressed separately from other resource uses and specifically allowed to continue. The relevant provision states: "Nothing in this proclamation shall be deemed to affect existing permits or leases for, or levels of, livestock grazing on federal lands within the monument; existing grazing uses shall continue to be governed by applicable laws and regulations other than this proclamation." Significantly, the proclamation only grandfathers existing livestock grazing uses; it does not sanction new grazing activities within the Monument. The FLPMA livestock grazing provisions (43 U.S.C. §§ 1751–53) and the Taylor Grazing Act (43 U.S.C. §§ 315–315r) continue to serve as the primary laws governing grazing activities within the Monument. Under these statutes, a grazing permit is not a constitutionally protected property interest (*Pankey Land & Cattle Co. v. Hardin*, 427 F.2d 43, 44 [10th Cir. 1970]), and the BLM may regulate stocking levels, designate foraging locations, establish seasonal timing restraints, and impose related restrictions to protect range resources. Violations of these regulatory limitations or other permit conditions are subject to enforcement actions. And given the BLM's protective management responsibilities for

Monument resources, it also has the authority to regulate or limit grazing activities that pose a direct threat to these resources.

Inholdings and Exchanges

Approximately 176,000 acres of state school trust lands are scattered throughout the new Monument. The federal government granted these lands to Utah upon statehood to support its public schools. Although state school trust lands are managed to maximize economic returns, management options are constrained by the scattered location of trust parcels and now by the new Monument designation (Evans, 1991). For the state, the principal option for addressing this problem is to exchange the state school sections located within the Monument for federal lands located outside the Monument, with the goal of "blocking up" contiguous tracts to maximize economic development potential. Under FLPMA (43 U.S.C. § 1716) and related case law (*Andrus v. Utah,* 446 U.S. 500 [1980]), federal land exchanges are governed by the equal value and public interest principles. Similarly, Utah law provides for equal value rather than equal acreage when state-owned lands are exchanged (Utah Code § 65A-7-7). The equal value determination is based upon fair market value, which raises the controversial question of whether the value of state trust lands can be enhanced by the presence of adjacent federal lands and resources. Due to the presence of mineral resources on federal and state lands within Monument boundaries, this fair market value issue must be addressed directly in any federal-state land exchange proposal. Absent an acceptable exchange agreement, the BLM is obligated to afford the state or its lessees reasonable access to state trust lands for economic development purposes (*Utah v. Andrus,* 486 F. Supp. 995 [D. Utah 1979]). Although the BLM can regulate this access to protect Monument resources, it cannot prevent access or make it so restrictive as to constitute a compensable taking.

Approximately 10,000 acres of privately owned land are within the new Monument. Private landowners also might find land exchanges an attractive option for ensuring an economic return on their property and investment. The same equal value and public interest legal principles govern federal-private land exchanges as apply to federal-state exchanges. Alternatively, private landowners might choose to retain their lands and pursue development options. In this event, access across the surrounding Monument lands is governed either by R.S. 2477 (for many pre-1976 roads), FLPMA right-of-way provisions (43 U.S.C. §§ 1761–70), or an Alaska National Interest Lands Conservation Act access provision (16 U.S.C. § 1323[b]). Regardless of which provision applies, the BLM retains regulatory authority over access routes and can impose reasonable but not prohibitive limitations to protect Monument resources (*e.g., Wilkinsen v. Department of Interior,* 634 F. Supp. 1265 [D. Colo. 1986]; *United States v. Vogler,* 859 F.2d 638, 642 [9th Cir. 1988]).

State or private inholdings located within the Monument boundaries are also potentially subject to federal regulation to protect Monument resources. Under the U.S. Constitution's Article IV § 2 property clause, the United States enjoys broad sovereign power over the public lands (*Camfield v. United States*, 167 U.S. 518 [1897]; *Kleppe v. New Mexico*, 426 U.S. 529 [1976]). Several courts have recognized that the federal government's regulatory authority extends beyond the boundaries of public lands to reach activities occurring on adjacent state or private lands that could potentially harm public lands or resources (*Minnesota v. Block*, 660 F.2d 1240 [8th Cir. 1981], *cert. denied*, 455 U.S. 1007 [1982]; *United States v. Lindsey*, 595 F.2d 5 [9th Cir. 1979]). Under the Antiquities Act as well as the proclamation, the Secretary of the Interior can draw upon broad regulatory powers to manage and protect Monument resources. Although an assertion of federal regulatory authority that extended beyond Monument boundaries would undoubtedly be politically controversial, the mere fact that the power exists could influence state and private land management decisions on Monument inholdings. To avoid a potential confrontation, the Monument planning process should be used to identify and address any potential land management conflicts resulting from these mixed ownership patterns.

Further Steps: Legislation or Regulations?

At this juncture, the Antiquities Act, the proclamation, and related laws provide only general guidance for management of the new Monument. Is additional legal guidance concerning management standards, planning procedures, and related matters necessary? If so, is this guidance necessary now or at the conclusion of the planning process? And should such guidance take the form of legislation or administrative regulations? The short answer to these questions is that additional guidance would be helpful and should probably take the form of regulations based on the Monument planning experience. Additional legislation is unnecessary, because the BLM has adequate authority to promulgate regulations establishing long term Monument management standards and procedures.

The proclamation authorizes the Secretary of the Interior to promulgate necessary management and planning regulations for the new Monument. Clearly, because the Grand Staircase–Escalante is the first BLM-administered national monument, the agency should commit itself to developing long-term management and planning regulations. Although interim regulations might help to structure the planning process and to address pressing valid existing rights claims, the BLM's limited resources would be better deployed focusing on specific Monument planning and resource management issues. Existing laws, including the Antiquities Act, the proclamation, FLPMA, and NEPA, should provide sufficient standards and guidance to keep BLM planners focused on designing management standards to protect the unique historical and scientific resources that led to the Monument's creation. As difficult legal questions arise during the planning process (*e.g.*, mineral exploration permit requests, access to state and private inholdings for development purposes), the BLM must be prepared to respond in a fair and consistent manner that promotes rather than undermines Monument management objectives. Moreover, the BLM must recognize that answers to these and related questions will inevitably establish important precedents with long-range man-agement implications. Once the planning process is completed, the BLM should proceed to transform its accumulated information and experience into governing regulations that establish clear Monument management standards and procedures.

The only proposed legislation addressing management of the new Monument con-tains several provisions that are contrary to well-established national monument manage-ment principles (S.357). Following other national monument designations, Congress has occasionally confirmed the designation by legislation or even converted the national monument to a national park. In the case of the Grand Staircase–Escalante, however, Utah senator Bob Bennett's legislative proposal (S.357) actually revises the proclamation and substantially alters the governing management standards. Senator Bennett's proposal would require traditional multiple-use management of Monument resources (including minerals, timber, and oil and gas), and it would require that Monument resources be managed "in a way that provides for economic sustainability of local communities." The proposed legislation also calls for establishment of an advisory committee composed exclusively of Utah representatives to advise the BLM on Monument management and planning decisions. While these provisions would obviously advance the state's interest in the new Monument, they deviate significantly from the protective standards contained in the Antiquities Act and the governing proclamation. Moreover, they could skew the planning process toward local concerns rather than the resource protection objectives that motivated the initial designation.

References

Bratt, C. S. 1989-90. VER–What's in a name? An essay on valid existing rights. JOURNAL OF MINERAL LAW & POLICY 5:383-89.

Coggins, G. C. and R. L. Glicksman. 1997. PUBLIC NATURAL RESOURCES LAW. Clark Boardman Callaghan, New York, NY.

Evans, S. T. 1991. Revisiting the Utah school trust lands dilemma: Golden Arches National Park. JOURNAL OF ENERGY, NATURAL RESOURCES, AND ENVIRONMENTAL LAW 11:347-67.

Hjelle, B. G. 1994. Ten essential points concerning R.S. 2477 rights-of-way. JOURNAL OF ENERGY, NAT-URAL RESOURCES, AND ENVIRONMENTAL LAW 14:301-22.

Laitos, J. G. 1989-90. The nature and consequence of "valid existing rights" status in public land law. JOURNAL OF MINERAL LAW & POLICY 5:399-430.

Lockhart, W. J. 1994. Federal statutory grants are not placeholders for manipulated state law: A response to Ms. Hjelle. JOURNAL OF ENERGY, NATURAL RESOURCES, AND ENVIRONMENTAL LAW 14:323-48.

Mansfield, M. E. 1991. On the cusp of property rights: Lessons from public land law. ECOLOGY LAW QUARTERLY 18:43-104.

CHAPTER ELEVEN

The BLM Planning Process

A. Jerry Meredith

Unique may be the most misused word in the English language. According to Webster's Dictionary, unique means "the only one of its kind." Unfortunately, the word is too commonly used to describe what is merely uncommon or unusual. In reality, few things are truly unique. However, the Grand Staircase–Escalante National Monument is one of those things.

The Monument is unique because it is the only national monument assigned to the Bureau of Land Management (BLM) to manage. This provides managers, planners, and others who are interested in the future of this spectacular landscape a tremendous opportunity to create something different. We do not have to pressure ourselves to think beyond a preconceived box, because there is no box. The BLM has never managed a national monument, either rightly or wrongly. Within the BLM there are no national monument molds to break, no national monument traditions to bind us, and no national monument habits to overcome.

It is true that the BLM has its own agency culture, some might call it baggage. Some of it is good, some bad. But the creation of the Monument gives the BLM an opportunity to start from scratch in managing this particular piece of land.

What a wonderful thing it is to be able to work with a clean canvas. The BLM is excited because the Monument has a unique proclamation. As a result, we have the opportunity to try out something different—a management style that is a bit more flexible and adaptive. The BLM has the chance to experiment with an approach that not only strives to protect the land but is truly inclusive and seeks to infuse the regional character, strength, and sense of place into the management regime. I think this is our chance to find a management regime that complements, but does not copy, what we have on neighboring federal lands and to create a flavor of federal land management. The rest of this paper focuses on some of the things we are doing to take advantage of this opportunity.

First, the rules we are using to develop the management plan for the Monument are minimal, and those we do have are flexible. The BLM has relied upon the Resource Management Plan as its typical planning document over the past several years. Like most agencies, the BLM has developed volumes of regulations, manuals, and guidance for the development of these plans. Just the program-by-program guidance issued as "supplemental program guidance" fills large binders with instructions and procedures for local planners.

But the management plan for the Monument will not be a traditional Resource Management Plan. Therefore, the BLM has decided that it will not be bound by every aspect of guidance that exists. At the same time, we recognize that we need a foundation for our work and therefore will take our basic direction from BLM's existing planning regulations. These regulations, found in 43 CFR 1610, implement authorities granted under a wide range of laws. They reflect such requirements as the development of planning criteria and alternatives, public participation, and interagency coordination and consistency. These regulations also specify the completion of an Environmental Impact Statement (EIS) under the requirements of the National Environmental Policy Act (NEPA). Despite these specifications, BLM's planning regulations are general enough to provide a great deal of flexibility.

Indeed, the BLM is looking at the development of the Monument management plan as an opportunity to rethink our current planning process. We are working closely with the BLM Planning Office in our national headquarters to experiment with various planning techniques and processes that may eventually become part of our national planning requirements.

Partly because we are not bound by existing BLM planning guidance, but mostly because this type of project has not been done before, we are also taking considerable license with the format and organization of the planning document. NEPA and BLM's planning regulations require that we discuss certain topics including the affected environment, an array of alternatives and the estimated effects of the various alternatives. However, the rest of the document has yet to be conceived. We may not know the final format of the planning document until the planning team for the Monument finishes writing. Indeed, we may want to make format changes to our initial draft of the document to better reflect the information the team has gathered during the public involvement process.

The composition of the planning team is unique as well. This planning team includes more than just BLM staff. Under an agreement between the Secretary of Interior and the governor of Utah, the state of Utah has been assigned five members to the team that will develop the management plan. These people include a geologist, wildlife biologist, paleontologist, economist, and historian and all have far broader experience than their titles can convey.

These people are not ex-officio, not part-time, and are they are not outside consultants or advisers. They are full-fledged, full-time members of the planning team. They have moved to Cedar City and will work with the planning staff as one, cohesive team. They add a mix of experience and talent that might not have been possible to duplicate if the team were made up of only federal employees.

But the presence of full-time team members who are not federal employees is not the only thing that makes this team different from other BLM planning efforts. Of the ten federal employees selected as team members to date, only four, including myself, were BLM employees prior to this assignment. We have selected two from the National Park Service, two from the National Forest Service, and two who have no prior federal experience.

Several of the team members have advanced degrees, including one who is a professor on sabbatical to participate in the planning process. A number of the team members have worked in private industry or for local or state government. Some team members have operated their own businesses. Some come from Utah, others are from around the nation; some were raised in small towns and others in big cities. All are well educated, well traveled, and highly skilled in their respective fields of expertise. This wide diversity of skills, backgrounds, work experience, and personalities gives us great hope that this process will end up as unique as the planning team and the Monument.

The BLM has always made an effort to coordinate planning with neighboring organizations. Actually, our planning regulations already require coordination with the plans of other federal agencies, state and local governments, and Indian tribes. This has usually occurred in two ways. First, BLM would obtain a copy of any planning documents that were available from these entities and ask its planners to review these plans. However, no matter how hard they tried, our planners could not understand and remember the details of these voluminous planning documents or recall those who had developed them. Second, the planning team would send copies of their draft plan to these various governmental entities during the public comment period, asking for comments and suggestions about consistency with other planning documents. The BLM would then review these comments and make efforts to incorporate them into the final plan.

While these steps have improved the BLM's coordination with other governments, the process can be improved. To further improve this process, we want invested agencies and governments to be partners in our work from the very start. Thus, we have asked these entities to appoint people who understand their planning documents as liaisons to our team. The state of Utah, Kane County, Garfield County, Forest Service, Park Service, and Indian tribes have all named people with whom we can work from the start.

This approach assumes that it will be much easier to coordinate the relevant planning considerations as we proceed, rather than trying to adjust an independently developed plan between a draft and final document. While it would undoubtedly take less time for these other government organizations to critique our work during the public review period two or three years from now, we are confident that this new approach will be well worth the effort.

We are also aware that we cannot please every partner with every decision we make. Some of our partners have conflicting missions or points of view. But this process will at least ensure that we understand and consider the planning efforts of relevant government entities as we develop our plan.

Public involvement is another important, yet controversial part of every planning effort. Given the wide diversity of opinion in the United States, it's unlikely that there will ever be a plan developed by a local, state, tribal, or federal entity that will appeal to everyone. Therefore, I do not believe that the plan for the Monument will be different. Yet the public has more than just a right to be involved; public involvement improves the chances that the planning document will succeed. Our team cannot think of every contingency and does not have exclusive access to every good idea. We need public input because our team does not represent every point of view. As a result, we are implementing various opportunities for public involvement.

My greatest concern is that if not done properly success in attracting a great deal of public involvement may backfire. The more people we attract to the planning process, the wider the range of views and opinions. Participating in planning can be like voting in an election. One participates in the plan or votes in the election, but may feel as though it were a waste of time if the plan does not turn out the way one hoped or if one's candidate does not win. We want to avoid leaving people with the feeling that their participation did not matter. Therefore, we are struggling to come up with a public involvement system that lets people know they have been heard and their ideas have been valued, even if the result of the involvement is not what they advocated.

Note that I used the phrase, "we are struggling to come up with a public involvement system." This does not mean that the BLM does not have any idea how to involve the public in the planning process, but rather that our public involvement strategy is not yet complete. In fact, no decisions on the process or even specific elements of the process are final. But, some of our basic philosophies and some of our ideas are in place.

First, we believe that this process should be more open and more interactive than any planning process BLM has ever conducted. We will do our best to let people know, with minimal effort on their part, what we are doing. We will also try to provide as much feedback as possible to those involved. Traditionally, we provided the public two or three chances to contribute to the planning process, but few opportunities to engage in two-way communication with planners. While time and staff resources are always limited, our goal is to engage in as much two-way communication as possible. The BLM's goal is to let people know that we have heard their comments and heard them correctly.

Too often planning agencies gather public input before starting the plan, but then offer no feedback to the public until a draft document comes out for public review. However, in planning for the Monument, the BLM plans to involve the public at several points along the way, not just during scoping and draft plan comment periods. We will, of course, start the process with a formal scoping period. During this time we will hold scoping workshops, meet with interested organizations of all types, and gather ideas through the mail and the Internet. But scoping will not be only a sixty- or ninety-day process. We are looking for ways to provide feedback on the input we receive during the formal scoping period, to allow the public to review what we think we have heard from them and to give individuals the opportunity to respond if they think we have misunderstood them.

The BLM also wants more than one way of providing regular updates to those interested in the planning process, so they know what we are doing and what we are working on. Periodic printed updates are certainly one alternative, but we are also looking at ways of using the Internet to make information available and to allow for public input along the way. We have also set up regular meetings with several groups that have expressed an interest in this process and are willing to meet with others. We are considering the idea of conference calls with groups that are distant, and would even consider video-teleconferences where practical.

The BLM is considering the addition of an entirely new area of public involvement when we reach the stage of developing management alternatives. Experience shows that the public is often frustrated by the choice of alternatives analyzed in the agency's planning documents. Therefore, we are looking for ways to open up the process of developing a range of analyzed alternatives to reduce the risk that this frustration will occur.

Throughout the process, the BLM is looking for opportunities to gather and share information that may have been overlooked during previous planning efforts. We are forming partnerships to share information about resources, social and economic conditions, and public values. The data we gather will be available for review and for use by all those interested in the Monument. And finally, we are looking for ways to use new technologies that we have not exploited in the past. We do not know whether our budget will allow us to do some of the things we would like; however, the following represent examples of what we wish to do.

The BLM hopes to set up a system that can be accessed through the Internet that allows anyone to look through all the data we have collected on the Monument. We are working closely with the state of Utah and the Utah Automated Geographic Reference Center to provide this information online.

The BLM is also investigating the feasibility of creating a computer-generated modeling system that would allow our planning team and the public to view the consequences of various management scenarios for the Monument. Users would be able to input their own management schemes and get feedback on the interactions and implications of those scenarios. This would allow people to test their own ideas about Monument management before suggesting them to us and even to see how their ideas might interact with ideas of others.

In sum, the above is an overview of some of the ways that the BLM can make this management plan as unique as the Monument. Our team is still not entirely in place and we still have a long way to go with some of these ideas whereas others are already in place and working. We believe we will have a planning process that will meet the regulatory requirements for public involvement. Far more important, we are well on our way to devising a communication system that will allow us to gather the best ideas from those who care, so that we can, together, build a common vision for the Grand Staircase–Escalante National Monument.

CHAPTER TWELVE

Utah and the National Monument Planning Process

Brad T. Barber

We have to look upon the Grand Staircase–Escalante National Monument as an opportunity; a chance to employ a new model for state and federal cooperation, and to make this national monument a showcase of environmental management for Utah and the United States. Governor Michael Leavitt

When President Clinton stood on the north rim of the Grand Canyon on September 18, 1996, and designated 1.7 million acres of land in Utah as the Grand Staircase–Escalante National Monument, he created an enormous challenge for public land management and planning in the state. The challenge was this: Despite the secrecy and the lack of public involvement in creating the Monument, could public land managers, elected officials, and local communities join to create a new model for environmental management and intergovernmental planning?

The seeds for a new model were planted in 1994 when federal, state, and local land managers jointly authored a concept paper titled, "Canyons of the Escalante: A National Ecoregion." That paper outlined a common management vision for the area, which preserved the natural setting while providing real and sustainable benefits to the local economy. Governor Leavitt has drawn from the concepts articulated in that paper to create his vision of the new Monument. He has also directed state and local leaders to be full partners in the planning process to make his vision a reality.

This paper describes the Monument planning process from the perspective of the state of Utah. This planning process has been designed jointly by the state and Department of the Interior to create a model for intergovernmental resource management. First, this paper addresses the demographic and economic setting of the surrounding areas to demonstrate the need for an inclusive and holistic planning process. Next, this paper articulates the state's overall vision for the Monument and proposes an implementation of this vision.

Demographic and Economic Setting

The Monument includes 1.7 million acres in Kane and Garfield Counties. Both of these counties are demographically and economically unique as is the outstanding natural environment that the Monument is designed to highlight and protect. A primary premise is that the planning process must address the needs of this local population. This is particularly important to balance the lack of public involvement in the Monument's designation. To address the needs of the local population, the planning process must first consider the economic and demographic realities of the surrounding area.

Demographics. Relative to the rest of the state, Kane and Garfield Counties have small, low-density populations with slow growth rates and a high median age. Approximately 10,400 people live in the area. According to the 1990 census, both counties have among the lowest population per square mile of any of the counties in Utah, with less than 1 person per square mile. The two largest cities in the area are Kanab, with approximately 3,300 people, and Panguitch, with approximately 1,600 people.

Population growth in the area has generally been lower than the state average. In Garfield County, net out-migration has occurred in six of the past ten years. Kane County's population has been increasing at a faster rate than that in Garfield County and net out-migration has occurred in only three of the past ten years. The average age of the population in both counties is among the oldest in the state. For instance, the median age in Garfield County, 31.3 years, is the fourth highest in the state, followed by Kane County, with a median age of 30.8.

These unique demographic characteristics are closely associated with the economic realities that both counties face. The population is small because there are relatively few employment opportunities for local residents. The population is older and net out-migration is common because many of those newly entering the labor force must leave the area to find work. Figure 12.1 provides an economic and demographic profile for both counties relative to the state.

Economics. The performance of the economies in Kane and Garfield Counties is cyclical and sluggish compared with the vibrant performance of the state's economy in recent years. Both counties struggle with unemployment rates higher than the state average, per capita personal income lower than the state average, and a lack of employment diversity. For instance, in Garfield County, where unemployment is currently the highest in the state at 12.3 percent, unemployment rates have been in the double digits in five of the past ten years. Per capita income in Garfield County is just 86 percent of the state average and 68 percent of the national average. Similarly, Kane County's per capita personal income of $16,400 is 90 percent of the state average and 71 percent of the national average.

Many of the economic problems in both counties can be explained by a general lack of economic diversity. The area relies heavily on the performance of just four major industries: agriculture, government, timber, and tourism. However, the opportunities for

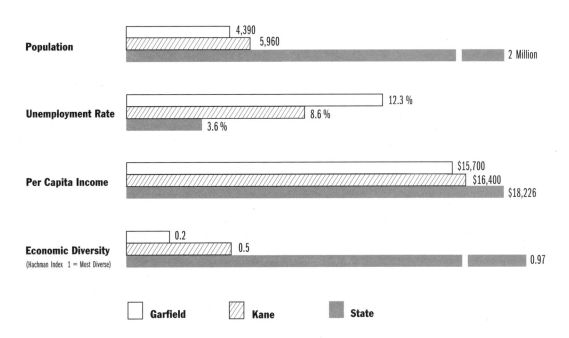

Figure 12.1. Demographic and economic profile of Kane and Garfield Counties.

employment in the first three of these industries are fairly stagnant or declining. For instance, while agriculture is an important economic resource to both counties, employment in this sector has not changed, and at times, has declined for many years. Employment in the timber industry has been cyclical and has declined as sawmills are downsized or closed. Employment in local, state, and federal government has been increasing, but slowly. It is only in the tourism industry that employment growth has been sustained. In fact, the economies' dependence on the tourism industry has steadily increased.

The economic data and trends lead to two distinct conclusions: First, many of the jobs in the communities adjacent to the Monument, such as agriculture, tourism, and resource extraction, are tied to the public lands. Second, the economies surrounding the Monument are struggling.

Because of the importance of the land to local economic performance and the struggling nature of the economies, *the Monument plan must focus on developing real economic opportunities for local residents in order to build a more healthy, diversified, and sustainable economy.* These opportunities should include promising ideas such as: (1) value-added sustainable timber and wood products; (2) environmentally sensitive ranching methods with higher-value beef and other products; (3) development of high-value destination tourism; (4) use of local guides and outfitters; (5) relocation of skilled professionals who can work in remote areas; (6) promotion of activities and industries that use local materials, local products, and local labor; and (7) development of industries such as recreation equipment that emphasize and capitalize on the proximity to unique landscapes.

Vision

The state's vision is to participate in a cooperative effort to make the Monument a showcase for innovative planning and management, while preserving the area's resources and providing benefits to the surrounding communities, the state of Utah, and the nation as a whole. This vision includes a plan for the Monument that is sensitive to the unique demographic and economic circumstances of the area just described. An added benefit of this cooperative process is that it can be a model for future state and federal partnerships in other multijurisdictional contexts.

The planning process and ultimate management of the Monument should attempt to achieve several broad goals: (1) establish a model for environmental management; (2) create a new standard for intergovernmental planning; (3) strengthen relationships among federal, state, and local governments; (4) maximize economic benefits for local residents; (5) increase the diversity and sustainability of the local economies; (6) capture sufficient government revenue from visitors to pay for the costs of services provided by local and state government; and (7) develop communities that are better places to live and work.

Implementation of the Vision

To implement the vision embodied in these broad goals requires extensive coordination. In the months since the designation of the Monument, the state of Utah, local government entities, and the federal government have worked to forge a cooperative three-year planning process. This process, along with several other important components that will help make the vision a reality, is addressed below.

Monument Planning Team. The state of Utah has significant capabilities that are essential to ensure interdisciplinary expertise in the development of the Monument plan. Accordingly, the state has assigned five people to work full-time on the Monument planning team in Cedar City. As fully integrated members of the planning staff, rather than visitors with occasional input, they will be an intrinsic part of the planning effort. As a result, the plan will benefit from their expertise and access to vital information. Also, to ensure local acceptance and involvement, a member from the Five County Association of Governments will join the team. The state members of the planning team include a wildlife biologist, geologist, paleontologist, historian/anthropologist, and community planner/socioeconomics expert. Figure 12.2 shows the planning process for the Monument, including the role of the planning team.

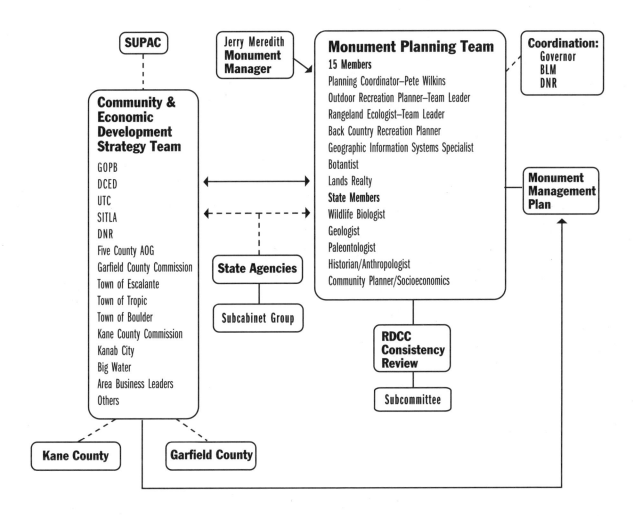

Figure 12.2. Grand Staircase–Escalante National Monument planning process.

Subcabinet Advisory Group. A subcabinet group of state officials will be formed to support and provide an interface between state agencies and the members of the planning team. Because the subcabinet group is a full partner in the planning process, all work done by any state agency with respect to the Monument will be done in conjunction with and reviewed before release by this subcabinet group.

Community and Economic Development Strategy Committee. The state of Utah, in partnership with local governments in Kane and Garfield Counties, proposes developing a community and economic development strategy for the land adjacent to the Monument and for other Monument planning issues that directly affect the surrounding communities. This effort would provide an opportunity to maximize short- and long-term benefits to local cities, counties, and other political entities. One of the major goals of this team is further consideration of economic, social, and community planning issues in the Monument management plan and promotion of compatibility between their economic strategy and the plan. One member of this strategy team with appropriate background and expertise would also serve as the state's representative on the Monument planning team. In addition, the Department of the Interior will provide assistance to this team, as will the governor and state agencies. The team would report to the Southwestern Utah Planning Authorities Council (SUPAC) to ensure coordination with all other governmental entities in the region. The members of the team would be appointed by the governor in consultation with local elected officials. Its membership would not exceed twenty-five members and would include representatives from the Southern Utah University, Governor's Office of Planning and Budget, Utah Department of Community and Economic Development, Utah Travel Council, Utah School and Institutional Trust Lands Administration, Utah Department of Natural Resources, Garfield County Commission, Kane County Commission, city mayors, Paiute Indian Tribe, area business leaders, and environmental groups. Ex-officio members will include representatives from the Bureau of Land Management, National Park Service, United States Forest Service, Rural Development Council, SUPAC, Utah State Legislature, and Utah's congressional delegation.

Existing Areas of Cooperation. The planning process must also capitalize on current state and federal agency coordination efforts. These include, but are not limited to: (1) the State Resource Development Coordinating Committee, which facilitates the governor's consistency review required by the Federal Land Policy and Management Act (FLPMA); (2) the recent assistance agreement between the BLM and Kane County for community participation in the Monument planning effort; (3) SUPAC, which coordinates the exchange of planning information between cities, counties, and state and federal agencies throughout southwestern Utah; and (4) the Five County Association of Governments planning office, which facilitates planning for counties and cities in southwestern Utah.

Data Exchange. The state and federal agencies should, whenever possible, facilitate the exchange of data between their agencies and other entities, both to ensure that the highest quality information is available to the planning effort and to enhance the public's knowledge and understanding of the Monument. This data exchange should include both tabular data and geographical (digital) data. Innovative telecommunications strategies such as those suggested by Governor Leavitt in other contexts should be employed, as well as electronic transfer capabilities.

Scientific Research. The state should participate in developing an organized and efficient approach to Monument research by identifying research needs that deserve attention from state agencies, federal agencies, academic institutions, and others.

Scientific research addressing the paleontologic, archaeologic, and energy or mineral resources is valuable to the state of Utah. The value of many of these resources is obvious, but the value of others may be known only to a handful of scientists involved in that field. Identification of these issues prior to the initial phases of the management plan development will ensure that the plan is based on sound scientific information. To accomplish this objective, the State Advisory Council on Science and Technology, which acts as a liaison to both academic and private scientific experts within the state, hosted a Scientific Forum in Cedar City during November 1997. The conference was designed to ensure focus on high priority research needs and cooperation in funding and project design, and to reduce the potential for duplication of effort. Figure 12.3 sets forth the objectives and goals of the Scientific Forum.

Primary Objectives
To focus on the natural history of the Monument, especially the geological, biological, archaeological, and paleontological resources of the area.
To assess the applicable data, research, and documentation of past and current research regarding the area.
To transfer that knowledge to the Monument planning team and to others through traditional channels and by utilizing emerging technological techniques.
To establish an interactive network of scientists, Monument staff, and others who have a continuing involvement in studies of the area.
To determine what additional scientific research may be needed in the short-term and long-term future, which pertains to the scientific resources of the Monument and surrounding environments.
Expected Outcomes
To increase visibility of scientific research and preservation as a major purpose of the Monument.
To compile pertinent materials and to serve as a forum for summarizing current and past research through presentations by noted scientists.
To establish and improve networking between scientists, planners, and managers.
To initiate an assessment of the Monument within the context of the Colorado Plateau, leading to a larger-scale understanding of the relationships within the region.
To develop a mechanism for incorporation of evolving scientific information through an adaptive management approach.
To identify short- and long-range science needs and set the stage for further data collection, research, and scientific documentation.
To support local educational activities in Kane and Garfield Counties through special teacher workshops and student programs.
To serve as the first in a periodic series of such collaborative conferences to promote and share scientific understanding of the Monument and surrounding ecosystems.

Figure 12.3. Goals and objectives of the Scientific Forum.

State School Trust Lands. There are approximately 176,000 acres of school trust lands within the Monument. These lands were deeded by the federal government to the state of Utah for the benefit of Utah's public schools. The board of trustees, School and Institutional Trust Lands Administration, and Governor Leavitt are united in protecting the value of the trust lands within the Monument and in protecting the purposes of the trust. This group will work to see either that the lands can be used for their purpose as the national economy permits, or that other federal assets will be available as compensation for the trust lands. The problem of school trust lands within federal parks and other reservations is an old and recurring one. Several exchanges are under way, including exchanges out of the Desert Tortoise Habitat Preserve near St. George and exchanges for the trust lands within national parks, Indian reservations, and national forests. These exchanges are a priority, and must be allowed to continue.

The trust lands within the Monument are also a priority. The trust lands administration, the board, and the governor are ready to work with the federal administration and Congress to accomplish these ends. Through the state's budgeting and appropriations process, monies have been set aside to work on the use or disposition of the trust lands within the Monument.

Conclusion

Despite the flawed process that led to its declaration, the Monument creates a unique opportunity to establish a new model for environmental management and intergovernmental coordination. Governor Leavitt has made his policy clear—the state will fully engage as a partner in the planning process. The state's commitment to the process arises from the unique economic and demographic setting of the communities adjacent to the Monument, whose economies are tied to public lands. The state's vision for the Monument is to preserve the area's resources while providing real and sustainable economic benefits to these surrounding communities. To implement this vision, the state is participating on the Monument planning team, working to ensure that Monument planning capitalizes on the existing areas of cooperation and that data are exchanged efficiently. Ultimately, the state would like to use this process to heal the wounds created with the formation of the Monument. The state will be successful if there is significant public participation such that all players can come away from the process feeling well served and proud of what has been created.

PART FOUR

The Long-Range Public Interest

Planning Issues

"I am somewhat skeptical of the fabled western self-reliance, because as I knew it, the West was a place where one depended on neighbors and had to give as well as get."

—*Wallace Stegner*
Where the Bluebird Sings to the Lemonade Springs

"We have to look upon the Grand Staircase–Escalante National Monument as an opportunity; a chance to employ a new model for state and federal cooperation…"

—*Michael Leavitt*
Governor of Utah

·Paria River Drainage

Photograph by Jerry Sintz, courtesy of the BLM, Utah State Office.

Previous page: Big horn sheep petroglyph from Calf Creek confluence, Site 3
from Kenneth B. Castleton, **Petroglyphs and Pictographs of Utah, Volume 2** *(1979).*

CHAPTER THIRTEEN

Monument Planning
Through an Economist's Eyes

R. Thayne Robson

Why is the management of public lands owned by the federal government such a contentious issue in Utah? My central thesis is as follows: The controversy over the Grand Staircase–Escalante National Monument is extremely important, not just because the Monument itself is extremely important, but because it forcibly illustrates that important segments of the Utah community and national interest groups have created an environment in which the democratic tradition of compromise that produces rational decisions is impossible. The political and economic incentives reward conflict and extremist positions, preventing decisions based on the democratic traditions of compromise that provide a foundation for moving forward. In today's environment, it would be difficult—if not impossible—to re-create the national parks, lay out a national highway system, or create a water reclamation program to facilitate the settlement of the West. It would be equally difficult to balance the needs of managing natural resources for recreation, resource development, and human and wildlife habitat, while offering some protection to scenic and fragile places.

As the debate rages on and positions become more entrenched, the parties involved become convinced that the future of everything dear is at stake, that these are life and death decisions at least as important as other wars fought in this century. Many seem to believe that evil and conspiratorial forces are aligned in a domino fashion behind the opposition—whoever they may be. In such an environment, economic issues become weapons, not for rational analysis, but for fortifying battle positions. Political issues can decide the fate of election outcomes, although elections have very little long-term consequence. The debate is said to determine the fate of the future education of small children, the very survival of communities, and the fate of the globe and the relationship of mankind to the state of nature. All of these contentions are very far removed from reality and any logical or reasonable assessment of scientific truth. The political climate that has been created has trapped politicians into a war that seemingly pays off in Utah elections, but which must eventually place Utah at serious odds with the federal government as well as much of the broader society. Utah people love to take every opportunity to pledge allegiance to the flag, but seldom reflect on the unique meaning of the words: "one nation, under God, *indivisible with liberty and justice for all.*" Right or wrong, the citizens of these United States own two-thirds of the land in Utah.

How did this contentious debate surrounding federal land management come about? The principal cause has been the willingness of rural and statewide leaders to blame the declining fortunes of agriculture, timber, and mining on the mismanagement of the federal government in general, and land management in particular. The fact that the fortunes of these industries have declined in almost all states independent of large federal landholdings, does not seem to register on those in the debate. These positions remind one of the old adage: "When you need an excuse, anything will do." Another cause has been the rise of national environmental policies, which has always been viewed as an attempt by outsiders to impose controls on Utah.

Since the 1960s, Utah politicians in both major political parties have tried to upstage each other in attacks on the federal government and federal land managers. As a consequence, nationally funded environmental groups have been able to raise significant resources to oppose the Utah political tides. These environmental efforts, as valuable as they may be, have only served to prod Utah political rhetoric to new heights of contentiousness. With few exceptions, Utah leaders in government, churches, and educational communities have found it best not to interfere, and simply go with the tide without serious thought about where this conflict would lead. Some have hoped that the issues might go away, or that some happy accident would resolve the conflict.

Where will another twenty-five to thirty years of conflict like we have known for the past thirty years take us? Maybe the republic of Utah can join the republic of Texas and secede from the Union. Or maybe extremist groups will take the law into their own hands and wars will settle the conflicting claims. But there is some reason for hope: Governor Leavitt gives some evidence of understanding where this conflict is leading, especially after the creation of the new Monument. Utah will surely learn that in a war with the federal government, the federal government always wins.

It may be that the only real solution to the contentious conflict is to auction off all public lands to the highest bidder with the courts left to settle the conflicting claims of private landowners. Maybe the Japanese or the Europeans will buy Utah, and the special interests of this region could find a new set of conflicts to fight about. Or maybe we can find a new set of incentives that would reward compromise instead of conflict and that would brush aside the false and misleading claims made by all interests.

* * * * * *

As an economist, I suggest several propositions regarding public land management for consideration in the Monument planning debates. Each point deserves much greater development than time and space will allow here.

1. The land mass of this globe appears relatively finite. As a resource, it deserves the wise stewardship of the human family.

2. There are numerous competing uses for land resources, and each generation must decide for itself how these resources should be managed. While everyone purports to know what is best for future generations, most of the postulates relating to the interests of future generations have little merit. Which future generation? Those 50 years hence or 200 years hence? Each generation cherishes the freedom to make its own decisions, while benefiting from the trees planted by the previous generation.

3. The amount of coal, oil, or gas consumed will not likely be altered by alternative sources unless those sources offer superior quality at a lower price. Despite the rhetoric, there is no shortage of low-sulfur, high-BTU coal in the western states. Expanded production in a new mine will likely reduce production from alternative mines. The same case can be made for oil and gas.

4. Public subsidies have already had a significant impact in skewing the location of production on federal lands. Further subsidies will not likely improve outcomes. In fact, further subsidies will only pit one community against another and thus reduce economic efficiency everywhere.

5. Natural resources on or below the earth's surface have been there for eons and will remain in their present condition unless someone decrees otherwise. Resources not developed today will be available for future development, when future generations can balance their interests and needs in light of conditions that exist in their time.

6. During the 20th century, increases in wealth and income, dramatic changes in technology, enhanced levels of educational attainment, and the expansion of human freedoms (coupled with the decrease in time and pecuniary costs) have given rise to a great set of activities called travel, tourism, and recreation. These human endeavors have altered land use patterns in urban and rural areas, and will continue to impose further changes. Increases in travel and tourism are occurring at surprising rates worldwide and in Utah. If the world's consumers choose to spend their money on travel, tourism, and recreation, then Utahns would be well advised to prepare to receive those expenditures by investing in an infrastructure that will accommodate, in an environmentally sound manner, the people who will visit. The old adage is true: "The better the service, the more people are willing to spend for it." But what will world tourism look like when the 2.5 billion people in Asia, from India to China, begin to show the same propensity to travel that we associate with the Japanese and the Americans?

7. Land use has changed dramatically since the outset of the industrial revolution and will undoubtedly change in even more significant ways over the next 200 years. Many old things, including highways, schools, churches, hotels, abandoned mines, barns, and piles of tailings, will be torn down, and some will be rebuilt. It is still possible that high-level nuclear waste will someday be stored well below ground rather than keeping it above ground as present wisdom seems to dictate.

8. Multiple-use and other flexible concepts need not be discarded for all times and all places for fear of setting political precedents that will bind humankind forever. For the most part, what man can do, man can undo. If land can be put in wilderness, it can be taken out of wilderness; resource development discouraged by one generation can be encouraged by another generation if conditions warrant a change. The wolf can be reintroduced into Yellowstone National Park, and the antelope can again roam on Antelope Island. Given time, resources, and modern technology, most things are reversible. Claims of nonreversible damage are frequently overstated. Just as it is possible to destroy rainforests, it is also possible to re-create rainforests. The rebirth of Yellowstone National Park after a devastating fire is a wonderful thing to watch.

9. Southern Utah has tremendous travel, tourism, and recreational potential. The people of the world will come, and it is highly doubtful that anyone can stop them. What they pay for their Utah experience is largely up to Utah private and public managers. The infrastructure that has emerged in northern Utah counties cannot be developed in southern Utah without a different set of incentives than presently exist.

10. Given present market conditions, the substantial coal reserves of the Kaiparowits Plateau cannot be feasibly developed, without a substantial public subsidy to help meet transportation costs. New subsidies for Kaiparowits coal development would lessen the value of production facilities elsewhere and would be a lose-lose situation.

11. The long-run tourism value of preserving the scenic and undeveloped character of the new Monument's 1.7 million acres will most likely exceed the value of all the resources now known to exist in the area many times over. Southern Utah communities will gain more wealth and income from travel, tourism, and recreation than they will ever gain from development of mineral or agricultural resources over a longer period of time. It is difficult, therefore, to explain the apparent local desire to return to a 19th-century natural resource economy when all indicators suggest that the economy of the 21st century will not be built upon a natural resource base. It may be possible, however, to capitalize on the potential values of both resource development and tourism attractiveness and at the same time preserve the land in a near natural state. Who is willing to raise this question in a serious and meaningful fashion? Why is it dismissed by so many so readily?

12. The mere existence of school trust lands in the new Monument should not govern Utah's decision making, because the value of these lands is a matter of alternative uses and tax policy. Under any of the alternatives now being discussed, the revenues from school trust lands will not finance much of Utah's education needs. Money from school trust lands does not generally benefit children as often claimed, rather it benefits their parents and other adults who pay for their education.

* * * * * *

Why is it that so many people get paid or benefit financially from creating conflict around these public land issues? Why do they demand that the interest they favor must win a total victory in public decision making? When will national, state, and local politicians understand that the strength of democracy and the welfare of Utah depends, to a significant degree, on being willing to work harmoniously on solutions, even at the expense of a few votes in the next election?

Immediately after the new Monument was created and a loud cry was heard all over Utah about the lack of consultation, I had a dream that I was invited to the White House for a visit with President Clinton. The president said to me: "Thayne, I'm thinking about creating the Grand Staircase–Escalante National Monument and I wonder if I should consult with Utah's political leaders. What do you think they would say about my plan?"

"Mr. President, they would tell you don't do it. But if they think you are going to do it anyway, they will call press conferences and explain the high-handedness of the federal government and impugn your honesty and integrity and moral character."

"Thayne, what would they say if I told them I was going to designate the new Monument no matter what they thought?"

"Mr. President, they would tell you to make it smaller—in fact, as small as possible."

"Thayne, if I asked them how the Monument ought to be managed, what would they say?

"Mr. President, they would tell you that the management should be turned over to the commissioners of Kane and Garfield Counties or to the state of Utah—but then that is saying the same thing."

"Well Thayne, what will I gain from consultation with the leaders of Utah?"

"Mr. President, absolutely nothing. They have said it all numerous times before, so do not ask for opinions that will be diametrically opposed to what you have determined to do. Remember that future generations will praise you for creating the Monument, just as present generations praise those who created the National Park System."

"Thayne, I must conclude that there is nothing to be gained from consulting with Utah's political leaders. Maybe after the fact, they will talk in more reasonable terms."

Did Utah political leaders have anything to say that had not already been said repeatedly? Has anything constructive been offered by those who decry the lack of consultation? Have they offered any advice that might have helped the president of the United States accomplish his objective?

Utah cannot afford to buy the federal lands in an open and competitive bidding process, nor can Utah afford to manage the lands in the way that the BLM, Forest Service, and the National Park Service now manage federal lands in Utah. All of which suggests, it is time for everyone to take the planning process—with its long-range implications—seriously and to begin addressing the new Monument's future with a view to regional economic realities.

CHAPTER FOURTEEN

Private Industry and Its Access Rights

Thomas W. Bachtell and Michael S. Johnson

The recently created Grand Staircase–Escalante National Monument covers 1.7 million acres in Kane and Garfield Counties. For industry, the major concern is access to the vast energy and mineral resources present within the Monument. Utilizing conservative methods of calculation, it is estimated that at least 11.3 billion tons of recoverable coal lie within the Monument boundaries. At current market value, this would translate into over $200 billion worth of recoverable coal. The Utah Geological Survey (UGS) believes that the actual amount of recoverable coal may be 50 percent higher. There are also significant recoverable quantities of coal bed gas, petroleum, and other minerals. The UGS estimates that the value of known and potential energy and mineral resources within the Monument is between $223 and $330 billion. Before the Monument was created, these energy and mineral resources were already the subject of numerous mining claims, mineral leases, and oil and gas leases issued by both the state and federal governments. Because industry is concerned with the fate of its prior existing rights in this area, this chapter will address the various rights that existed in the Monument prior to its creation, the action taken by the president in creating the Monument, and the status of those rights in light of the president's actions.

The President's Proclamation

The president is empowered by the Antiquities Act of 1906 to create national monuments by proclamation to protect objects of historic or scientific interest that are situated on federal lands (16 U.S.C. § 431). As a general matter, valid existing rights or claims are expressly or impliedly recognized by the Antiquities Act itself, by acts of Congress establishing or authorizing monuments, and by presidential proclamations (RMMLF, 1982:333). President Clinton's proclamation creating the Grand Staircase–Escalante National Monument is no exception; it expressly states that "the establishment of this Monument is subject to valid existing rights."

Valid Existing Rights within the Monument

The area within the Monument is subject to numerous preexisting mining claims, coal leases, and oil and gas leases. It is hornbook law that such claims and leases are "valid existing rights" (Watson, 1983:42–43, RMMLF, 1982). While the withdrawal of lands for the Monument will prevent the location of any new mining claims or the issuance of any new mineral or oil and gas leases, such withdrawal does not affect prior valid claims and leases. Many companies are concerned, however, that the drilling, construction, and other surface permits necessary to develop subsurface rights will not be granted given the area's new Monument status. These concerns will either be borne out or put to rest at the end of the three-year Monument management planning period. Because the various preexisting rights within the Monument are property rights protected against an unlawful "taking" without just compensation under the Fifth Amendment of the U.S. Constitution, industry will have no choice but to go to federal court to protect its rights if prior claims and leases are not honored.

Mining Claims. A mining company's interest need not amount to a mineral lease or a patented mining claim to come within the proclamation's savings clause. Unpatented mining claims are recognized as valid existing rights. The Antiquities Act protects tracts "covered by a bona fide unperfected claim held in private ownership" (16 U.S.C. § 431). The U.S. Supreme Court has taken the position that a "valid existing right" obviously means something less than a vested right, since a vested right would require no exception to ensure its preservation (*Stockly v. United States*, 260 U.S. 532 [1922]). Clearly, the owner of a mining claim on which an adequate discovery was made prior to the effective date of the proclamation has a valid existing right (RMMLF, 1982:§ 2.62).

Therefore, the question is to what extent will these "valid existing rights" and the rights of access and surface occupancy necessary to enjoy them be protected? Based upon statements made by Secretary of the Interior Babbitt and others, industry is concerned that it will be deprived of the benefit of its subsurface rights within the Monument through the BLM's refusal to grant the permits necessary to develop those rights. Yet it is well settled that federal patented and unpatented mining claims are "private property" enjoying the full protection of the Fifth Amendment (*Kunkes v. United States*, 78 F.3d 1545, 1551 [Fed. Cir. 1996]; *Swanson v. Babbitt*, 3 F.3d 1348, 1353 [9th Cir. 1993]; *United States v. Bagwell*, 961 F.2d 1450, 1456 [9th Cir. 1992]; *Webb v. Hodel*, 878 F.2d 1252, 1258 [10th Cir. 1989]). If the administration effectively precludes the owners of existing mining claims within the Monument from developing their rights under those claims, it will have to compensate those interest holders for the "taking" of their property interests.

Federal Mineral Leases. The recoverable coal reserves lying within the Monument's boundaries were already subject to numerous coal leases when the Monument was created. Federal mineral leases, such as coal leases, also create valid existing rights, which are defined in their scope by the terms of the leases themselves (*Eastern Minerals Int'l, Inc. v. United States*, 26 Fed. Cl. 541, 548 [1996]; Watson 1984:42–43). If leaseholders are precluded from enjoying their rights under these leases, they will be entitled to compensation for the taking of their property.

The president has suggested that coal leaseholders trade their leases within the Monument for other sites outside its boundaries. While this option sounds reasonable in theory, finding alternative sites is a problematic and uncertain process. The lack of detailed geologic knowledge in the absence of exploration and development makes it hard to ensure that new sites will be as useful as those within the Monument.

Federal Oil and Gas Leases. Numerous federal oil and gas leases have been issued within the boundaries of the Monument. Standard federal oil and gas leases contain provisions subjecting the leases to regulations existing at the time of issuance as well as those subsequently promulgated. This is only true, however, to the extent such subsequent regulations are not inconsistent with the provisions and purposes of the lease (RMMLF, 1996:§ 9.06). Current federal leaseholders are concerned that they will be prevented from developing their interests under these leases within the Monument.

As with mining claims and coal leases, federal oil and gas leases are interests in real property protected by the Fifth Amendment (*F.D.I.C. v. Hulsey*, 22 F.3d 1472, 1483 [10th Cir. 1994]; *State of Utah v. Babbitt*, 830 F. Supp. 586, 594 n.14 [D. Utah 1993]). If the federal government through its management of the Monument effectively prohibits these leaseholders from enjoying the benefits of their leases, they will be entitled to compensation for the taking of their leases.

State Mineral and Oil and Gas Leases. The Monument encompasses approximately 176,000 surface acres belonging to the state of Utah. Additionally, 200,700 mineral acres owned by the state of Utah are surrounded by the Monument. These lands are managed by the School and Institutional Trust Lands Administration (SITLA) for the benefit of Utah's schools. State mineral and oil and gas leases have been issued on these trust lands. The UGS estimates that the value of the recoverable coal on the school trust lands located within the Monument boundaries is at least $17 billion and could be as high as $25 billion or more.

State leaseholders are concerned that BLM's management of the surrounding Monument lands might effectively preclude them from enjoying their rights. These state leaseholders will likewise be entitled to compensation from the government for a taking if they are prevented from developing their leases.

Road Rights-of-Way and Other Access Issues

Existing roadways and other rights-of-way within the Monument boundaries spring from several sources. State school trust lands benefit from an implied right-of-access granted when the trust lands were given to the state. Additionally, under the R.S. 2477 rights-of-way provision, the counties enjoy the use of numerous road rights-of-way established prior to the passage of the Federal Land Policy Management Act in 1976.

Implied Grant of Access to School Trust Lands. Because the Monument surrounds numerous state school trust tracts, SITLA and its private lessees are concerned that the BLM's management of the surrounding federal lands will effectively preclude development of these mineral and oil and gas leases. The BLM, however, can not regulate federal lands within the Monument so as to deny access to the trust lands for purposes of economic development without effecting a taking. A Utah federal court has upheld the rights of the state and its lessees to access school lands surrounded by federal lands. In 1979, the United States sued a Utah state lessee of school trust lands to prevent construction, road building, and other surface activities on federal land surrounding the school trust tract (*State of Utah v. Andrus*, 486 F. Supp. 995 [1979]). The court noted that the school trust lands were granted to Utah by Congress for the purpose of generating revenue for the state's school system. The court recognized that the state and its lessees enjoyed an easement over surrounding federal lands to reach the school trust land tracts. According to the court, while the federal government could regulate the manner of access across its lands to the trust land tracts, such regulation could not be so restrictive as to render the land incapable of full economic development. The court stated that if regulation of surrounding federal lands seriously impinged on "investment-backed expectations" on the state trust lands, such regulation would constitute a taking.

The president has suggested exchanging Utah school lands within the Monument for lands of equal value outside the Monument. SITLA has recently adopted a formal policy statement questioning whether any such exchange will be equitable (SITLA, 1997). The policy statement first notes the state's right of access to the vast and valuable mineral resources underlying the trust lands within the Monument (*Id.* at 2). The statement then recognizes that these lands have been leased to various companies and that such leases qualify as "valid existing rights." Finally, it notes major problems with the federal government's methods of valuation, namely the failure to consider undiscovered mineral resources and the general lack of detailed geological knowledge of the area's resources due to restrictive federal management (*Id.* at 5-7). The policy statement calls for consideration of litigation to protect access rights and to seek compensation for takings that might occur (*Id.* at 8).

R.S. 2477 *Road Rights-of-Way*. Prior to passage of the Federal Land Policy Management Act (FLPMA) in 1976, rights-of-way for the construction of roads over public lands could be obtained pursuant to section 8 of the 1866 Mining Law (14 Stat. 257, 43 U.S.C. § 932). When FLPMA was enacted, these prior R.S. 2477 rights-of-way were expressly protected and exempted from FLPMA's provisions as "valid existing rights" (43 U.S.C. §§ 701 note [a], 701[h]). Rights-of-way established under R.S. 2477 could be obtained without application to the federal government and were effective upon construction of a road in accordance with state law (*Sierra Club v. Hodel*, 848 F.2d 1068, 1078 [10th Cir. 1988]). The scope of these rights-of-way is defined by the uses to which they were put prior to October 21, 1976, and include the right of the county to make reasonable and necessary improvements within the right-of-way boundaries (*Id.* at 1086).

In other words, R.S. 2477 rights-of-way were acquired prior to 1976 through the action of state and local governments. They were also acquired without government action where roadways were put to public use for ten years (Utah Code Ann. § 27-12-89).

Because FLPMA recognized these rights-of-way as "valid existing rights," they will likewise be valid existing rights for purposes of the Monument (*Schultz v. Department of Army*, 10 F.3d 649, 654 [9th Cir. 1993]; *Sierra Club v. Hodel*, 848 F.2d 1068, 1087-88 [10th Cir. 1988]). However, the managers of these road rights-of-way are concerned that their rights may be taken as a result of BLM management of the Monument.

Water Rights

Prior to the Monument's establishment, water rights within the area now covered by the Monument could be acquired pursuant to state law. While the Monument designation withdrew these lands from subsequent operation of state water laws, it did not affect existing vested water rights (*Fallini v. Hodel*, 725 F. Supp. 1113, 1119–20 [D. Nev. 1989]). These water rights are property rights protected by the Fifth Amendment (*Hage v. United States*, 35 Fed. Cl. 147, 172 [1996]; *Fallini v. Hodel*, 725 F. Supp. 1113, 1119–20 [D. Nev. 1989]).

Conclusion

Now that the Monument has been established, industry's primary concern is whether existing mineral, oil and gas, access, water, and other rights within the Monument will be honored as stated in President Clinton's proclamation. These rights are property rights protected by the Fifth Amendment and may not be taken without just compensation. The owners of these rights are skeptical that proposed exchanges and buyouts will be equitable given the lack of detailed geological knowledge in this relatively unexplored and undeveloped area and given the history of such exchanges. If valid existing rights are not honored or if their value is not recognized, federal takings claims may be the only resort for the owners of these rights.

References

Rocky Mountain Mineral Law Foundation (RMMLF). 1982. AMERICAN LAW OF MINING. Denver, CO.

Rocky Mountain Mineral Law Foundation (RMMLF). 1996. LAW OF FEDERAL OIL AND GAS LEASES. Denver, CO.

School and Institutional Trust Lands Administration Board of Trustees. 1997. POLICY STATEMENT NO. 97-04, CAUSE NO. 1.

Watson, John, L. 1984. *Mineral and oil and gas development in wilderness areas and other specially managed federal lands in the United States*. 29 ROCKY MOUNTAIN MINERAL LAW INSTITUTE 37.

CHAPTER FIFTEEN

Protecting Environmental Values

Scott Groene

The Grand Staircase–Escalante National Monument was born out of the turmoil over Utah Bureau of Land Management (BLM) wilderness in the 104th Congress. The Utah congressional delegation tried to pass legislation (H.R. 1745 and S. 884) that would have opened millions of acres of undeveloped BLM lands to development. Thousands of citizens from Utah and elsewhere responded with a grassroots campaign directed toward legislators from outside Utah, which eventually stopped these antiwilderness bills. In losing, Utah's politicians managed to lift Utah's Redrock Wilderness into the national spotlight, a goal that had eluded environmentalists for years. President Clinton responded by creating the new Monument on September 18, 1996.

There has been some fury in Utah over the Monument, driven by political interests. But the Grand Staircase–Escalante National Monument is not the first area to be protected in Utah by presidential proclamation. Natural Bridges National Monument, Cedar Breaks National Monument, Hovenweep National Monument, Timpanogos Cave National Monument, Arches, and Capitol Reef and Zion National Parks were all created under the Antiquities Act by authority delegated to the president by Congress.

The political posturing surrounding the Grand Staircase–Escalante National Monument mirrors that which took place when past monuments were designated in Utah. The 1969 Salt Lake Tribune headline—"Bennett Blasts LBJ Land Grab to Expand 2 Monuments in Utah"—referred to former Utah senator Wallace Bennett's opposition to the expansion of Capitol Reef and Arches National Monuments. At that time, the community of Boulder passed a resolution renaming the town Johnson's Folly, claiming that expansion of Capitol Reef National Monument would turn the community into an "inevitable ghost town." *The Salt Lake Tribune* editorialized against the "arbitrary land grab," and decried the loss of "rich hydrocarbon deposits" in the Capitol Reef area. After the Arches expansion, hearings were held in Moab where some residents told Utah politicians that "it is the tax dollar of mining and livestock that built this county, not the promised tourist dollar." In 1961, when Secretary of the Interior Stewart Udall placed 1 million acres proposed for Canyonlands National Park under interim protection, Utah politicians objected that the Canyonlands action "robs Utah schoolchildren of millions of dollars." They charged that "one of the most mineral rich [areas] in the United States" was "lock[ed] up" by Udall's action.

The same thirty-year-old antimonument rhetoric is repeated today by Utah politicians and dutifully reported by the media. Once again, schoolchildren are used as political tools, and exaggerated claims are made about lost mineral resources. Apparently Utah's politicians have learned little from history. Moab thrives as a tourist destination, largely due to Arches National Park after the mining industry collapsed and the livestock industry became of negligible importance. Rather than becoming a ghost town, Boulder now struggles to cope with rapid growth brought on by newcomers attracted by the area's scenic beauty, not oil industry jobs. In fact, all of the areas established as national monuments under the Antiquities Act are now very popular. When the State Institutional Trust Lands Administration threatened to develop state sections within Arches National Park a few years ago, it was stopped by an outcry from Utah citizens. In short, creation of the monuments enhanced, rather than harmed, local economies. With time the Monument will also gain favor with Utahns, both rural and urban.

President Clinton's proclamation creating the Monument controls management of the area. The proclamation leaves the Bureau of Land Management (BLM) as manager of the Monument, the only monument managed by this agency. The proclamation requires the Secretary of the Interior to prepare a management plan for the Monument within three years. The primary issue to be addressed in the plan is simply how to best protect the values for which the Monument was established: the geological, paleontological, archeological, biological, and historical wonders of the area.

The proclamation withdrew the area from "entry, location, selection, sale, leasing, or other disposition under public land laws, other than by exchange that furthers the protective purposes of the monument." This prohibits future leasing of oil, coal, and gas, and closes the area to future mining claims. Assuming the BLM adheres to the proclamation and prevents the development of energy resources in the area, the greatest threats to Monument values are grazing and tourism-related impacts.

The proclamation states that "existing grazing uses shall continue to be governed by applicable laws and regulations." Grazing is causing damage to the area, in part because the BLM has never considered the issue in a comprehensive plan. The area is currently managed under two dated management framework plans that do not comport with the Federal Land Policy Management Act of 1976 (FLPMA). Although the BLM had started to prepare FLPMA-mandated resource management plans, that effort has now been replaced with preparation of the Monument plan. Thus, the grazing issue should be included within the Monument management plan, otherwise it will never be considered.

Approximately 176,000 acres of Utah trust lands are located within the Monument area. The state of Utah should be fairly compensated for school trust sections within the Monument. In the best interest of the school trust and the Monument, these lands should be exchanged for federal revenues or lands located elsewhere. The trust lands are difficult to manage and do not produce much revenue, largely because of where the parcels are located. Under the Utah Enabling Act of 1894, the state was granted four numbered sections out of each township, resulting in scattered and isolated parcels, many without road access or water availability.

Little revenue has been generated from the 176,000 acres of Utah trust lands within the Monument. In fact, the direct contribution from the entire 3.8 million acres of Utah trust lands generated less than half of 1 percent (0.33 percent) of Utah's total education budget in 1996. It is questionable whether the Monument trust lands have provided enough revenue to cover management costs or the value of resources taken from them. Due to a lack of industry interest, much less than half of the state land within the Monument is currently leased for energy resource speculation, whether for coal, oil, or coal bed methane. Despite a lack of legal restraints, state lands within the Monument and wilderness areas have not been developed for energy resources over the past century, simply because it is not profitable.

There have been claims that state lands in the Monument contain extremely valuable coal deposits. These claims ignore the reasons the fuel has been left in the ground over the past century. As explained in a recent U.S. report on the economic feasibility of mining coal in the Monument, the Kaiparowits coal is on the average higher in sulfur and lower in BTU quality than coal found elsewhere in Utah. Due to the costs of mining this lower-quality coal, including transportation from the remote location, the study concluded the coal could not be profitably mined in the future.

Creation of the Monument did not place any legal limitation on the development of state lands. But such development threatens the values that the Monument was established to protect, even if only some state sections are developed for commercial purposes while the bulk of the acreage remains in a natural state. The principal factor limiting revenue generation on these lands is the economic feasibility of developing scattered parcels, not the Monument designation. However, the Monument designation may provide the political impetus to trade the state parcels for federal lands elsewhere in Utah that would actually generate revenue for education.

Industry and various political entities have sought to obfuscate the purposes of the Monument by promoting local tourism development. Either deliberately or inadvertently, these groups have misrepresented the proclamation's intent by suggesting it includes the same bedeviling mandate pursued by some national park managers: try to preserve natural values while accommodating rising visitation. But unlike legislation creating national parks, the proclamation cuts short arguments for building tourist infrastructure. Rather, the Monument was created solely for the purpose of protecting natural and historic values. The proclamation recognized that "remoteness, limited travel corridors, and low visitation have all helped to preserve intact the monument's important ecological values," including wildlife, fossils, archaeology, and wilderness. BLM's management plan for the region must therefore perpetuate those conditions.

BLM's plan must prohibit the construction of tourist infrastructure inside the Monument, and disallow any improvement of existing dirt roads. Fragmentation of habitat remains one of the greatest threats to the Monument's biological values, and road access facilitates both inadvertent and deliberate damage to archaeological sites. The national park experience instructs that if new roads are built, people will come in great numbers. The Monument is likely to face enormous recreational pressure, especially in the Escalante region. Paving over currently rutted and rocky roads will speed the crowds into the canyons, threatening the Monument's natural values. New highways would encourage off-road vehicles to venture farther into the backcountry, tracking over sensitive soil crusts and disturbing wildlife.

Although some rural county commissioners support such development, there is common ground here between environmentalists and local communities. If the towns surrounding the Monument choose to make tourism a component of their economy, the chambers of commerce should encourage visitors to stay in their communities, rather than advocate for roads to hasten tourists out of town and into the Monument. Paving Smoky Mountain Road would create a bypass around Kanab. Upgrading the dirt Cottonwood Wash Road would bring RVs into now lonely canyons, rather than into campgrounds built adjacent to towns. Slathering asphalt on the Hole-in-the-Rock route will only pile more hikers into the already overused Escalante side canyons, not add to motel receipts. Instead, tourist interests should take advantage of the nearly 100 miles of existing paved roads in the Monument, especially along the Highway 12 corridor where the towns are. Any public funds appropriated for tourist facilities should be directed to enhancing the surrounding small communities, not developing the Monument. The President said protect it, not pave it.

Unfortunately, county commissioners have already begun to call for new roads. At a March 4, 1997, House Appropriations Interior Subcommittee meeting, a Garfield County commissioner asked for $2 million for county road construction in the Monument.

The county commissioners, however, may be headed toward the same mistakes that occurred in Moab during nearly ten years of enormous growth in visitation. During that period, some Moab political leaders continued to place their economic hopes in revitalized oil and gas and mining industries, fighting efforts at environmental protection and wilderness designation, even as a tourism economy was developing. Little effort was made to ensure that local residents and businesses were prepared to take advantage of the changing economies. Local political leaders were reluctant to impose zoning that would control growth, fearing it would either stifle economic revenues or undermine private property rights. As a result, growth proceeded haphazardly, while knowledgeable businesspeople from other cities and states moved to the area and established successful tourism businesses. Outside financial interests and national chains either replaced existing local businesses ill-equipped for changing consumer desires, or filled niches that might have gone to local businesses. Many in the local community were frustrated, feeling that they had little control over the changes wrought by a shifting economy that brought economic growth along with increased housing costs and crowding.

Although the Monument was not established to assist local economies, it can be useful for that purpose. National monuments in other locations have had such an effect. But the opportunity will be missed unless Utah's politicians redirect their efforts toward acquiring the capital and training necessary to prepare communities for a growing tourism industry. Wasting energy trying to legislate the Monument out of existence, or appropriating funds for tourist roads and infrastructure within the Monument rather than in the local communities, will not help rural economies in the long run.

A great deal of land located in three distinct areas within the Monument qualifies as wilderness: the Escalante Canyon region to the east, the Kaiparowits Plateau in the center, and the Grand Staircase (or Pariah River drainage) to the west. These three areas cover nearly 1.3 million acres of wilderness proposed for protection under the citizens' legislative proposal, America's Redrock Wilderness Act. This includes 355,000 acres of proposed wilderness in the Escalante area, 650,000 acres in the Kaiparowits, and 268,000 acres in the Paria Canyons area. Because the Monument designation did not resolve the wilderness issue, the Utah Wilderness Coalition's goal remains legislation to protect the full 6 million acres of remaining Utah BLM wilderness, including the 1.3 million acres in the Monument. The BLM must recognize and protect wilderness within the Monument as a tool to protect the values delineated in the proclamation.

Currently, 900,000 acres inside the Monument are protected as wilderness study areas (WSAs). Under section 603 of FLPMA, these areas must be protected for their wilderness characteristics absent congressional legislation otherwise. Despite unfounded contrary claims, the WSAs remain in effect under the Monument proclamation, and the Monument plan must reflect this fact.

Although the direction of Monument management is clear under the proclamation, the Monument is faced with myriad political threats. Utah senator Bennett has introduced legislation (S. 357) that would contravene the proclamation by allowing mining and oil development, dam construction, and road construction, while also creating a management board dominated by development interests. This bill, if made into law, may eliminate protections now in place for WSAs within the Monument. The bill would also make it difficult to pursue a beneficial exchange of state land within the Monument. It is unlikely, however, that the bill will ever serve as more than a political hammer for Senator Bennett to publicly pound the new Monument, as his father did with Arches and Capitol Reef National Monuments thirty years ago.

Several groups have filed lawsuits in federal court challenging the creation and size of the Monument. Initially, wise-use groups filed two separate actions, which were subsequently allowed to lapse. The Utah Association of Counties has a pending case challenging the Monument designation on the basis that FLPMA repealed the Antiquities Act. In a separate action, the State Institutional Trust Lands Administration (SITLA) has filed a case claiming that the Monument designation is invalid because the Antiquities Act is not a land management tool. Governor Leavitt has set aside funds to pay for the SITLA litigation.

Kane and Garfield Counties celebrated creation of the Monument by illegally running road graders through proposed wilderness areas. The road graders were stopped, perhaps only temporarily, by litigation filed by the Southern Utah Wilderness Alliance and the United States. The road work accomplished little other than scarring the land. Both counties, however, continue to threaten road construction activities within the Monument under claims of authority granted by the Mining Law of 1866, which was repealed in 1976. Senators from Alaska and Utah unsuccessfully sought to include language within an emergency supplemental appropriations bill that would allow counties to gain rights-of-ways across public lands, including the Monument, by claiming that off-road vehicle trails and cow paths qualify as "constructed highways."

Conoco Inc., a subsidiary of DuPont, has an application pending with BLM to drill for oil in the heart of the Monument, a region recently determined by *Car and Driver* magazine to be the most remote in the lower forty-eight states. The state of Utah has already granted Conoco a permit to drill on a state section near the same area. Conoco is planning to drill a 14,000-foot well in previously untested strata. The corporation hopes to use its leases for a taxpayer funded buyout or develop an oil field that would require new roads, waste pits, and pipelines.

With its new Monument management responsibilities, the BLM faces the task of overcoming its history of kowtowing to the livestock and extractive industries. Management of the Monument will be a publicly scrutinized test of whether the agency is capable and willing to heed federal land management law, unlike its miserable performance in carrying out wilderness inventory tasks in the 1980s. The first indication of BLM's capability as an administrator will be its response to Conoco's effort to transform quiet canyons into an oil field industrial zone. If BLM allows oil drilling in the Monument, we will need a new manager.

The new Monument holds a wealth of wildlife, archaeology, and wilderness for future generations. It may provide the impetus to trade school lands that generate little or no income for others that do. The values of the area can be protected by directing development resources away from the Monument and to surrounding towns to benefit economies there. With time, the Monument will be viewed as a treasure by citizens of Utah and the United States.

CHAPTER SIXTEEN

The Utah Travel Division and Tourism Planning

Dean Reeder

In the proclamation establishing the Grand Staircase–Escalante National Monument, President Clinton describes Utah's newest national monument as a "vast and austere landscape [that] embraces a spectacular array of scientific and historic resources ... a high, rugged and remote region, where bold plateaus and multi-hued cliffs run for distances that defy human perspective ... a place with a long and dignified human history where one can see how nature shapes human endeavors in the American West, where distance and aridity have been pitted against our dreams and courage..." (Clinton, 1996). While agreeing that the region is beautiful, Garfield County commissioner Louise Liston observes that most of the area "is typical of millions of acres of western land" (Woolf, 1997). A similar wide spectrum of viewpoints and emotions including elation and dismay, accompanied the monumental designation. "It is an unfortunate irony that a land offering so many unique opportunities for tranquillity and renewal, a natural setting lending itself to seemingly what is best in the human spirit, is the stage of such pronounced and deeply rooted contention" (Barber and Clark, 1996).

Nevertheless, Gov. Michael O. Leavitt believes that Utahns still share a common love of the land: "There is disagreement on how to protect sensitive lands, but a common desire to preserve them. For decades our efforts have revolved around our conflicts, and it is now time to build on what unites us" (Leavitt, 1996). For the Grand Staircase–Escalante National Monument, this means beginning the process of planning to preserve the regional setting while providing real and sustainable economic benefits to the local economy (Barber, 1996).

As public interest in the new Monument accelerates, the Utah Division of Travel Development is encouraging communities in the proximity of the Monument to view the challenges of increasing tourism visitation as opportunities. Rather than seeing tourists as part of the problem, well-planned tourism can become part of the solution. If low-paying, seasonal positions, which are usually associated with tourism are undesirable, then higher-paying, higher-quality alternatives might be created by the way a community chooses to develop tourism.

Additionally, the division believes that with proper planning, the new Monument can become a model for responsible development throughout the nation. In 1994 the division helped develop a concept paper titled "Canyons of the Escalante: A National Ecoregion," which provides the foundation for such a national model. The management philosophy of the ecoregion concept emphasizes the integration of human processes and natural systems: Since humans are a part of the natural process and have the ability to fundamentally alter the setting, they have a responsibility as stewards of the natural setting to protect and sustain the resources while utilizing them for their human needs (GOPB, 1994). Using this model, the division has created the state's first ever, long-range strategic plan for tourism development, which includes the following mission statement: *Make Utah a better place to live by increasing the economic contribution of tourism.* The division's primary focus is on quality of life and extracting greater economic benefits, which emphasizes destination tourism rather than "windshield" tourism, quality earnings rather than numbers of visitors, and career employment rather than "pass-through" or seasonal employment. Other division objectives are tax burden relief for Utah citizens and protection of natural resources.

Also in 1994, Governor Leavitt introduced a policy that identified the economic resettlement of rural Utah as one of his administration's primary objectives. Accordingly, the division emphasizes extending the prosperity of the Wasatch Front to Utah's rural communities in its strategic plan, which includes encouraging forms of tourism that are more likely to achieve greater economic benefits. However, before higher earnings can be realized, an investment in infrastructure must take place. Tourists need more opportunities to spend money on lodging, dining, attractions, and other value-added services. In many areas of rural Utah, this infrastructure does not exist.

This paper begins by briefly examining the challenges posed by increasing tourism in Kane and Garfield Counties. The paper then sets forth a vision for sustainable tourism development, which emphasizes quality earnings and jobs, quality of life, resource protection, and enhanced visitor experience. Applying these sustainable tourism concepts to the new Monument, the paper then outlines three implementation strategies to achieve this vision: (1) appropriate destination development; (2) visitor management tactics; and (3) maintenance of community values and quality of life. These ideas represent a starting place for turning challenges into opportunities.

Tourism Challenges Presented by the Grand Staircase–Escalante National Monument

In rural Utah, many communities are experiencing changes that raise questions about maintaining community identity and quality of life, attracting quality jobs and quality capital investments, achieving economic diversification, and protecting fragile ecosystems, landscapes, and cultural resources. In 1994 a southern Utah resident encouraged his community to not make the same mistakes made in other areas of the state: "This is one of the last great places, so let's consider carefully how we develop the infrastructure and not overbuild" (Conine, 1994). With this sentiment in mind, community leaders, county officials, and local business leaders face difficult decisions about how to best shape the economic, environmental, and cultural future of their communities.

Economic Challenges in Kane and Garfield Counties

Between 1970 and 1995, the resource-based sectors of the economy in Garfield and Kane Counties, including agriculture, mining, and lumber, decreased significantly both in terms of earnings and employment. At the same time, the service sector, mainly due to tourism, increased to become the largest sector, followed by government and trade. Unemployment levels have remained relatively high in the two counties compared with statewide averages, paralleled by low average wage levels for all sectors of Kane and Garfield economies. However, 1994–95 data show that Kane and Garfield Counties experienced relatively high rates of growth in per capita personal income and average monthly nonagricultural wages (Utah Department of Employment Security, 1996), primarily due to increases in the construction, manufacturing, and service sectors. Current trends in tourism and recreation withstanding, those sectors most closely related to this industry, such as service, trade, and construction will most likely continue to increase in importance.

As in many rural areas, high unemployment rates and volatile local economies have led to an out-migration of youth in search of career opportunities elsewhere, with ensuing wear on the social fabric. Since 1960 Garfield County has experienced several years of zero or negative population growth, mainly due to out-migration. Kane and Garfield Counties face an ongoing challenge to provide enough quality jobs and earnings for the area's youth, to find alternatives for displaced workers, and to diversify increasingly service-based economies.

Social, Cultural, and Environmental Challenges in Garfield and Kane Counties

With 40 to 60 percent of total employment due to travel and recreation-related tourism, Kane and Garfield Counties have one of the highest proportions of travel and recreation-related employment in the state (Utah Division of Travel Development, 1996). Since 1990, spending by travelers has increased on average 8 percent per year in Garfield County and 10 percent in Kane County, compared with 5.9 percent average annual growth for the rest of the state. Visitation to the region has increased steadily, especially to area state parks. Nearby Zion National Park and Glen Canyon National Recreation Area received close to 2.5 million visitors in 1995. According to visitor counts at the Escalante Interagency Office, Escalante area visitation has increased significantly (35 percent) since 1993. Since the Monument designation, visitation numbers have grown, but it is too soon to detect exactly how the designation will affect area visitation.

For two counties with combined populations of less than 10,000 people, the prospect of supporting hundreds of thousands of tourists with lodging, food, and services while paying the costs for search and rescue, garbage collection, sewer, roads, and natural resources protection may seem daunting. The community's desire to maintain its cultural identity will also be tested in the face of booming visitation. Small communities face strong short-term pressures to meet increasing demands and these pressures are exacerbated without a long-term vision for how new development should fit into a community's cultural and historical identity.

Since Utah was settled, in the late 19th century, the extraction of natural resources has been a principal economic activity. Today, tourism may be the single largest factor affecting the future of rural Utah. This is especially true of the areas within the Colorado Plateau, including the Grand Staircase–Escalante National Monument in Kane and Garfield Counties where travel and recreation-related jobs represent a large portion of total employment. To avoid the difficulties that such tourism dependency can pose, tourism should be developed as part of a balanced mix of economic opportunities. The challenge for communities surrounding the new Monument is to create a tourism vision that maximizes income while minimizing costs, without degrading the opportunity for unique visitor experiences, the values inherent to rural communities, or the region's fragile ecosystems.

Sustainable Tourism Development

Tourism—especially ecotourism—is being promoted as an industry compatible with sustainable development goals (Burr et al., 1995, McIntosh et al., 1995). However, to meet these goals, tourism must include a vision for maintaining cultural and natural resources for current and future generations. "The interest in sustainable tourism development then is in protecting, using carefully and benefiting the human cultural, as well as the natural heritage of an area, implying active participation and leadership by local people, organizations and government" (Burr et al., 1995). Tooman (1997) advocates a "deliberate acceptance of slower growth through planning" in order to ensure that vulnerable cultural, historical, and environmental assets that attract visitors are not degraded or dislocated.

Sustainable development represents a new paradigm for balancing community economic development with wise resource use. Sustainable development refers to "development that meets the needs of the present without compromising the ability of future generations to meet their own needs" (WCED, 1987, McIntosh et al., 1995). A sustainable development strategy must contain a number of principles: Development must grow from within, not be imposed from the outside; it must provide the basic necessities of life and promote equity; and it must be compatible with and rely on sustainable forms of resource use (Burr and Walsh, 1994).

The product that supports tourism in Utah—the natural landscape—is a "common good," vulnerable to overuse and undervaluation (Hardin, 1968, Healy, 1994, Daily, 1997). According to Hardin in "The Tragedy of the Commons," unrestricted access to a common resource, such as a grazing common, or a landscape, or public lands, leads users to "harvest" as much as possible, because any remaining value will be taken by the others (Hardin, 1968). Since "harvesters" receive little marginal return, they have little incentive to invest in maintaining the "grazing common" (Healy, 1994). To protect "the tourism commons," management mechanisms to prevent overuse and to mitigate impacts are required, such as user fees, backcountry permits, use of knowledgeable guides, multiple-use zones, and visitor management to protect core areas.

The concepts of sustainable tourism development and "protecting the commons" are not always understood or adopted by local planning efforts. Especially in the West, which has a long history of protecting individual property rights, the preservation of community character and values will often lose out to private interests. Strong leadership, vision, and planning tools are required for communities to mold tourism development to fit their vision. To address these problems in the Grand Staircase–Escalante region, three implementation strategies and related planning tools might be used by the affected communities.

Destination Development and Sustainable Tourism

What Is Destination Tourism?

The Utah Division of Travel Development has labeled the brand of tourism that existed in much of rural Utah until recently as "windshield tourism." This kind of tourism is characterized by families traveling in their personal cars and briefly visiting as many sites as possible (perhaps all five Utah national parks) during their vacations. Edward Abbey described the windshield tourist in the following excerpt from *Desert Solitaire*:

> They roll up incredible mileages on their odometer, rack up state after state in two-week transcontinental motor marathons, knock off one national park after another, take millions of square yards of photographs, and endure patiently the most prolonged discomforts: the tedious traffic jams, the awful food of roadside eateries, the nocturnal search for a place to sleep or camp, the dreary routine of One-Stop Service.... They are being robbed and robbing themselves. So long as they are unwilling to crawl out of their cars they will not discover the treasures of the national parks and will never escape the stress and turmoil of the urban-suburban complexes which they had hoped, presumably, to leave behind for a while (Abbey, 1968).

The vast majority of jobs generated by windshield tourism are gas stations, motels, fast-food restaurants, and grocery stores. Obviously, windshield tourism still exists in Utah and continues to be the dominant form of tourism in Kane and Garfield Counties.

In recent years, however, destination tourism has emerged and offers many desirable characteristics for the state. Unlike family vacations of the past, where the important part of the trip was getting somewhere, the primary focus of the trip in destination tourism is the final place of arrival. The emphasis is on quality over quantity; fewer sites are visited, and visitors remain in one location for longer periods of time.

> A man on foot, on horseback or on a bicycle will see more, enjoy more in one mile than the motorized tourists can in a hundred miles. Better to be idle through one park in two weeks than try to race through a dozen in the same amount of time (Abbey, 1968).

Why Destination Tourism Is Preferable to the Windshield Model

Less focus on quantity in exchange for quality. Since developing its long-range strategic plan, the Division of Travel Development is concentrating its efforts on destination tourism to encourage higher tourism revenues. This emphasis on quality tourism acknowledges that attractions in the state, particularly outside the Wasatch Front, are heavily weighted toward the low-end (in terms of spending potential) offerings. The division's goal is to increase product development and long-range capital investment throughout the state.

Destination tourists are desirable guests because they contribute to higher-quality earnings by spending more money, both per day and in total during their trip. Skiers, for example, are destination travelers who spend on average $226 per day compared with a pass-through summer visitor, who spends $70 per day (Wikstrom, 1997; D. K. Shifflet, 1997). Destination visitors desiring a guided experience in the new Monument could spend $115 per day for a full-service backpacking/camping trip or $185 per day for a guided bike trip (Red Rock n' Llamas, 1997, Western Spirit Cycling, 1997) whereas Bryce Canyon visitors spend an average $50 per person per day (DRRT, 1993). Destination visitors emphasize shopping, use local guides and outfitters, often visit heritage and cultural sites, and generate a somewhat different mix of jobs in the local economy. These jobs have potential for higher-quality earnings and provide meaningful nonmonetary compensation, such as enjoyable outdoor employment with recreational benefits and opportunities to meet interesting people. Moreover, destination travelers often report a higher degree of satisfaction with their vacations than do their windshield counterparts. This increased satisfaction helps develop a "sense of place." Once developed, the practice of repeat visitation and place loyalty is set.

Preserved sense of place. A sense of place is represented by those aspects of a community that make it unique and prevent it from becoming homogenized into Anywhere, USA. It is a relationship that occurs between people and their environment as they assign meaning to a setting (Motloch, 1991). Developing and maintaining a sense of place can be interpreted differently by residents and visitors.

When community members talk about maintaining quality and a way of life, they are referring to preserving the community as home and those elements that provide roots and a connection to their heritage. A Kane County resident recently summarized these concerns:

> This little county in the State of Utah is comprised of people that have made this area their home for generations. In fact there are many individuals still living here who are descendants of the original settlers. Life doesn't change much here. Since its earliest settlement, we have recognized our dependence upon the land and have tried to be good stewards. We feel that we have done a good job.... We love this country. We have worked its soil. Our ancestors are buried in its ground. We have sweated and added our own blood to the soil making it rich, red and productive (Carter, 1996).

Clearly, changes in a community resulting from increased tourism can threaten feelings of security and well-being. But before a community can preserve its character, it must define itself and identify those elements of the environment that it wishes to protect and preserve. This evaluation of these specific community aspects is one that the locals must do themselves; it should not be determined by state government or outsiders.

For many visitors, it is a sense of place that differentiates one tourism offering from another and attracts them to a specific destination. Attracting visitors who value distinction can translate into higher earnings, particularly if a community develops its assets so visitors can do more than pass through the area or buy a meal at a fast-food franchise. "The challenge for communities is to provide a unique, special, and participatory tourist experience that will bring with it jobs and economic development" (McNulty, 1989). Greater economic benefits can be realized by offering value-added services to the visitor based on local handicrafts, historic sites, art, music, architecture, cuisine, festivals, and events (Utah Division of State History, 1995). Visitors who are treated hospitably develop a propensity for repeat visitation based on a sense of place by being comfortable in a strange place. A repeat visitor will often return for other activities or in different seasons of the year.

Creating Destinations

Establishing gateway developments. The concept of developing gateways or staging areas from which visitors can base their activities will ultimately provide benefits to both the communities surrounding the new Monument and the natural resources within it. If it is desirable to concentrate visitors in specific areas to protect historical sites, fragile ecosystems, or community privacy, then infrastructure and services should be located accordingly. By encouraging development on the periphery of the Monument rather than inside, visitors will be more dependent on local lodging facilities, eating establishments, retailers, and guides and outfitters. And by promoting such services with the destination concept in mind, several benefits follow, including resource protection, economic benefits for local businesses, and enhanced visitor experiences.

Developing products for unmet demand. In several Utah tourism segments, demand and interest should support more destination-oriented products and attractions. A specialized heritage tourism product—traditionally known as a dude ranch—has thrived for over seventy years in neighboring Colorado, Wyoming, and Montana. Utah, however, has been slow to respond to demand for this small-scale, high-quality destination attraction, despite its comparable western flavor and hospitality. Currently, most lodging properties in Kane and Garfield Counties provide limited services and offer visitors overnight accommodations for between $50 and $75 per night. In contrast, the Dude Ranch Association (DRA) reported that 1996 weekly guest prices in member properties averaged $1,076 per adult guest based on double occupancy (DRA, 1997). This revenue translates into an average of $154 per person per day spending for a guaranteed seven-day stay.

The value-added element is the key to creating an opportunity for higher earnings. For example, the Lazy H Guest Ranch in Colorado offers outdoor activities, including hay rides, a mountain man's camp, Native American entertainment, line dancing, and a wonderful musician storyteller. Such value-added experiences and opportunities are underutilized and possibly undervalued in Utah. The communities in Garfield and Kane Counties can be proud of their pioneer, ranching, and even outlaw heritage and still share it in appropriate ways with visitors. However, the Utah ranch recreation industry is not yet well developed and represents an area where supply is not meeting demand. Although the DRA does not currently represent any Utah properties, it has received numerous inquiries about ranch vacations in Utah.

Ecotourism is another area for expanded tourism activity. Since much of the new Monument's appeal is based on its spectacular natural scenery, the area must be maintained in a pristine condition. Ecotourism combines the ideals of a strong commitment to nature and a sense of social responsibility. It is a form of tourism that is "responsible travel to natural areas, which conserves the environment and improves the welfare of the local people" (Western, 1993). As an economic matter, the quality of life for local people can be improved through economic diversification, high dollar expenditures, demand for local goods and services, foreign exchange earnings, long-term stability, longer visitor stays, and infrastructure development (GOPB, 1995).

The Monument region offers a wide variety of activities for outdoor enthusiasts, including camping, backpacking, hiking, fishing, wildlife viewing, and scenic drives, that are compatible with ecotourism development. Birdwatching, for example, produces high-quality returns. In Utah, birdwatchers spent an estimated $140 million in 1991 on birding activities, including travel and equipment (USDI, 1991). The reintroduction of the California condor near the Utah-Arizona border represents an ecotourism opportunity that Monument area communities could potentially capitalize on.

The Monument also displays incredible geological activity and erosional forces. Visitors can view sandstone arches, natural bridges and windows, sheer cliffs, deep canyons, and other unusual rock formations. Guides and outfitters could provide services to educate visitors on the area's geology, anthropology, paleontology, and heritage. They could also teach environmental sensitivity and appropriate methods of interacting with the land (GOPB, 1994).

In sum, ranch recreation and ecotourism are two tourism products that can be appropriately developed in or adjacent to the new Monument. These forms of tourism represent higher-quality earnings and focus on protecting the resources that attract visitors.

Quality Capital Investments. The development of destination-oriented tourism products in the area of the new Monument will require significant capital investment, which is readily available for windshield developments, because high highway traffic counts and franchise affiliations' convenience-based products are perceived as less risky investments. But windshield development does not maintain unique community character and values, meet demand for higher-quality destination products, or provide quality jobs in all seasons. Attention should therefore be paid to reducing the risk faced by small-scale destination developments.

Government economic development tools effectively provide coverage for financial risk in other segments of the economy. The special needs of rural Utah, coupled with the need to protect sensitive resources, represent a special case for applying these tools. But public economic development programs are controversial and must address competitive claims of perceived unfairness and "corporate welfare arguments."

Visitor Management Tactics

The concept of visitor management can help community planners address the effects of visitors on infrastructure and sensitive ecosystems. If a tourism site is developed as a particularly alluring attraction, visitors are more likely to follow a designated path and avoid sensitive areas. In the Sand Flats Recreation Area in Grand County, local and federal partners have worked together to provide education, services, and protection for the land. Campsite clusters were created to concentrate visitors to limit land destruction and to protect larger tracts of surrounding vegetation.

Entry fees, recreational user fees, search and rescue insurance, and market-based pricing are also useful visitor management tools. If visitors can access public lands and experiences for free, they may perceive the experience as having less value, making it difficult to foster respect and appreciation. A federal Fee Demonstration Program will begin in 1997 to facilitate natural resource protection, improve infrastructure maintenance, and enhance visitor experience. The Sand Flats Recreation Area and Millcreek Canyon along the Wasatch Front are two sites that have already achieved successful results through joint partnerships and visitor fees. In 1994 the "Canyons of the Escalante: A National Ecoregion" document proposed a multi-tier user fee at two entry points on Highway 12 in Garfield and Wayne Counties. The fee system could be implemented on a sliding scale to accomplish the following objectives: (1) exempt locals from paying the fee, (2) offer Utah residents an annual pass at a significant discount, (3) assist counties with visitor impacts on local services infrastructure development, and (4) help control and reduce the use of highly sensitive areas.

Guides and outfitters can serve as a useful visitor management tool that also meets quality earnings and quality job objectives of destination tourism. The tourism guide is a counselor, mentor, teacher, and leader. Guiding can provide a viable career option for rural Utahns who prefer to remain close to home. For the visitor, guided visitation represents a high-quality, value-added experience. More often than not, people come to Utah to fill their minds, as well as their eyes. They want to be shown things they otherwise would not find. They want to learn how things in nature have come to be. They want to treat the resource more respectfully. And they want to have someone else handle all the details. Guides can encourage a quieter, softer, more introspective association with the land.

Identifying and Retaining Community Values and Quality of Life

Preservation of Values: Economic and Community Heritage

Utah's rural communities, including those surrounding the Grand Staircase–Escalante National Monument, uniformly desire to retain that rural lifestyle. The question is how can communities identify a common vision to preserve that lifestyle, maintain quality of life, and plan for the type of tourism that will accommodate this vision. By identifying and projecting their unique characteristics, communities can attract a higher-quality tourism, either as part of a diversified economic strategy or to supplement agriculture and ranch-based incomes. Heritage tourism, ecotourism, and agriculture or ranch-based recreation are examples of destination-type tourism that are compatible with rural lifestyles and offer quality jobs.

But only when community development strategies are community driven, (i.e., defined and agreed to by community members) are they likely to prove long lasting. Communities inevitably face conflicts between special interests, individual property rights, and the right to define a lifestyle vision. External assistance and resources may be necessary to implement community development strategies, but may also be detrimental in terms of loss of local influence and control (Burr and Walsh, 1994). By creating an interactive setting, where individuals and community leaders can participate actively in visioning and planning, groups and individuals may be less inclined to pursue special interests, and more inclined to meet the established vision of the community as a whole (Burr and Walsh, 1994). Two distinctive Utah communities—Midway and Springdale—are examples for observation and evaluation.

The alternative to a coordinated approach usually leads to lower quality, nondistinctive rural towns without safeguards for preserving rural lifestyles and character. By lining their points of entry with homogenized, convenience-based businesses, the opportunity for a unique sense of arrival is lost.

Strategies for Identifying Uniqueness

All communities have a distinguishing characteristic-perhaps natural or man-made assets, a historical event, cultural phenomenon, or folklore. Week-long festivals that draw thousands (and even millions) of visitors have been constructed around such themes as unique birds, local harvests, cowboy poetry, rodeos, and local music.

How can a community undertaking a visioning process identify a special characteristic and then reap the benefits by projecting that image? Successful visioning processes are usually conducted through an interactive process involving all parties in the dialog. One effective approach is to bring individuals together around a community project and to focus on the relationships (or sense of community) that develops as they work together (Burr and Walsh, 1994). Four communities in Sanpete County, for example, are working together to forge an identity as a heritage destination. This approach can be particularly helpful where conflict has arisen due to a recent influx of new residents with different values, as is true in Kane and Garfield Counties.

Once a community's characteristics have been identified, both formal and informal tools can be used to develop economic strategies based on this "uniqueness." Formal strategies include zoning requirements, county ordinances, architectural and historical standards, and building codes. Informal strategies include historical, cultural and business associations (i.e., Historic Main Street programs, arts cooperatives). Marketing can then be used to *promote* areas or seasons for visitation. Likewise, "demarketing" techniques can be used to move visitors away from fragile sites that are not prepared or intended for visitors, or to emphasize other seasons that may not receive as much visitation. Gateway communities can be marketed to manage and control unwanted development in national and state parks. Ultimately, however, gateway communities must adopt a proactive approach in planning for development.

Above all, the process of identifying and retaining community values should emphasize a coordinated approach based on local input and decision making. The process should build a sense of community, opening itself to outside ideas without allowing external recommendations or opportunities to dictate. Moreover, identifying community uniqueness is a natural way to plan and assign markets. Rather than trying to outdo the town next door, communities should seek a unique niche that works. Given the opportunity, individuals who share a common locality and other ties and interests will naturally seek to achieve common goals. Tourism can provide opportunities for supplementing rural incomes while maintaining rural lifestyles, values, and quality of life. However, the onus is on community leaders and individuals to make it happen the way they envision. As Steve Puro from Kane County Travel Council observes: "We are standing here receiving the ripples when we should be throwing the rocks."

Conclusion

With or without the new Monument, Kane and Garfield Counties are making a transition from traditional, resource-based economies to ones supported by service-sector jobs, many of which are seasonal. Such change is inevitable, and tourism is only one part of the new equation. Communities must face the changes brought by increasing visitors and turn them into opportunities. They will more likely succeed by creating sustainable tourism development opportunities that address the needs of the present *and* the future, as well as of man *and* the environment.

Economic diversification will continue to be critical in the quest for sustainable solutions. As in extractive industries, tourism is subject to the inevitable ups and downs of a typical business cycle. Even when profitable, communities should not depend solely on tourism to maintain a healthy local economy, but should see it as a cornerstone of a balanced, diversified economic mix.

The Division of Travel Development believes that destination tourism—with its focus on quality over quantity, higher earnings and better jobs, appropriate and sustainable development, a well-developed sense of place, and carefully selected locations—is the best way to establish a strong cornerstone. Visitor management tactics are also a critical element of the planning equation for the new Monument, to preserve and protect the area's fragile ecosystems. And priority must be placed on retaining community values and improving quality of life. Tourism development must enhance communities *first* for the people who live there and then for those who visit.

Wallace Stegner describes a paradox: "We may love a place and still be dangerous to it." This sentiment appropriately applies to the creation of the Grand Staircase– Escalante National Monument in southern Utah. Some love the land encompassed within the new Monument because it rejuvenates the spirit to experience it; others because it provides sustenance for one's family and traditional way of life. But without proper care and forethought, the lover can become a peril to the beloved.

References

Barber, B. T. 1996. *A partnership approach to public lands planning.* UTAH TRAVEL BAROMETER. Utah Division of Travel Development, Salt Lake City, UT.

Barber, B. T. and A. P. Clark. 1996. RECONCILING ENVIRONMENTAL PRESERVATION AND ECONOMIC SUSTAINABILITY OF UTAH'S COLORADO PLATEAU. Governor's Office of Planning and Budget, Salt Lake City, UT.

Burr, S., and J. Walsh. 1994. *A hidden value of sustainable rural tourism development.* TRENDS, SUSTAINABLE RURAL TOURISM DEVELOPMENT, 31(1). U.S. Department of the Interior, National Park Service.

Carter, R. 1996. Speech delivered at the Loss of Rights Rally, Kanab High School, Kanab, UT.

Clinton, President W. J. September 1996. *Establishment of the Grand Staircase–Escalante National Monument: A proclamation by the President of the United States of America.* The White House, Washington, D.C.

Conine, D. August 1994. Tourism Planning Community Meeting, Torrey, UT.

Daily, G. 1997. NATURE'S SERVICES. Island Press, Washington, D.C.

D. K. Shifflet & Associates, Ltd. 1997. 1996 UTAH VISITOR PROFILE. McLean, VA.

D'Amore, L. J. 1993. *A code of ethics and guidelines for socially and environmentally responsible tourism.* JOURNAL OF TRAVEL RESEARCH 31: 64-66.

Department of Resource, Recreation and Tourism (DRRT). 1993.BRYCE CANYON VISITOR SURVEY. University of Idaho, Moscow, ID.

Dude Ranch Association. 1996. Fact Sheet. LaPorte, CO.

Dude Ranch Association. 1996. THE ORIGINS OF DUDE RANCHING AND THE DUDE RANCHER'S ASSOCIATION. LaPorte, CO.

Governor's Office of Planning and Budget. 1994. CANYONS OF THE ESCALANTE: A NATIONAL ECOREGION. Salt Lake City, UT.

Governor's Office of Planning and Budget. 1995. EDA TITLE IX SUSTAINABLE DEVELOPMENT PROJECT TO ASSIST WITH AN ADJUSTMENT STRATEGY IN GARFIELD AND EMERY COUNTIES. Salt Lake City, UT.

Governor's Office of Planning and Budget. 1995. 1995 UTAH ECONOMIC AND DEMOGRAPHIC PROFILES, GOVERNOR'S OFFICE OF PLANNING AND BUDGET. Salt Lake City, UT.

Governor's Office of Planning and Budget. 1997. 1997 ECONOMIC REPORT TO THE GOVERNOR, GOVERNOR'S OFFICE OF PLANNING AND BUDGET. Salt Lake City, UT.

Hardin, G. 1968. *The tragedy of the commons.* SCIENCE 162:1243-48.

Healy, R. G. 1994. *The common pool problem in tourism landscapes,* ANNALS OF TOURISM RESEARCH. 21(3): 596-611.

Leavitt, Governor M. O. 1996. *Memo to the cabinet: Direction on public land issues in Utah.* Salt Lake City, UT.

McIntosh, R. G., and C. R. Brent. 1995. TOURISM PRINCIPLES, PRACTICES AND PHILOSOPHIES. Seventh Edition. John Wiley & Sons, Inc. New York, NY.

McNulty, R. 1989. SYMPOSIUM ON CULTURAL TOURISM. University of Calgary, Alberta, Canada.

Motloch, J. L. 1991. INTRODUCTION TO LANDSCAPE DESIGN. Van Nostrand Reinhold, NY.

Office of Energy and Resource Planning. 1995. UTAH COUNTY ECONOMIC PROFILES. State of Utah Department of Natural Resources, Salt Lake City, UT.

Red Rock n' Llamas. 1997. GUIDES AND OUTFITTERS SURVEY, UTAH DIVISION OF TRAVEL DEVELOPMENT. Department of Community and Economic Development, Salt Lake City, UT.

Salt Lake Tribune. March 22, 1997. *No break for rescuers, Garfield: Hikers may pay search costs.* Salt Lake City, UT.

Tooman, A.. 1997. *Tourism and development.* JOURNAL OF TRAVEL RESEARCH 35(3): 33-44.

United States Department of Interior, Fish & Wildlife Service, and U.S. Department of Commerce, Bureau of the Census. 1991. 1991 NATIONAL SURVEY OF FISHING, HUNTING AND WILDLIFE-ASSOCIATED RECREATION. U.S. Government Printing Office, Washington DC.

Utah Department of Employment Security. 1996. KEY LABOR MARKET INFORMATION FOR UTAH. Labor Market Information Division, Salt Lake City, UT.

Utah Division of State History. 1995. PRESERVING OUR PAST THROUGH HERITAGE TOURISM. Department of Community and Economic Development, Salt Lake City, UT.

Utah Division of Travel Development. 1996. 1996 ECONOMIC AND TRAVEL INDUSTRY PROFILES FOR UTAH COUNTIES. Department of Community and Economic Development, Salt Lake City, UT.

Western Spirit Cycling. 1997.GUIDES AND OUTFITTERS SURVEY. Utah Division of Travel Development, Department of Community and Economic Development, Salt Lake City, UT.

Wikstrom Economic & Planning Consultants, Inc. 1997. 1996-97 UTAH SKIER SURVEY. Salt Lake City, UT.

Williams, P. 1991. *Ecotourism management challenges.* FIFTH ANNUAL TRAVEL REVIEW CONFERENCE PROCEEDINGS: 83-87.

World Commission on Environment and Development. 1987. OUR COMMON FUTURE. Oxford University Press, New York, NY.

Woolf, J. 1997. *Monument site isn't unique, say backers of oil drilling.* SALT LAKE TRIBUNE. Salt Lake City, UT.

Appendix

GARFIELD COUNTY

For Garfield County, population 4,308 in 1995, growth in manufacturing, government, construction, agriculture, transportation and utility services remained fairly constant between 1970 and 1995. A brief boom in the mining sector in the late 1970s and early 1980s, which declined dramatically in 1982 and 1983, provided a number of jobs and "echo booms" in the construction and manufacturing sectors. Following this boom, manufacturing and construction have remained fairly stable, increasing somewhat in 1994 and 1995. The service sector, considered one of the most tourist-dependent categories, remained relatively stable until the early 1990s when it outpaced the government sector as the largest employment category in the county. Unemployment rates, averaging 12 percent since the 1970s, have consistently remained well above the state's 6 percent average, except briefly during the "mining boom" of the late seventies. A second drop in unemployment, to 8 percent, occurred again in the late 1980s, due to rapid growth in the service sector. Unemployment rates in the 1990s have fluctuated between 9 and 14 percent, with 10.1 percent unemployment in 1996 (Utah Department of Employment Security).

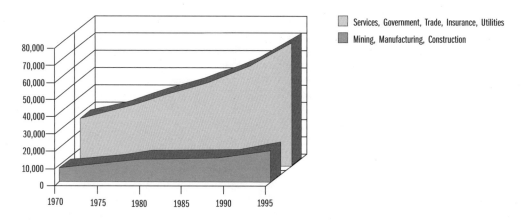

Figure 16.1. Statewide nonagricultural employment.

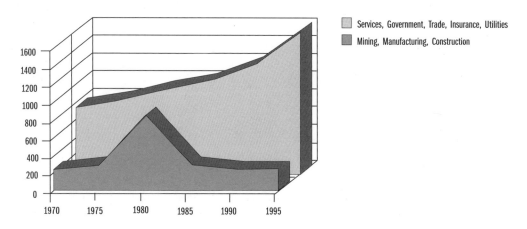

Figure 16.2. Garfield County nonagricultural employment.

KANE COUNTY

Kane County, population 5,900 in 1995, experienced a similar decline in the resource-based sectors between 1970 and 1995. The mining boom that shook Garfield County in the late seventies did not occur in Kane County, which also experienced lower unemployment (8 percent on average) during 1970 and 1995. Steady increases in the service and government sectors accounted for most of the economic growth and lower unemployment rates in Kane County compared with Garfield County. Unemployment in Kane County for 1996 was 7 percent. In 1995, the service sector was the largest employment sector, representing 33.2 percent of all jobs in the county, followed by 31.7 percent for trade and 24.7 percent for the government sectors.

EARNINGS IN KANE AND GARFIELD COUNTIES

Earnings, alongside employment rates, provides another important indicator of local economic health. Wage levels in Garfield and Kane Counties have been among the lowest in the state for all sectors: $1,347 for Garfield and $1,184 for Kane, compared with the state average $1,867. Exceptions can be found in the construction sector in Garfield County, where the average monthly nonagricultural wage in 1995 was $2,208, compared with the state average $2,042. Although not indicative of a trend, total personal income increased at a greater rate between 1994 and 1995 in Kane and Garfield counties, by 13.7 percent and 11.7 percent respectively, compared with the statewide average, 8.5 percent. This increase can be partially explained by a steeper increase in payroll wages in Garfield and Kane Counties compared with the rest of the state, and partially due to nonwage earnings. Nonwage earnings, such as dividend and transfer payments, account for a greater part of total personal income than for the state as a whole. This probably indicates a growing retirement population, or individuals whose income is based on property and dividend payments.

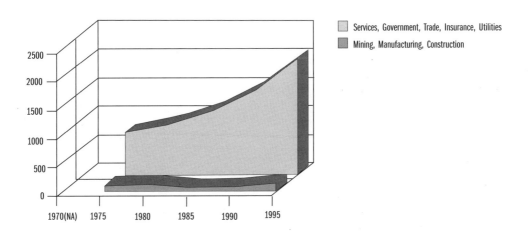

Figure 16.3. Kane County nonagricultural employment.

Appendix Sources

Governor's Office of Planning and Budget. 1995. 1995 UTAH ECONOMIC AND DEMOGRAPHIC PROFILES. Salt Lake City, UT.

Governor's Office of Planning and Budget. 1997. 1997 ECONOMIC REPORT TO THE GOVERNOR. Salt Lake City, UT.

State of Utah Natural Resources, Office of Energy and Resource Planning. 1995. UTAH COUNTY ECONOMIC PROFILES. Salt Lake City, UT.

State of Utah, Division of Travel Development. 1996. 1996 ECONOMIC AND TRAVEL INDUSTRY PROFILES FOR UTAH COUNTIES.

Travel Industry Association of America. 1997. 1997 OUTLOOK FOR TRAVEL AND TOURISM. Salt Lake City, UT.

Utah Department of Employment Security, Labor Market Information Division. 1996. KEY LABOR MARKET INFORMATION FOR UTAH. Salt Lake City, UT.

CHAPTER SEVENTEEN

Maintaining Local Communities

Scott Truman

It is my observation, as an old cowboy once commented, "Timing has a lot to do with the outcome of a rain dance" (Bender, 1992). Just prior to September 18, 1996, there must have been some mighty fine dancing going on, because in the minds of the residents of Garfield and Kane Counties they experienced a real cloudburst, a gully-washer, a flood that is most capable of breaking ditches. I am referring, of course, to President Clinton's proclamation creating the Grand Staircase–Escalante National Monument. I think that the timing is opportune to explore and implement new collaborative management approaches that go beyond what we traditionally have done. Accordingly, we need to mend the ditches and begin a new rain dance to bring the light steady rains that will cause the crops to grow and flourish.

During the summer of 1994, when Governor Leavitt addressed the Utah state legislature, he identified six critical issues facing the state. One of these challenges was to "become a generation of planners—not compulsive regulators, but dedicated planners, always following the rule and fighting for the principle that the more local the decision the better," thus ensuring consideration of the human dimension along with the landscape (Leavitt, 1994). One concern facing everyone in Garfield and Kane Counties, as they hope to become part of the Grand Staircase planning and decision-making process, is that it not become an effort of regulation but rather an effort of great vision and foresight.

* * * * * *

Over the years, volumes of planning documents have been written. Unfortunately, the result behind many of those efforts was to create regulatory documents rather than documents that would guide a community, a county, a state, a resource area, or an ecosystem into the next decade and beyond.

In the case of communities and counties, part of the problem is that plans often are created as a reaction rather than an action. That is, they are created to meet a requirement for state or federal funding or in reaction to a federal or state planning effort that requires consideration of local plans.

On a state or federal level, problems can be traced to the process itself. Scoping sessions are held but generally attract little interest. Considerable time, money, and effort are expended (not without claim to ownership and pride of authorship) before a draft document is released for public comment. The public, accordingly, is suspicious and even nonsupportive before comments on the draft are taken. Their attitude is reflected in a shrug of the shoulders and a comment of "What's the use, they have already made the decision."

Those writing the draft are defensive, and justifiably so, of any criticisms. They have just spent a significant amount of time studying, analyzing, and justifying their recommendations. To be told that they have missed the point is an affront to their abilities and their intentions.

Current planning and management of our various resources, whether federal, state, or local, is done without much interagency or intergovernmental coordination. It is solicitous of input from others, but it does not involve others in the actual planning process. Too often, planning and management efforts are conducted independently rather than in conjunction with one another.

This approach to planning and management has often fostered hostility. According to professor Robert H. Nelson: "In the rural West, the federal government functions as a local planning and zoning board" (Nelson, 1996:17). This federal role is both unwanted and unappreciated: "Historic federal dominance has kept much of the West in a condition of political and economic adolescence" (*Id.* at 19). Most residents of Garfield and Kane Counties would not be so kind in their expressions.

In the spirit of exploring and finding collaborative approaches in our planning efforts, we need to create a process for planning coordination at all levels of government. This is a strong local area of concern in the Grand Staircase planning process. In the minds of the "locals," the jury is still out on the Monument planning team and on the governor's economic development team.

* * * * * *

Let me relate a personal experience. In 1982, while serving as a city councilman in Ferron, Utah, I first became involved in economic development. With the construction of the power plants in Emery County, the county and the city had both experienced substantial growth. By 1982 that upward spiral of growth had peaked and the decline began. There were construction lay-offs, and housing shortages became housing surpluses. Unemployment levels, which had been extremely low, were showing double-digit levels. We found that we were subject to swings in the local economy, just as the state and the nation experienced ups and downs. Prior to this, we had come to think that we were somewhat invincible. We were the suppliers of power to all of the state with a guaranteed demand for our high-quality coal that should insulate us from swings in the economy.

We did not foresee that conservation measures would reduce the demand for power and that technology would make it possible to mine greater amounts of coal with fewer people. We found that we were indeed vulnerable. Accordingly, the city fathers assigned me the responsibility for economic development.

The county almost simultaneously determined that it needed to be involved in economic development. Shortly, I was hired as county economic development director. One of my first assignments was to send a proposal to General Motors encouraging them to locate their Saturn plant in Emery County. After all, we had previously geared up to accommodate the construction of the Huntington and the Hunter power plants.

Many other communities and counties throughout rural America extended similar efforts. Economic development committees and offices were established; industrial parks were funded and built. Prisons, waste dumps—anything that would create a job was a hot item. For what? To create jobs so "our children would not have to leave or so they would have something to which to come home ... so our communities would not shrivel up and die."

Those concerns still exist. There are few people in rural Utah (or urban Utah or even urban America), who do not have hopes and desires for a good-paying job to support themselves and their families, and to provide an opportunity for their children to go to college and then to come home and make a decent living. Many rural Utahns, however, are now concerned with the question of "for whom are we developing?" If we do develop and grow, will what we create be what we want our children to come home to, or will they want to come home? Most rural residents are beginning to examine "quality of life" issues closely and what growth might mean to their particular quality of life. They view economic development as community development, stressing capabilities not deficiencies. Moreover, they realize that quality community development is based on "how we make a living—not how we create jobs."

Rural Utahns are painfully aware that a low-paying service-sector job for the primary wage earner does not mean quality of life for a family. We are also aware that if that same service-sector job is a secondary job to a family, the quality of life will be greatly enhanced.

Do the residents of Garfield and Kane Counties want jobs in their communities? Do they believe in the economic resettlement that Governor Leavitt champions? The answer is a resounding yes, but with reservations and unanswered questions: (1) What impact will these new jobs or the resettlement have? (2) What will be the cost? (3) How will we pay for it? (4) Can it be controlled? (5) Will it happen in spite of us? (6) Will we have a say? These same questions need to be asked about the Monument and its planning process. According to rural development specialist Jerry Wade: "People want to be involved in the decision making. If you do something for the public, you take something away from them. If you do something with them, you create strength."

*   *   *   *   *   *

Several years ago, I attended an uncle's funeral at which my cousin, the oldest son of that family, spoke. He and his father had not always gotten along very well. Part of the reason for the strained relationship was that they were both in the farming and ranching business. Each owned his own operation, but they shared equipment, as many families do.

(This scenario is similar to the not always peaceful coexistence of the long-term "local" and the environmental community as they confront sharing the Grand Staircase.)

My cousin operates his farm and ranching operation as a modern business. He keeps meticulous records and has largely computerized his operation. He is tied to marketing networks, and follows the futures market. His ranch sustains him well. His father, on the other hand, operated out of a notebook he sometimes kept. Over the years, he gained enough savvy to pay his bills on time, to send those that wanted of his ten children to college, and to buy what they needed when necessary. There were not many vacations other than to the mountains or the desert and occasionally to the city. And there were few luxuries other than a television.

Quite different planning and management styles, yet both were in their own ways successful. So why didn't they get along? The equipment. My cousin observed in his tribute: "My dad operated on the premise that if it ain't broke, don't fix it; and if it still moves, it ain't broke."

So what is the point? There are two. First, there are different ways of doing things and there may not be a right or a wrong way, but there might be a better way. Second, looking at the equipment, is it still moving?

In the past, land use and resource management planning processes relied primarily upon the data of scientific studies and expert opinion to develop and implement plans. Little consideration was given to the people dimension, to the social aspects and implications of planning decisions on the local populace. "Outside" experts rarely considered either the technical or social information generated from years of local experience as a valid database to use in planning efforts. (Not surprisingly, creation of the new Monument has done little to dispel this perception.) These outside experts moved into town or into a resource area, as one old rancher phrased it, "with an insult on their lips and an injunction in their hands." Their mission, according to an environmental writer, was to protect "the ecologically devastated western landscape." Yet they also expected to be accepted.

In contrast, the locals like my uncle, depended upon their own observations and lessons from years of experience (i.e., their savvy or good judgment) to support their resource and community management efforts for their livelihood. Unfortunately, that "good judgment, `savvy,' comes from experience, and a lot of that sometimes comes from bad judgment" (Bender, 1992:29).

In fairness, bad judgment has perhaps given the outside expert reason not to consider local input. Prior to the Taylor Grazing Act, there were obvious grazing abuses, and it has taken a number of decades to rectify them. In the minds of some, this abuse is still occurring, and past abuses have not been corrected.

The point, however, is not to debate the past, it is to suggest that there are different ways of doing things (i.e., my cousin's and uncle's ranching experience), and that we should seek these better ways regardless of our frame of reference. And we should realize that although the equipment "ain't broke," it certainly "ain't moving very fast."

There are two planning scenarios in which locals often feel entrapped. First, data from scientific studies and expert opinions are used to develop and implement plans. Second, local stakeholders are included in the planning process, but only after outside experts have developed the draft management plan and presented it to the public for comment. Although local involvement is sought in public scoping meetings, the rural stakeholder perception is that the first real local involvement occurs during the public comment process on the proposed plans. And even then the comments delivered by the locals to the planning entity are often outweighed by more professional comments from outsiders.

There are, however, solutions to keep the machinery moving and to ensure the long-range public interest.

1. A desired outcome would be to engage in a planning effort that is truly cross- jurisdictional and inclusive of all concerned. Such an effort would help to meet Governor Leavitt's challenge that we "become a generation of planners" dedicated to locally based decision making (Leavitt, 1994:3). Such an effort would need to broaden the understanding and definition of "local," which would mean the local rancher, the local elected official, the local land manager and his local staff, and the local environmentalist. Residency would not necessarily require being a local, but it would presume a grassroots involvement in the process, ensuring that the broad local community has a vested interest and input in the planning process and will assume authorship of the product. It would assume that these grassroots participants would be empowered to make decisions independent of some distant oversight group, committee, or individual. It would also assume that those so involved would individually and collectively be responsible and answerable for the decisions. The decision makers could not draft policy and leave, leaving the implementation and consequences to a new manager. The drafters and implementors would be the same, and they would have to live with the consequences and benefits of their decisions.

2. We need to look at a more holistic and sustainable approach to management of federal lands and waters. In his 1995 address to the Utah Rural Summit, Gary Tomsic made the following observation: "We pretend that we can effectively plan for ... change as though we are separate independent ... units instead of being what we really are—part of an interdependent economy with many components." We can no more separate the local community with its various components [i.e., the environmental community, the county, the state, and the federal government in our public land states] than we can separate and distinguish between economic and community development and public land planning and management, trying to treat them as separate activities. They are in fact one and the same. They are part of an interdependent order with many components.

3. Locals are a marvelous resource in planning for sustainability because they have the most to win or to lose. I have had the opportunity, working in community development for over fifteen years, to help plan, design, finance, and construct two golf courses in rural Utah (in locations where they probably should not have been built). While doing so I learned some valuable lessons.

One lesson is captured in a quote from Bix Bender in his book *Don't Squat With Yer Spurs On! A Cowboy's Guide to Life*: "If yer ridin' ahead of the herd, take a look back every now and then to make sure it's still there" (Bender, 1992:41). It took some real backtracking to gather support for a project that depended heavily upon volunteer labor, machinery, and donations. I really did not realize how far out in front of the herd I was until after the grass came up and my wife admitted to me that she, too, wondered if grass would ever grow. Garfield County and Governor Leavitt found how difficult it is to be too far in front of the herd through the Canyons of the Escalante National Eco-Region proposal.

Another lesson learned was the value of outside experts. After we locals had done everything we could, we hired a contractor who specialized in golf course construction to do the finish work. The first thing he asked was where he could keep his horse. The second was, "Where do they rope?" We really began to wonder if we had sent some good money chasing after bad, but in a matter of two weeks he had silenced more naysayers than had any of our public meetings and hearings. With the second golf course, I followed the same procedure, but my roper/contractor came on board much earlier. And we learned much sooner about soil conditions, water table levels, salinity, who had equipment, and who would help.

And that leads to a third lesson: The outside expert is much more effective as a local. Accordingly, the BLM resource manager, the area forester, the district ranger, the FWS, and the environmentalist need to be a part of the community. They need to coach Little League, be on community committees, join the PTA, rope with the ropers, and drink coffee at the local cafe. Besides, "Every quarrel is a private one. Outsiders are never welcome" (Bender, 1992:3). As locals we can better resolve our differences among ourselves.

4. Finally, the locals need to be empowered to make decisions. Regional planning groups—a movement instigated by Governor Leavitt in Utah that includes the Southwestern Utah Planning Authorities Council (SUPAC), the Canyon Country Planning Partnership, and the Emery County Public Lands Council—are (or have been) in various stages of joint coordination and collaboration. These efforts were established to create a strong base for collaboration. They operate on a simple premise: Those involved are engaging in a collaborative process to find solutions to problems by being proactive rather than reactive (Tichy and Sherman, 1993). They are finding that by working together they can find common ground. They are finding that by being "candid and forthcoming" and using "face-to-face constructive conflict as a way to make key decisions" (Tichy, 1993:372), they have a basis for collaboration and for finding common ground. It is critical, however, that the key players and networks are present, empowered, and willing to make things happen.

*   *   *   *   *   *

As noted earlier, "Timing has a lot to do with the outcome of a rain dance" (Bender, 1992:2). This is an opportune time to enter into collaborative efforts to develop a more effective planning and management process. Not only is it opportune, but it is necessary and the need may be revolutionary. You may ask, "Isn't a call for revolutionary change a little extreme?" And I would answer, "No," and quote from *Control Your Own Destiny or Someone Else Will:*

> If you don't believe [me], look at what has happened to so many of America's greatest corporations, from GM to IBM to Westinghouse, to American Express, to Sears. Even Apple Computer, regarded not long ago as the epitome of entrepreneurial vigor has fallen from grace. The failure to adapt has unseated CEOs, destroyed hundreds of thousands of jobs, and caused billions of dollars in losses. Investors who believed their money was safe were brutally punished: During the two decades ending in 1992, the combined market value of IBM, Sears, and GM plunged $21 billion (Tichy and Sherman, 1993:xxii).

The change that was called for in the private sector must also be called for in our collective communities. This includes our environmental communities, business communities, local communities, counties, state, and federal public land management agencies. The demands on our public lands and on our rural communities are much different today than they were twenty or twenty-five years ago. These demands mandate a different way of doing business, because the variety and multitude of demands are accelerating. We need to be engaged in local- and state-based, action-oriented joint planning that deals with the landscape as well as the social and human dimension, and that is not limited to a one-time, three-year planning effort, but represents an ongoing and responsive effort.

Such an effort would be in the public interest by meeting the interests and needs of the communities of Garfield and Kane Counties as well as the needs of our state, national, and global community.

References

Bender, T. B. 1992. Don't Squat With Yer Spurs On! A Cowboy's Guide to Life. Peregrine Smith Books, Salt Lake City, UT.

Leavitt, M. O. 1994. *Utah's niche: Quiet quality.* Excerpts of address to the Utah State Legislature, Logan, UT.

Nelson, R. H. 1996. Transferring Federal Lands in the West to the States. How Would it Work? Western Wire-Western Rural Development Center.

Tichy, N. M., and S. Sherman. 1993. Control Your Own Destiny or Someone Else Will. Doubleday, NY.

Tichy, N. M. 1993. *Handbook for Revolutionaries.* In N. Tichy and S. Sherman, Control Your Own Destiny or Someone Else Will. Doubleday, NY.

Tomsic, G. R. 1995. Comments to the September 6–8, 1995 Utah Rural Development Conference.

CHAPTER EIGHTEEN

Through Turquoise Eyes:
A Hopi Perspective

Wilfred Numkena

Dawa (the sun) and Spider Woman looked upon the vast void of darkness that was the night. Together, they saw there needed to be life so Spider Woman said she would create life forms in the void of darkness, while Dawa would create light, which would give life to all that which would be created. Spider Woman went forth to create the mineral world from elements of the void of darkness. She looked upon the mineral world, found it was good, and filled with elements that would nourish all that would be created. She went forth to create the plant world, plants of all kinds to nourish the earth and that which was still to be created. Then she went forth to create the animals, fish of the sea, birds of the sky, and insects of every kind to live upon the earth. Finally, she created people from soil of the earth to walk upon the land. When she looked upon all she had created, she smiled and found all was good. Spider Woman returned to Dawa inviting him to see all she had created.

Together they looked upon all that was created by Spider Woman and found it was good. Dawa turned to Spider Woman then said, "All you have created must have life," so Dawa breathed life into elements of the mineral world, giving them the power to nourish and give strength to all that was created; he then breathed life into the plant world, giving plants the power to nourish, to create air, to control movement of air, to heal the body, and give strength to all that was created; he then breathed life into the animal world, the fish, birds, and insects giving them the powers of organization, to teach, and to balance life; lastly, he breathed life into the people, giving them the power to reason, giving them spiritual power and instructing them to be caretakers of all that was created.

Dawa and Spider Woman, blessed all that was created and given breath of life, for it was all good. Dawa's breath of life bound all things together in creation, making all things to be connected and interdependent upon each other. Together Dawa and Spider Woman have continued the cycle of life and blessed all that was created for they are the source of life.

Creation stories teach us of our origins, the connection we have with our ecosystem, the interdependence of all things, as well as the spiritual value of all that was created. The spiritual value of all creation is paramount to the Hopi people. Understanding the spiritual dimension of all that was created is what develops the relationship we have with our environment, a spiritual kinship with the earth, as well as with the greater of creation, the cosmos. This relationship helps us to view the earth as our mother, for the earth nurtures the plants, animals, birds, fish, insects, and the people.

Spiritual philosophies of the Hopi people are melded into their lifeways as they live them daily through their customs, dances, songs, rituals, ceremonies, and prayers. Hopi thought ponders the interdependence of all things in life. It is a way of life that consciously connects one in a holistic way with the whole of creation, to find your spiritual connection to all that is in front of you, to the left of you, to the right of you, behind you, above you, below you, and within you. When this introspective spiritual foundation has been established, then life is in balance and harmony.

Hopi people are taught tenets of spiritual philosophies through which to live. These tenets help us to develop a personal foundation, a role, and acceptance of responsibilities in life, a spiritual connection and relationship with our environment. We are taught that all things upon this earth are alive, that the minerals have spirits, trees and grass have spirits, birds have spirits, fish have spirits, insects have spirits, animals have spirits, and people have spirits. The Creator instructed us to care for this earth, therefore, we are stewards having responsibility to care for all the plants and all living things upon the earth. We are taught to be mindful of how we use the natural resources, continually being admonished to maintain balance and harmony, not to be wasteful, destructive, or avaricious.

Today the culture of Hopi people is still vibrant, very much alive in practice. The Elders, those who have lived a rich harmonious life, who are now with age showing upon their face, with streaks of gray in their hair, teach the traditions of tribal lifeways to their grandchildren. Spiritual leaders asseverate the effectualness of tribal spiritual philosophies through conducting rituals and ceremonies for the people. The practice of these lifeways shapes the spiritual character and foundation of the Hopi person, how the person sees, thinks, hears, feels, and articulates the world about him, as well as how the Hopi person connects with all creation. Hopi ties with the earth are rooted in the acquisition, practice, and internalization of spiritual knowledge. It is an actualization of the kinship to all things.

Ties with the land are one of tradition, transmitted by oral history from generation to generation and preserved by what is written upon the rocks. Such a coherent body of precedents still influences the Hopi way of life. The value of these traditions continues to impress firmly upon our spirits the responsibilities that we have to care for the earth. The traditions remind us to respect the spirit of creation and the breath of life that exists in all things created, and to use spiritual wisdom in the performance of our role as stewards. If the people are not mindful of their responsibilities as caretakers of this earth, then we shall reap the consequences of our negligence, for being remiss in complying with the Creator's instructions.

For the Hopi, oral history imparts our origins and traces the migratory footprints of our ancestors, and it is validated by writings upon red rock canyon walls. The rock art writings affirm the passage of clans through various regions of the land as related in the migration stories, thus giving the Hopi a historic connection with the land where their forebears lived and left footprints. Our ancestors (the hisat' sinom) left their mark upon the land through their rock art, settlements, pottery shards, and sacred sites; they are buried in the canyons and plateaus of the Grand Staircase. Their spirit voices silently echo through the canyons, while the soft canyon breezes whisper to remind us of the sacredness of the land. Our spiritual core, as well as our ancestral ties, are in these very canyons which have been set aside as a national monument.

All that is upon, around, and within the land is holy and dedicated to a sacred purpose by the Creator. This has been fulfilled by the high order of the Rattle Snake Priests, the Flute Clan priests, as well as by the One Horned and Two Horned Priests who have performed the sacred ceremonies as recorded in the rock art. We need only trace the footprints of the hisat' sinom, to understand the sacredness of the land and to perform the responsibilities that are incumbent upon us.

Elements of two dissimilar belief systems can be antithetical to each other, causing a divergence from a common cause. Hopi spiritual philosophies, including the precepts for understanding land and its use, are very different from the Anglo-American economically based philosophies of land and its use. The Hopi people view Anglo-American precepts as one of exploiting natural resources for monetary gain and of owning the land. The Hopi see this as a sign of neither understanding nor respecting the spiritual dimension of the earth. This difference of lifeway views and understandings has led to impasse and to distrust of the Anglo-American. It is important, therefore, for Indian tribes to be direct participants in developing plans, policies, and regulations for the Grand Staircase–Escalante National Monument. The Hopi and other Indian people are still spiritually connected to this land—the ancient ruins of settlements that existed in the canyons, the sacred sites that are still visited, and the spirits of ancestors buried within the canyons.

A Hopi observes with great interest the non-Indian activities of hiking and camping in order to see and to walk over the land in wonderment and awe. The moment of visitation may be recorded by camera, creating an amusing memory that may be imprinted in the mind. But during the visitation, there has been no spiritual connection with the land, nor with the life-forms that inhabit the landscape. On the other hand, a Hopi person's experience is of a spiritual nature, beginning with the preparation of paho (prayer feathers) and sacred cornmeal. He arrives in humility and feels contrite while descending into the canyons to seek the appropriate place to make an offering to the ancestral spirits. There is a peaceful connection: One feels the spiritual joy of the ancestors at the visitation of one's grandchildren. There is respect for the ancestors and understanding of the sacredness of the land that they inhabit. This reflects the embodiment and wholeness of Hopi ties with the land and ancestors who have long since gone.

Despite these differing views and understandings, the Indian and non-Indian must search for a common understanding in protecting and preserving the land. The Grand Staircase–Escalante National Monument contains the ancestral roots of the Hopi, as well as those who have followed. Do not desecrate the sacredness of the land, the sacred sites, and the burial sites of our ancestors. Understand the delicateness of the land and all life-forms upon it; they are all connected and each has its purpose. Do not allow politics or laws to be the sole driving forces, for they are the frailty of man. Man does not own the land. Have respect for one another, seek the Creator's guiding hand, then together we can honor and preserve the sanctity of the land.

Afterword

Robert B. Keiter

Since the preceding chapters were first written, the BLM's planning for the Grand Staircase–Escalante National Monument has proceeded apace. Monument manager Jerry Meredith has assembled a 20 member, interdisciplinary planning team that is actively soliciting public participation in the planning process (See Appendix D). As part of the initial scoping process, the team has prepared and disseminated a visions kit, asking interested parties to provide ideas related to Monument values, management strategies, and the role of local communities. A related series of public workshops has been held throughout Utah and elsewhere. The team is now reviewing the responses and beginning to develop alternative management strategies with the goal of publishing a draft management plan in the fall of 1998. During November 1997, the Monument planning team, in cooperation with the Utah Advisory Council on Science and Technology and Southern Utah University, hosted a Scientific Forum to gather information about the Monument's resources and to identify necessary additional research. The proceedings of the Scientific Forum will be published and the information will be used in the Monument planning process.

Controversy continues to swirl around the Monument's potential mineral resources. Shortly after the Monument was designated, Andalex Resources announced that it would cease work on its proposed Kaiparowits Plateau coal mine and seek to negotiate an exchange with the federal government for its coal leases within the Monument boundaries. Conoco, Inc., which holds 59 federal oil and gas leases on 108,000 acres within the Monument, has recently announced that it will not drill an exploratory well on its Reese Canyon lease. In a controversial decision, the BLM had earlier granted Conoco permission to drill at this location, and the Interior Board of Land Appeals sustained that decision in an administrative appeal filed by environmental opponents (141 IBLA 86). Conoco, however, completed an exploratory well on a nearby state lease within the Monument and failed to discover sufficient reserves to justify further exploration in the Reese Creek area. Nonetheless, Conoco has expressed interest in exploring on its other leases in the southern portion of the Monument. In December 1997, the General Accounting Office released a report placing the value of the Monument's mineral resources at $223-331 billion (GAO/RCED-98-5D), a figure that was based on the

Utah Geological Survey's preliminary estimates. Both federal officials and environmental groups have criticized this estimate, asserting that it fails to take account of market fluctuations and production costs, and is not based on standard appraisal methods. In addition, Congress recently appropriated one million dollars to help the State Institutional Trust Lands Administration pay for "appraisals, resources, studies, and other expenses" related to the exchange of state school trust lands located within the Monument (H.R. 2264).

The American public appears to have discovered the Monument. The Escalante Interagency Office has recorded a significant increase in visitors to the Monument region: 25,740 people visited during 1997, compared to 16,322 people in 1996 and 15,140 people in 1995. Not surprisingly, local officials are beginning to examine how they might participate effectively in the Monument planning process and to adjust local economic development plans to account for the new Monument's popularity.

The acrimony that accompanied President Clinton's decision to designate a new national monument in southern Utah has triggered congressional hearings and legislative activity. The House Resources Subcommittee on National Parks and Public Lands, under the chairmanship of Utah Representative James Hansen, has conducted an inquiry into the Monument designation decision and issued a report entitled "Behind Closed Doors: The Abuse of Trust and Discretion in the Establishment of the Grand Staircase–Escalante National Monument" that criticizes the designation process. The report, which was dismissed by administration officials as political posturing, suggests that the Antiquities Act procedure was used improperly to avoid the public involvement requirements of other public land laws and that the Monument was established to curry political favor with environmental constituents before the 1996 election even though the lands being protected were not facing any imminent threat. In December 1997, the House of Representatives passed the "National Monument Fairness Act of 1997" (H.R. 1127) by a 229-197 vote. The bill would amend the Antiquities Act by prohibiting the President from designating national monuments in excess of 50,000 acres without consulting with the affected state's governor and securing congressional approval. The Senate has not yet acted on related legislation (S. 477), but the President is expected to veto the bill if it reaches him. Utah Senator Robert Bennett's bill (S. 357), which would mandate multiple-use management in the new Monument, has been referred to the Senate Committee on Energy and Natural Resources and not yet made any further progress.

At the same time, three lawsuits are pending in Utah federal district court challenging the legality of the President's initial national monument designation decision. Brought by the Utah Association of Counties, the State Institutional Trust Lands Administration, and Mountain States Legal Foundation, the lawsuits allege that the President's monument designation decision violated the Antiquities Act by not designating the "smallest area compatible with the proper care and management of the objects to be protected," the Federal Land Policy and Management Act by making an illegal withdrawal of public land without congressional consultation, the National Environmental Policy Act by not employing the EIS public involvement process, and the Federal Advisory Committee Act by involving nonfederal employees in the designation process. A decision in this litigation is not expected before 1999, and any ruling will almost certainly be appealed by the losing party.

Clearly, controversy is nothing new in the establishment of national monuments. While the Grand Staircase–Escalante is no exception to this historical reality, the new Monument may nevertheless portend a significant shift in federal preservation policy. First, the sheer size of the Monument represents an effort to preserve the region's important historical and scientific resources on an ecosystem scale. Second, the BLM—not the National Park Service—has been charged with managing the new Monument and preserving its resources while also allowing some traditional multiple-use activities to continue. Third, the state of Utah and local communities have been encouraged to play an active role in the planning process. According to Secretary of the Interior Bruce Babbitt, "[W]e are determined to work together in innovative ways to pool all relevant information about the land and the resources within the Monument, protect the environment and the special treasures of the Grand Staircase–Escalante, help citizens and local government participate in the management plan, and encourage economic development in the towns surrounding the Monument." If the BLM can bring that vision to reality and ensure the ecological integrity of the new Monument while integrating local concerns into the planning process, the Grand Staircase–Escalante designation could presage a new approach to federal preservation efforts on the public domain.

Appendix A

Proclamation No. 6920   3 C.F.R. 64 (1997)
September 18, 1996   1996 USCCAN A73

ESTABLISHMENT OF THE GRAND STAIRCASE–ESCALANTE NATIONAL MONUMENT

. . . .

BY THE PRESIDENT OF THE UNITED STATES OF AMERICA

A PROCLAMATION

The Grand Staircase–Escalante National Monument's vast and austere landscape embraces a spectacular array of scientific and historic resources. This high, rugged, and remote region, where bold plateaus and multi-hued cliffs run for distances that defy human perspective, was the last place in the continental United States to be mapped. Even today, this unspoiled natural area remains a frontier, a quality that greatly enhances the monument's value for scientific study. The monument has a long and dignified human history: it is a place where one can see how nature shapes human endeavors in the American West, where distance and aridity have been pitted against our dreams and courage. The monument presents exemplary opportunities for geologists, paleontologists, archeologists, historians, and biologists.

The monument is a geologic treasure of clearly exposed stratigraphy and structures. The sedimentary rock layers, are relatively undeformed and unobscured by vegetation, offering a clear view to understanding the processes of the earth's formation. A wide variety of formations, some in brilliant colors, have been exposed by millennia of erosion. The monument contains significant portions of a vast geologic stairway, named the Grand Staircase by pioneering geologist Clarence Dutton, which rises 5,500 feet to the rim of Bryce Canyon in an unbroken sequence of great cliffs and plateaus. The monument includes the rugged canyon country of the upper Paria Canyon system, major components of the White and Vermilion Cliffs and associated benches, and the Kaiparowits Plateau. That Plateau encompasses about 1,600 square miles of sedimentary rock and consists of successive south-to-north ascending plateaus or benches, deeply cut by steep-walled canyons. Naturally burning coal seams have scorched the tops of the Burning Hills brick-red. Another prominent geological feature of the plateau is the East Kaibab Monocline, known as the Cockscomb. The monument also includes the spectacular Circle Cliffs and part of the Waterpocket Fold, the inclusion of which completes the protection of this geologic feature begun with the establishment of Capitol Reef National Monument in 1938 (Proclamation No. 2246, 50 Stat. 1856). The monument holds many arches and natural bridges, including the 130-foot-high Escalante Natural Bridge, with a 100 foot span, and Grosvenor Arch, a rare "double arch." The upper Escalante Canyons, in the northeastern reaches of the monument, are distinctive: in addition to several major arches and natural bridges, vivid geological features are laid bare in narrow, serpentine canyons, where erosion has exposed sandstone and shale deposits in shades of red, maroon, chocolate, tan, gray, and white. Such diverse objects make the monument outstanding for purposes of geologic study.

The monument includes world class paleontological sites. The Circle Cliffs reveal remarkable specimens of petrified wood, such as large unbroken logs exceeding 30 feet in length. The thickness, continuity and broad temporal distribution of the Kaiparowits Plateau's stratigraphy provide significant opportunities to study the paleontology of the late Cretaceous Era. Extremely significant fossils, including marine and brackish water mollusks, turtles, crocodilians, lizards, dinosaurs, fishes, and mammals, have been recovered from the Dakota, Tropic Shale and Wahweap Formations, and the Tibbet Canyon, Smoky Hollow and John Henry members of the Straight Cliffs Formation. Within the monument, these formations have produced the only evidence in our hemisphere of terrestrial vertebrate fauna, including mammals, of the Cenomanian-Santonian ages. This sequence of rocks, including the overlaying Wahweap and Kaiparowits formations, contains one of the best and most continuous records of Late Cretaceous terrestrial life in the world.

Archeological inventories carried out to date show extensive use of places within the monument by ancient Native American cultures. The area was a contact point for the Anasazi and Fremont cultures, and the evidence of this mingling provides a significant opportunity for archeological study. The cultural resources discovered so far in the monument are outstanding in their variety of cultural affiliation, type and distribution. Hundreds of recorded sites include rock art panels, occupation sites, campsites and granaries. Many more undocumented sites that exist within the monument are of significant scientific and historic value worthy of preservation for future study.

The monument is rich in human history. In addition to occupations by the Anasazi and Fremont cultures, the area has been used by modern tribal groups, including the southern Paiute and Navajo. John Wesley Powell's expedition did initial mapping and scientific field work in the area in 1872. Early Mormon pioneers left many historic objects, including trails, inscriptions, ghost towns such as the Old Paria townsite, rock houses, and cowboy line camps, and built and traversed the renowned Hole-in-the-Rock Trail as part of their epic colonization efforts. Sixty miles of the Trail lie within the monument, as does Dance Hall Rock, used by intrepid Mormon pioneers and now a National Historic site.

Spanning five life zones from low-lying desert to coniferous forest, with scarce and scattered water sources, the monument is an outstanding biological resource. Remoteness, limited travel corridors and low visitation have all helped to preserve intact the monument's important ecological values. The blending of warm and cold desert floras, along with the high number of endemic species, place this area in the heart of perhaps the richest floristic region in the Intermountain West. It contains an abundance of unique, isolated communities such as hanging gardens, tinajas, and rock crevice, canyon bottom, and dunal pocket communities, which have provided refugia for many ancient plant species for millennia. Geologic uplift with minimal deformation and subsequent downcutting by streams have exposed large expanses of a variety of geologic strata, each with unique physical and chemical characteristics. These strata are the parent material for a spectacular array of unusual and diverse soils that support many different vegetative communities and numerous types of endemic plants and their pollinators. This presents an extraordinary opportunity to study plant speciation and community dynamics independent of climatic variables. The monument contains an extraordinary number of areas of relict vegetation, many of which have existed since the Pleistocene, where natural processes continue unaltered by man. These include relict grasslands, of which No Mans Mesa is an outstanding example, and pinon-juniper communities, containing trees up to 1,400 years old. As witnesses to the past, these relict areas establish a baseline against which to measure changes in community dynamics and biogeochemical cycles in areas impacted by human activity. Most of the ecological communities contained in the monument have low resistance to, and slow recovery from, disturbance. Fragile cryptobiotic crusts, themselves of significant biological interest, play a critical role throughout the monument, stabilizing the highly erodible desert soils and providing nutrients to plants. An abundance of packrat middens provides insight into the vegetation and climate of the past 35,000 years and furnishes context for studies of evolution and climate change. The wildlife of the monument is characterized by a diversity of species. The monument varies greatly in elevation and topography and is in a climatic zone where northern and southern habitat species intermingle. Mountain lion, bear, and desert bighorn sheep roam the monument. Over 200 species of birds, including bald eagles and peregrine falcons, are found within the area. Wildlife, including neotropical birds, concentrate around the Paria and Escalante Rivers and other riparian corridors within the monument.

Section 2 of the Act of June 8, 1906 (34 Stat. 225, 16 U.S.C. 431) authorizes the President, in his discretion, to declare by public proclamation historic landmarks, historic and prehistoric structures, and other objects of historic or scientific interest that are situated upon the lands owned or controlled by the Government of the United States to be national monuments, and to reserve as a part thereof parcels of land, the limits of which in all cases shall be confined to the smallest area compatible with the proper care and management of the objects to be protected.

NOW, THEREFORE, I WILLIAM J. CLINTON, President of the United States of America, by the authority vested in me by section 2 of the Act of June 8, 1906 (34 Stat. 225, 16 U.S.C. 431), do proclaim that there are hereby set apart and reserved as the Grand Staircase–Escalante National Monument, for the purpose of protecting the objects identified above, all lands and interests in lands owned or controlled by the United States within the boundaries of the area described on the document entitled "Grand Staircase–Escalante National Monument" attached to and forming a part of this proclamation. The Federal land and interests in land reserved consist of approximately 1.7 million acres, which is the smallest area compatible with the proper care and management of the objects to be protected.

All Federal lands and interests in lands within the boundaries of this monument are hereby appropriated and withdrawn from entry, location, selection, sale, leasing, or other disposition under the public land laws, other than by exchange that furthers the protective purposes of the monument. Lands and interests in lands not owned by the United States shall be reserved as a part of the monument upon acquisition of title thereto by the United States.

The establishment of this monument is subject to valid existing rights.

Nothing in this proclamation shall be deemed to diminish the responsibility and authority of the State of Utah for management of fish and wildlife, including regulation of hunting and fishing, on Federal lands within the monument.

Nothing in this proclamation shall be deemed to affect existing permits or leases for, or levels of, livestock grazing on Federal lands within the monument; existing grazing uses shall continue to be governed by applicable laws and regulations other than this proclamation.

Nothing in this proclamation shall be deemed to revoke any existing withdrawal, reservation, or appropriation; however, the national monument shall be the dominant reservation.

The Secretary of the Interior shall manage the monument through the Bureau of Land Management, pursuant to applicable legal authorities, to implement the purposes of this proclamation. The Secretary of the Interior shall prepare, within 3 years of this date, a management plan for this monument, and shall promulgate such regulations for its management as he deems appropriate. This proclamation does not reserve water as a matter of Federal law. I direct the Secretary to address in the management plan the extent to which water is necessary for the proper care and management of the objects of this monument and the extent to which further action may be necessary pursuant to Federal or State law to assure the availability of water.

Warning is hereby given to all unauthorized persons not to appropriate, injure, destroy, or remove any feature of this monument, and not to locate or settle upon any of the lands thereof.

IN WITNESS WHEREOF, I have hereunto set my hand this eighteenth day of September, in the year of our Lord nineteen hundred and ninety-six, and of the Independence of the United States of America the two hundred and twenty-first.

WILLIAM J. CLINTON

Appendix B

ANTIQUITIES ACT OF 1906 (As amended)
(16 U.S.C. §§ 431-33)

§ 431.   National monuments; reservation of land; relinquishment of private claims

The President of the United States is authorized, in his discretion, to declare by public proclamation historic landmarks, historic and prehistoric structures, and other objects of historic or scientific interest that are situated upon the lands owned or controlled by the Government of the United States to be national monuments, and may reserve as a part thereof parcels of land, the limits of which in all cases shall be confined to the smallest area compatible with the proper care and management of the objects to be protected. When such objects are situated upon a tract covered by a bona fide unperfected claim or held in private ownership, the tract, or so much thereof as may be necessary for the proper care and management of the object, may be relinquished to the Government, and the Secretary of the Interior is authorized to accept the relinquishment of such tracts in behalf of the Government of the United States.
June 8, 1906, c. 3060 § 2, 34 Stat. 225.

§ 431a.   Limitation on further extension or establishment of national monuments in Wyoming

No further extension or establishment of national monuments in Wyoming may be undertaken except by express authorization of Congress.
Sept. 14, 1950, c. 950, § 1, 64 Stat. 849.

432.   Permits to examine ruins, excavations, and gathering of objects; regulations

Permits for the examination of ruins, the excavation of archaeological sites, and the gathering of objects of antiquity upon the lands under their respective jurisdictions may

be granted by the Secretaries of the Interior, Agriculture, and Army to institutions which they may deem properly qualified to conduct such examination, excavation, or gathering, subject to such rules and regulations as they may prescribe: Provided, That the examinations, excavations, and gatherings are undertaken for the benefit of reputable museums, universities, colleges, or other recognized scientific or educational institutions, with a view to increasing the knowledge of such objects, and that the gatherings shall be made for permanent preservation in public museums. The Secretaries of the departments aforesaid shall make and publish from time to time uniform rules and regulations for the purpose of carrying out the provisions of this section and sections 431 and 433 of this title.
June 8, 1906, c. 3060, §§ 3, 4, 34 Stat. 225.

433.   American antiquities

Any person who shall appropriate, excavate, injure, or destroy any historic or prehistoric ruin or monument, or any object of antiquity, situated on lands owned or controlled by the Government of the United States, without the permission of the Secretary of the Department of the Government having jurisdiction over the lands on which said antiquities are situated, shall, upon conviction, be fined in a sum of not more than $500 or be imprisoned for a period of not more than ninety days, or shall suffer both fine and imprisonment, in the discretion of the court.
June 8, 1906, c. 3060, § 1, 34 Stat. 225.

Appendix C

NATIONAL MONUMENTS

Established by Presidential Proclamation:

Name & Date	Location	Legal Reference*
Ackia Battleground NM Oct. 25, 1938	Mississippi	Proc. No. 2307 53 Stat. 2494
Admirality Island NM Dec. 2, 1980	Alaska	Proc. No. 4611 93 Stat. 1446
Andrew Johnson NM Apr. 27, 1942	Tennessee	Proc. No. 2554 56 Stat. 1955
Aniakchak NM[1] Apr. 27, 1942	Alaska	Proc. No. 4612 93 Stat. 1448
Arches NM[2] Apr. 12, 1929	Utah	Proc. No. 1875 46 Stat. 2988
Aztec Ruins NM Jan. 24, 1939	New Mexico	Proc. No. 1650 42 Stat. 2295
Badlands NM[3] Jan. 25, 1939	South Dakota	Proc. No. 2320 53 Stat. 2521
Bandelier NM Feb. 11, 1916	New Mexico	Proc. No. 3388 39 Stat. 1764
Becharof NM Dec. 1, 1973	Alaska	Proc. No. 4613 93 Stat. 1450
Bering Land Bridge NM[4] Dec. 1, 1978	Alaska	Proc. No. 4614 93 Stat. 1451
Big Hole Battlefield NM[5] June 23, 1910	Montana	Proc. No. 2339 53 Stat. 2544
Black Canyon of Gunnison NM[6] Mar. 2, 1933	Colorado	Proc. No. 2033 47 Stat. 2558
Bryce Canyon NM June 8, 1923	Utah	Proc. No. 1664 43 Stat. 1914
Buck Island Reef NM Dec. 28, 1961	Virgin Islands	Proc. No. 3443 76 Stat. 1441

Cabrillo NM Oct. 14, 1913	California	Proc. No. 1255 38 Stat. 1965
Canyon De Chelly NM Apr. 1, 1931	Arizona	Proc. No. 1945 47 Stat. 2448
Cape Krusenstern NM[7] Dec. 1, 1978	Alaska	Proc. No. 4615 93 Stat. 1453
Capitol Reef NM[8] Aug. 2, 1937	Utah	Proc. No. 2246 50 Stat. 1856
Capulin Volcano NM[9] Aug. 9, 1916	New Mexico	Proc. No. 1340 39 Stat. 1792
Carlsbad Cave NM[10] Oct. 25, 1923	New Mexico	Proc. No. 1679 43 Stat. 1929
Casa Grande NM Aug. 3, 1918	Arizona	Proc. No. 1470 40 Stat. 1818
Castillo de San Marcos NM[11] Oct. 15, 1924	Florida	Proc. No. 1713 43 Stat. 1968
Castle Pinckney NM Oct. 15, 1924	South Carolina	Proc. No. 1713 43 Stat. 1968
Cedar Breaks NM Aug. 22, 1933	Utah	Proc. No. 2054 48 Stat. 1705
Chaco Canyon NM[12] Mar. 11, 1907	New Mexico	Proc. No. 740 35 Stat. 2119
Channel Islands NM[13] Apr. 26, 1938	California	Proc. No. 2281 52 Stat. 1541
Chesapeake & Ohio Canal NM Jan. 18, 1961	Maryland	Proc. No. 3391 75 Stat. 1023
Chiricahua NM Apr. 18, 1924	Arizona	Proc. No. 1692 43 Stat. 1946
Cinder Cone May 6, 1907	California	Proc. No. 753 35 Stat. 2131
Colonial NM[14] May 6, 1907	Virginia	Proc. No. 1929 46 Stat. 3041
Colorado NM May 24, 1911	Colorado	Proc. No. 1126 37 Stat. 1681
Craters of the Moon NM May 2, 1924	Idaho	Proc. No. 1694 43 Stat. 1947
Death Valley NM[15] Feb. 11, 1933	California & Nevada	Proc. No. 2028 47 Stat. 2554
Denali NM[16] Dec. 1, 1978	Alaska	Proc. No. 4616 93 Stat. 1455
Devil Postpile NM July 6, 1911	California	Proc. No. 1166 37 Stat. 1715
Devils Tower NM Sept. 24, 1906	Wyoming	Proc. No. 658 34 Stat. 3236

Dinosaur NM Oct. 4, 1915	Utah	Proc. No. 1313 39 Stat. 1752
Edison Laboratory NM[17] Sept. 5, 1962	New Jersey	Proc. No. 3148 70 Stat. c49
Effigy Mounds NM Oct. 25, 1949	Iowa	Proc. No. 2860 64 Stat. A371
El Morro NM Dec. 8, 1906	New Mexico	Proc. No. 695 34 Stat. 3264
Fort Jefferson NM Jan. 4, 1935	Florida	Proc. No. 2112 49 Stat. 3430
Fort Laramie NM[18] Apr. 29, 1960	Wyoming	Proc. No. 2292 74 Stat. 84
Fort Marion NM[19] June 5, 1942	Florida	Proc. No. 1713 43 Stat. 1968
Fort Matanzas NM Oct. 15, 1924	Florida	Proc. No. 1713 43 Stat. 1968
Fort Niagara NM Sept. 5, 1925	New York	Proc. No. 1745 44 Stat. 2582
Fort Pulaski NM Oct. 15, 1924	Georgia	Proc. No. 1713 43 Stat. 1968
Fort Wood NM Oct. 15, 1922	New York	Proc. No. 1641 42 Stat. 2286
Fossil Cycad NM Oct. 21, 1922	South Dakota	Proc. No. 1641 42 Stat. 2286
Gates of the Arctic NM[20] Dec. 1, 1978	Alaska	Proc. No. 4617 93 Stat. 1457
Gila Cliff-Dwellings NM Nov. 16, 1907	New Mexico	Proc. No. 781 35 Stat. 2162
Glacier Bay NM[21] Feb. 26, 1925	Alaska	Proc. No. 1733 43 Stat. 1988
Grand Canyon NM[22] Jan. 11, 1908	Arizona	Proc. No. 794 35 Stat. 2175
Grand Staircase–Escalante NM Sept. 18, 1996	Utah	Proc. No. 6920 3 C.F.R. 64
Gran Quivira NM[23] Nov. 1, 1909	New Mexico	Proc. No. 882 36 Stat. 2503
Great Sand Dunes NM Mar. 17, 1932	Colorado	Proc. No. 1994 47 Stat. 2506
Holy Cross NM[24] May 11, 1929	Colorado	Proc. No. 1877 46 Stat. 2993
Hovenweep NM Mar. 2, 1923	Colorado	Proc. No. 1654 42 Stat. 2299
Jackson Hole NM[25] Mar. 15, 1943	Wyoming	Proc. No. 2578 57 Stat. 731

Jewel Cave NM Feb. 7, 1908	South Dakota	Proc. No. 799 35 Stat. 2180
Joshua Tree NM[26] Aug. 10, 1936	California	Proc. No. 2193 50 Stat. 1760
Katmai NM[27] Sept. 24, 1918	Alaska	Proc. No. 1487 40 Stat. 1855
Kenai Fjords NM[28] Dec. 1, 1978	Alaska	Proc. No. 4620 93 Stat. 1463
Kobuk Valley NM[29] Dec. 1, 1978	Alaska	Proc. No. 4621 93 Stat. 1462
Lake Clark NM[30] Dec. 1, 1978	Alaska	Proc. No. 4622 93 Stat. 1465
Lassen Peak NM[31] May 6, 1907	California	Proc. No. 4622 35 Stat. 2132
Lava Beds NM Nov. 21, 1925	California	Proc. No. 1618 42 Stat. 2260
Lehman Caves NM[32] Jan. 24, 1922	Nevada	Proc. No. 1618 42 Stat. 2260
Lewis & Clark Cavern NM May 11, 1908	Montana	Proc. No. 807 35 Stat. 2187
Marble Canyon NM Jan. 20, 1969	Arizona	Proc. No. 3889 83 Stat. 924
Meriwether Lewis NM[33] Feb. 6, 1925	Tennessee	Proc. No. 1730 43 Stat. 1986
Misty Fjords NM[34] Dec. 2, 1980	Alaska	Proc. No. 4623 93 Stat. 1466
Montezuma Castle NM Sept. 8, 1906	Arizona	Proc. No. 696 93 Stat. 3265
Mound City Group NM Mar. 2, 1923	Ohio	Proc. No. 1653 42 Stat. 2298
Mount Olympus NM[35] Mar. 2, 1909	Washington	Proc. No. 869 35 Stat. 2247
Muir Woods NM Jan. 9, 1908	California	Proc. No. 793 35 Stat. 2174
Mukuntuweap NM[36] July 31, 1909	Utah	Proc. No. 877 36 Stat. 2498
Natural Bridges NM Apr. 16, 1980	Utah	Proc. No. 804 35 Stat. 2183
Navajo NM May 20, 1909	Arizona	Proc. No. 873 36 Stat. 2491
Noatak NM[37] Dec. 1, 1978	Alaska	Proc. No. 4624 93 Stat. 1468
Ocmulgee NM[38] Dec. 23, 1936	Georgia	Proc. No. 2212 50 Stat. 1798

Old Kasaan NM[39] Oct. 25, 1916	Alaska	Proc. No. 1351 39 Stat. 2497
Oregon Caves NM July 12, 1909	Oregon	Proc. No. 876 36 Stat. 2497
Organ Pipe Cactus NM Apr. 13, 1937	Arizona	Proc. No. 2232 50 Stat. 1827
Papago Saguaro NM Jan. 31, 1914	Arizona	Proc. No. 1262 38 Stat. 1991
Perry's Victory & Int'l Peace Memorial NM July 6, 1936	Ohio	Proc. No. 2182 50 Stat. 1734
Petrified Forest NM[40] Dec. 8, 1906	Arizona	Proc. No. 697 34 Stat. 3266
Pinnacles NM Jan. 16, 1908	California	Proc. No. 796 43 Stat. 1911
Pipe Spring NM May 31, 1923	Arizona	Proc. No. 1663 43 Stat. 1913
Rainbow Bridge NM May 30, 1910	Utah	Proc. No. 1043 36 Stat. 2703
Russell Cave NM May 11, 1961	Alabama	Proc. No. 3413 75 Stat. 1058
Saguaro NM[41] Mar. 1, 1933	Arizona	Proc. No. 2032 47 Stat. 2557
Santa Rosa Island NM May 17, 1939	Florida	Proc. No. 2337 53 Stat. 2542
Scotts Bluff NM Dec. 12, 1919	Nebraska	Proc. No. 1547 41 Stat. 1779
Shoshone Cavern NM[42] Sept. 21, 1909	Wyoming	Proc. No. 880 36 Stat. 2501
Sieur de Monts NM July 8, 1916	Maine	Proc. No. 1339 39 Stat. 1785
Sitka NM[43] Oct. 18, 1972	Alaska	Proc. No. 959 36 Stat. 2601
Statute of Liberty NM Oct. 15, 1924	New York	Proc. No. 1713 43 Stat. 1968
Sunset Crater Volcano NM[44] May 26, 1930	Arizona	Proc. No. 1911 46 Stat. 3023
Timpanogos Cave NM Oct. 14, 1922	Utah	Proc. No. 787 35 Stat. 2168
Tonto NM Dec. 19, 1907	Arizona	Proc. No. 2230 50 Stat. 1825
Tumacacori NM[45] Sept. 15, 1908	Arizona	Proc. No. 821 35 Stat. 2205
Tuzigoot NM July 25, 1939	Arizona	Proc. No. 2344 53 Stat. 2548

Verendrye NM June 29, 1917	North Dakota	Proc. No. 1380 40 Stat. 1677
Walnut Canyon NM Nov. 30, 1915	Arizona	Proc. No. 1318 39 Stat. 1761
Wheeler NM Dec. 7, 1908	Colorado	Proc. No. 831 35 Stat. 2214
White Sands NM Jan. 18, 1933	New Mexico	Proc. No. 2025 47 Stat. 2551
Wrangell-St. Elias NM[46] Dec. 1, 1978	Alaska	Proc. No. 4625 93 Stat. 1470
Wupatki NM Dec. 9, 1924	Arizona	Proc. No. 1721 43 Stat. 1977
Yucca House NM Dec. 19, 1919	Colorado	Proc. No. 1549 41 Stat. 1781
Yukon-Charley NM[47] Dec. 1, 1978	Alaska	Proc. No. 4626 93 Stat. 1472
Zion NM[48] Jan. 22, 1937	Utah	Proc. No. 2221 50 Stat. 1809

Established by Congress:

Name & Date	Location	Legal Reference
Agate Fossil Beds NM June 5, 1965	Nebraska	Pub.L. 89-33 79 Stat. 123
Alibates Flint Quarries NM Aug. 31, 1965	Texas	Pub.L. 89-154 79 Stat. 587
Congaree Swamp NM Aug. 31, 1965	South Carolina	Pub.L. 94-545 90 Stat. 2517
El Malpais NM Dec. 31, 1987	New Mexico	Pub.L. 100-225 101 Stat. 1539
Florissant Fossil Beds NM Dec. 31, 1987	Colorado	Pub.L. 91-60 83 Stat. 1069
Fossil Butte NM Oct. 23, 1972	Wyoming	Pub.L. 92-537 86 Stat. 1069
Hagerman Fossil Beds NM Nov. 18, 1988	Idaho	Pub.L. 100-696 102 Stat. 4575
Hohokam Pima NM Oct. 21, 1972	Arizona	Pub.L. 92-525 86 Stat. 1047
John Day Fossil Beds NM Oct. 26, 1974	Oregon	Pub.L. 93-486 88 Stat. 1461
Kill Devil NM[49] Mar. 2, 1927	North Carolina	Ch. 251 44 Stat. 1264
Little Bighorn Battlefield NM Dec. 10, 1991	Montana	Pub.L. 102-201 105 Stat. 1631-1633
Mount St. Helens Volcanic NM Aug. 26, 1982	Washington	Pub.L. 97-243 96 Stat. 301
Newberry Volcanic NM Nov. 5, 1990	Oregon	Pub.L. 101-522 104f Stat. 2288
Pecos NM[50] June 28, 1965	New Mexico	Pub.L. 89-54 79 Stat. 195
Petroglyph NM June 27, 1990	New Mexico	Pub.L. 101-313 104 Stat. 272
Poverty Point NM Oct. 31, 1988	Louisiana	Pub.L. 100-560 102 Stat. 2803
Salinas Pueblo Missions NM Dec. 19, 1980	New Mexico	Pub.L. 96-550 94 Stat. 3231

Notes

*The legal reference is to the initial proclamation designating the national monument. In many instances, the initial proclamation has been amended or modified by subsequent proclamations. A complete list of the amended proclamations is available in the annotations following 16 U.S.C.A. § 431.

1   See 16 U.S.C. § 410hh(1).

2   Monument abolished and redesignated Arches National Park in 1971, 16 U.S.C. § 272.

3   Redesignated Badlands National Park, Jan. 25, 1939, 16 U.S.C. § 441e-1.

4   Redesignated Bering Land Bridge National Preserve in 1980, 16 U.S.C. § 410hh(2).

5   Redesignated Big Hole National Battlefield, June 23, 1910, 16 U.S.C. § 430uu.

6   See also 16 U.S.C. § 401.

7   See 16 U.S.C. § 410hh(3).

8   Monument abolished and redesignated Capitol Reef National Park, Aug. 2, 1937, 16 U.S.C. § 273.

9   Changed from Capulin Mountain National Monument to Capulin Volcano National Monument in 1987, 16 U.S.C. § 460uu-46(g).

10 Redesignated Carlsbad Caverns National Park in 1930, 16 U.S.C. § 407.

11 Redesignated Castillo de San Marcos National Monument in 1942, 56 Stat. 312.

12 Monument abolished and redesignated Chaco Culture National Historical Park in 1980, 16 U.S.C. § 410ii-1(a).

13 Monument abolished and incorporated in Channel Islands National Park in 1980, 16 U.S.C. § 410ff.

14 Monument redesignated Colonial National Historical Park in 1936, 16 U.S.C. § 81.

15 Monument abolished and incorporated in Death Valley National Park in 1994, 16 U.S.C. § 410aaa-1.

16 See 16 U.S.C. § 410hh-1(3).

17 Redesignated Edison National Historic Site in 1962, 76 Stat. 428.

18 Redesignated Fort Laramie Historic Site in 1960, 74 Stat. 84.

19 Redesignated Castillo de San Marcos National Monument in 1942, 56 Stat. 312.

20 Redesignated Gates of the Arctic National Park in 1980, 16 U.S.C. § 410hh(4).

21 Redesignated Glacier Bay National Park in 1980, 16 U.S.C. § 410hh-1.

22 Abolished and mostly incorporated into Grand Canyon National Park in 1975, 16 U.S.C. § 228a.

23 Redesignated Salinas National Monument in 1980, 94 Stat. 3231, and then redesignated Salinas Pueblo Missions National Monument in 1988, 102 Stat. 2797.

24 Monument abolished in 1950, 64 Stat. 404.

25 Monument abolished and incorporated in Grand Teton National Park in 1950, 16 U.S.C. § 406d-1.

26 Monument abolished and incorporated in Joshua Tree National Park in 1994, 16 U.S.C. § 410aaa-22.

27 Redesignated Katmai National Park in 1980, 16 U.S.C. § 410hh-1(2).

28 Redesignated Kenai Fjords National Park in 1980, 16 U.S.C. § 410hh(5).

29 Redesignated Kobuk Valley National Park in 1980, 16 U.S.C. § 410hh(6).

30 Redesignated Lake Clark National Park in 1980, 16 U.S.C. § 410hh(7).

31 Incorporated into Lassen Volcanic National Park in 1916, 16 U.S.C. § 201.

32 Monument abolished and lands redesignated Great Basin National Park in 1986, 16 U.S.C. § 410mm(d).

33 Monument included in Natchez Trace Parkway in 1961, 16 U.S.C. § 460-1.

34 Monument established within Tongass National Forest in 1980, 94 Stat. 2399.

35 Monument abolished and lands incorporated in Olympic National Park in 1938, 16 U.S.C. § 251.

36 Redesignated Zion National Monument by Proc. No. 1435, Mar. 18, 1918, 40 Stat. 1760, and later redesignated Zion National Park in 1919, 16 U.S.C. § 344.

37 Redesignated Noatak National Preserve in 1980, 16 U.S.C. § 410hh(8).

38 See also 16 U.S.C. § 447a.

39 Monument abolished and incorporated in Tongass National Forest in 1955, 69 Stat. 380.

40 Monument disestablished on establishment of Petrified Forest National Park in 1958, 16 U.S.C. § 119, 444.

41 Monument incorporated into Saguaro National Park in 1994, 108 Stat. 3467.

42 Monument abolished in 1954, 68 Stat. 98.

43 Redesignated Sitka National Historical Park in 1972, 86 Stat. 904.

44 Changed from Sunset Crater National Monument to Sunset Crater Volcano National Monument in 1990, 104 Stat. 3222.

45 Monument abolished and incorporated in Tumacacori National Historical Park in 1990, 16 U.S.C. § 410ss.

46 Redesignated Wrangell-Saint Elias National Park in 1980, 16 U.S.C. § 410hh(9).

47 Redesignated Yukon-Charley Rivers National Preserve in 1980, 16 U.S.C. § 410hh(10).

48 Monument combined with Zion National Park into a single national park unit in 1956, 16 U.S.C. § 346b.

49 Renamed Wright Brothers National Memorial in 1953.

50 Redesignated Pecos National Historical Park in 1990, 16 U.S.C. § 410rr-1.

Appendix D

THE MONUMENT PLANNING TEAM

Grand Staircase–Escalante National Monument
337 South Main, Suite 010, Cedar City, Utah 84720
Phone (435) 865-5100   Fax (435) 865-5170
http://www.ut.blm.gov/monument

Jerry Meredith   (435) 865-5100   jmeredit@ut.blm.gov
Monument Manager

Kate Cannon   (435) 865-5162   kcannon@ut.blm.gov
Associate Monument Manager

Pete Wilkins   (435) 865-5161   p1wilkin@ut.blm.gov
Planning Coordinator

Elizabeth Ballard   (435) 865-5104   eballard@ut.blm.gov
Backcountry Recreation

Bob Blackett   (435) 865-5103   rblacket@ut.blm.gov
Geology/Minerals

Andrew Dubrasky   (435) 865-5131   adubrask@ut.blm.gov
GIS Specialist

Marietta Eaton   (435) 865-5114   meaton@ut.blm.gov
Cultural/Earth Sciences Lead

Alden Hamblin   (435) 865-5115   ahamblin@ut.blm.gov
Paleontology

Joel Haynes   (435) 865-5109   jrhaynes@ut.blm.gov
Computer Specialist

Clair Jensen   (435) 865-5110   fcjensen@ut.blm.gov
Wildlife

Tom Leatherman   (435) 865-5107   tleather@ut.blm.gov
Botany

Cara Mollenkopf Administrative Assistant	(435) 865-5101	emollen@ut.blm.gov
Kezia Nielsen Writer/Editor	(435) 865-5106	knielsen@ut.blm.gov
Dennis Pope Biological Lead	(435) 865-5111	dpope@ut.blm.gov
Lorraine Pope Lands/Realty	(435) 865-5108	lpope@ut.blm.gov
Gabrielle Renshaw External Affairs	(435) 865-5102	grenshaw@ut.blm.gov
Jerry Sempek Data Management	(435) 865-5130	jsempek@ut.blm.gov
Barb Sharrow Recreation/Visitor Services Lead	(435) 865-5112	bsharrow@ut.blm.gov
Ken Sizemore Community Planning/Economic Analysis	(435) 865-5113	ksizemor@ut.blm.gov
Kathleen Truman History/Community Involvement	(435) 865-5105	ktruman@ut.blm.gov

Contributors

M. Lee Allison is the state geologist and director of the Utah Geological Survey.

Thomas W. Bachtell is the president of the Pruitt, Gushee and Bachtell law firm in Salt Lake City, Utah.

Brad T. Barber is deputy director of the Utah Governor's Office for Planning and Budget and state planning coordinator.

Ralph Becker is a principal of Bear West, an environmental consulting firm, adjunct professor of geography at the University of Utah, and a representative in the Utah state legislature.

Jayne Belnap is a research ecologist in the Biological Resources Division of the United States Geological Survey.

Gail Blattenberger is an associate professor of economics at the University of Utah.

Sarah B. George is director of the Utah Museum of Natural History and adjunct associate professor of biology at the University of Utah.

David D. Gillette is state paleontologist for the Utah Geological Survey.

Scott Groene is the issues director for the Southern Utah Wilderness Alliance.

Michael S. Johnson is an attorney at the Pruitt, Gushee and Bachtell law firm in Salt Lake City, Utah.

Robert B. Keiter is the James I. Farr professor of law at the University of Utah College of Law, and director of the Wallace Stegner Center for Land, Resources and the Environment.

David Kiefer is a professor of economics at the University of Utah.

John D. Leshy is the solicitor for the U.S. Department of the Interior.

Dean L. May is a professor of history at the University of Utah.

A. Jerry Meredith is manager of the Grand Staircase–Escalante National Monument for the Bureau of Land Management.

Duncan Metcalfe is curator of archaeology for the Utah Museum of Natural History and associate professor of anthropology at the University of Utah.

Wilfred Numkena, formerly executive director of the Utah Division of Indian Affairs, is executive director for the Hopi tribe Board of Education, Kykotsmovi, Arizona.

Dean Reeder is director of the Division of Travel Development in the Department of Community and Economic Development for the state of Utah.

R. Thayne Robson is director of the Bureau of Economic and Business Research and professor of business at the University of Utah.

Edward J. Ruddell is associate professor of parks, recreation and tourism at the University of Utah.

Scott Truman is executive director of the Utah Rural Development Council, vice chair of the Southwestern Utah Planning Authorities Council, and Rural Liason to Southern Utah University.

Joro Walker is associate director of the Wallace Stegner Center for Land, Resources and the Environment at the University of Utah College of Law.